WILL FOR CHILDREN

"I refuse to accept that the shackles of slavery can ever be stronger than the quest for freedom."

WILL FOR CHILDREN

Kailash Satyarthi
(Nobel Peace Prize Winner)

No part of this publication can be reproduced, stored in a retrieval system or transmitted in any form or by any means, electronic, mechanical, photocopying, recording or otherwise, without the prior permission of the author and the publisher.

Published by
PRABHAT PRAKASHAN PVT. LTD.
4/19 Asaf Ali Road,
New Delhi-110 002 (INDIA)
e-mail: prabhatbooks@gmail.com

ISBN 978-93-86300-35-5
WILL FOR CHILDREN
by Kailash Satyarthi

© Reserved

Paperback Edition
2025

Price
₹ 600.00 (Rupees Six Hundred only)

Printed at
R-Tech Offset Printers, Delhi

Author's Note

This book is a compendium of seeds of thoughts, sparks of conversations, and a few foundational pieces. Written over a period of time, in the years after 1980s, these articles formed the basis of principles and practices on the topics of, inter alia, child labour, child trafficking, sexual exploitation, and education. This also includes my earliest articles on children's rights. I think these will be quite useful not only for lay readers but for research scholars as well.

Recently, my associates gathered a few of my old articles. Now, neither my organisation nor I had ever made such a compilation in a methodical fashion—which is why, most of them remain lost to this day. Of those that could be recovered, a select few have been compiled for this book. In all humility, I can say that these were historical documents that have fomented a movement against child labour, not only in India but all over the world. These writings created a sense of urgency amongst the public as well as intellectuals, and the policy makers to the United Nations. Over 36 years, I have seen the power of these thoughts take form via the establishment of organisations and institutions, the creation of various government departments, as well as sparking interest in new research studies, informing the policies of the corporate world, national and international legislation, and impacting the budgetary allocation within the governments.

Many of these articles were written even as I lay wounded after being attacked by those who had subjected children to slavery. Other articles were written at a time when I did not have enough money to buy milk for my son. With the money earned through writing for newspapers, my wife and companion in this movement, Sumedha*ji*, managed to run the household. I had written a short book in those days, when the mafia gangs engaged in child slavery attacked my home and, later, threatened to kidnap and kill my little daughter. At the same time, other pieces reflect my musings on the joyful faces of thousands of rescued children residing at our boys' rehabilitation homes for former child labourers *Mukti Ashram* and *Bal Ashram*, as well as our work in the villages involved in the child-friendly villages project (*Bal Mitra Gram*).

The following incident is from 1959. It was my first day at school. Like any other child, I had on new shoes and clothes, a bag of books, and my dreams. I was filled with excitement. The school's name was Durg, a government primary school in my hometown, Vidisha. As I was entering through the gates, I caught sight of a child of my age, sitting on the ground and polishing shoes right outside the school. His father sat alongside, mending shoes and *chappals* (sandals). I stopped short for a moment. I might have seen kids working like this before, but had not paid much attention to them. This was the first time that the irony of the juxtaposition hit me: Here we were, my friends and I, about to start school, whereas that child could not. He kept looking at our shoes. Our shoes were new and, as such, did not need polishing.

After the introduction of students in my class was over, I summoned up my courage and asked the teacher: "Master *Sahib*, why is one child sitting outside and polishing shoes? Why is he not with us in class?" The teacher explained to me that this is nothing new. After all, children of the poor work as labourers. Later, I talked to the headmaster of my school as well as with my family members. All of them tried to make me understand the same thing in different ways. Maybe I would have understood. But every single day, whilst going to and returning from school, I would feel upset whenever I saw the child. This went on for a week or so. Nevertheless, I kept gathering the strength from within.

One day, as I was returning from school, I stood near the father-son duo. I asked the father why he did not send his son to school. At first, he was taken aback. But then he considered it for a moment and said, "*Babuji,* I never thought about this. Nor has anyone ever asked. This is what our forefathers have been doing. I have been mending shoes since childhood." Then, joining his hands together, he said, "*Babuji,* you don't know, we are born to do labour!" That was an answer for him, but for me, it was an issue and the challenge of a lifetime. How was I, a five or six-year-old kid, to understand the issues of upper caste versus lower caste, the rich versus the poor, or other forms of social inequalities? But somewhere, something was wrong—that much I understood. This incident allowed me to look at society and life with a new perspective. With the eyes of a child, I learned to differentiate between right and wrong. And, to date, I have tried to preserve those eyes in my innermost being.

Fifty-five years ago today, I had ignored the cultural norms and values held by my teachers and parents. Even today, I strongly reject those concepts and assumptions which preach double standards about children. I started my fight against child slavery with tangible action. In the early part of the 1980s, when our small group of activists started rescuing children from agricultural fields, brick kilns, stone quarries, factories, restaurants and homes, our friends used to make fun of us, because child labour was hardly an issue in the country or the world at that time. Child rights had not even been conceived back then. The United Nations adopted the Declaration of the Rights of Child in 1989, almost a decade after the beginning of our on-the-ground struggle. Independent India had no laws of its own on child labour. No political party had ever held any political debates or discussions on this issue. Forget a book or research, op-eds or articles were not even visible in the newspapers.

Likewise, education was considered merely a part of governmental programmes or devotional activity. When a few people like us attempted to make it a human rights issue in India and other parts of the world, rarely did we find people ready to listen and understand what we had to say. During my engineering studies and a few years of teaching, I learnt about the value of having a rational approach towards arguments and the importance of analysing the basic principles of any issue. Given that I was active in various social movements as a student, I had also studied, to some extent, the ideological basis of those movements. I was always interested in writing and studying. Even before I started *Bachpan Bachao Andolan* (BBA – Save the Childhood Movement), I used to write articles on social, cultural and spiritual issues in several newspapers and magazines in India. Against this backdrop, I took recourse to facts, arguments and analyses in formulating my campaign to save childhoods into a mass movement. I wrote several articles in newspapers and journals. I also wrote all kinds of pamphlets and had them printed and distributed. This was the first literature related to the atrocities on children and the practical solutions to their issues to be published in India. And as the issue evolved, I too, kept advancing my thoughts along its various dimensions—through the medium of my pen.

This thought journey of mine has been inspired, on one side, by deep compassion and faith in the need for childhood and freedom, and on another, by practical action and struggle. I do not gaze upon anyone with pity—in writing, speech or even day-to-day life. Nor do I engage in any form of beneficence. My relationship with children has been one of empathy, equality, respect and friendship. While rescuing a child, the thought never crossed my mind that I am doing them a favour. The first smiles of freedom on the faces of these children are, for me, a glimpse of God. So, it is the children who have done me a favour. I have faith in solutions, not problems. Right from the beginning, it has been my belief that the solution to every problem is cradled within its womb. That is why the articles included in this book have solutions and suggestions based on experience. Those who just sit the whole night, lamenting the darkness, often fall asleep by the time of dawn. But the people who find a way to light a lamp with the spark of their self-confidence and creativity—no darkness can ever diminish their shine. The light from a tiny lamp can keep the hope of a great sunrise alive. So, it is my belief that the concept of childhood freedom will emerge victorious one day.

Even now, approximately 168 million children all over the world are occupied in child labour. Sixty million have never been to a school and 120 million are forced to drop out before they complete their primary education. Eighty-five million children are victims of slavery, prostitution, child-trafficking, forced begging and child labour in hazardous industries. These are huge challenges before us. But the good thing is that the government, society and the corporate world can no longer ignore the atrocities on our children. Raising public awareness, legislating strict laws and their proper enforcement, the engagement of civil society, and the provision of sufficient budgetary allocation by the government to education, health and the protection of children—these are some measures that can help end all forms of violence against children.

I acknowledge the contribution of my colleagues in collecting and translating these articles, including Eirliani A. Rahman for her help in editing the English version.

I dedicate this anthology to you, with an appeal to save the childhood of each and every child in India and the entire world.

—Kailash Satyarthi

28th Nov., 2016

Contents

Contents

PROTECTING CHILDHOOD

THE CHAINS OF SLAVERY WILL BREAK

EDUCATION IS THE KEY TO FREEDOM

CHILDREN AND RELIGION

THE DREAM OF FREEDOM

"My dream in life is to see every child being free to be a child."

The novel concept of Bal Mitra Gram **(Child-friendly Village) was started in 2001 by** Bachpan Bachao Andolan **(BBA – Save the Childhood Movement) with the objective of ending social ills, such as child labour, child trade and illiteracy. The fundamental aim is to keep children as the focal point and, under their leadership, establish a child-friendly society through democratic processes and actions.**

- **More than 400 villages in 11 states of India have been made into** Bal Mitra Gram**.**
- **Almost 50% of the** Bal Sarpanch **(Head of the Child Council) in** Bal Mitra Gram **are girls.**
- **Under the** Bal Mitra Gram **programme, nearly 200,000 children have been pulled out of labour and enrolled in schools between the years 2001 and 2015.**
- **Through their efforts,** Bal Panchayat **(Children's Council) have implemented about two dozen welfare schemes of central and state governments in their villages. More than 10,000 people have directly benefitted from this.**
- **Under the** Bal Mitra Gram **programme, the democratic principle has been inculcated in more than 4,000 children and they have been brought into leadership roles in the village schools.**

Saving Childhood

This article, written in the year 1990, was the first milestone in creating social awareness about child labour and establishing a mass movement. It is an extension of the facts and experiences described in the pamphlets distributed during the author's campaign on creating public awareness in the 1980s. In later years, several facts were added and it was published in the form of a booklet. Multiple editions of this were published between 1992 and 1999. Civil society organisations, governments and international organisations such as UNICEF got it translated into many languages and distributed the copies amongst hundreds of thousands of people. As a result, child labour emerged as a major issue in India for the first time. The last edition of the booklet was published in 1994, the same is published here.

—Editor

It was evening, sometime in March 1982. I still remember with a heavy heart, the last words of Gulabo, a 14-year-old child slave, who took her final breath in my lap. She had been desperately imploring her mother: *"Mujhe bacha le Amma*!" (Save me, Mother!), before she slept, for the last time. I still feel bogged down by the weight of Gulabo's lifeless body, even though she was emaciated.

The girl's father, Subey, and I took her to the capital's Ram Manohar Lohia Hospital, where the doctors declared her dead and sent the body for post-mortem. Baffled by what had happened, Subey could not believe that Gulabo was no more. When we took her body to the electric crematorium for the last rituals, Subey, who had lost one hand while working in a kiln, tried in vain to wake her up with his only hand.

The stony look on Subey still haunts my thoughts, and his questions: "For what fault did my daughter have to burn her body everyday in the brick kiln? Why is she being burnt again?" still send shivers down my spine.

Due to prolonged work in brick kilns, Gulabo had contracted tuberculosis. She had been working as a child slave along with 32 others in a brick kiln in Kurukshetra, in the state of Haryana. We had approached the Supreme Court and procured orders for their release. When we arrived at the site with the Commissioner, the employer had already whisked them away to some secret hideaway. After a frantic search, we finally located them at midnight, dumped along the roadside in heavy rain. We brought them to our office in Delhi, one question ringing in my head: How many Gulabos are dying everyday? Why do they have to die everyday? That night, I had no answers.

I do not lay claim to being a scholar of esoteric compilations of religious books but I have certainly observed that all holy scriptures categorically declare that children are precious gifts of God; that they are the very embodiment of divinity. We have umpteen number of legal instruments protecting the rights of the child besides the UN Declarations on Human Rights, the Conventions on the Rights of the Child, all vying with one another to safeguard the healthy growth and overall development of children. The future of humanity is at stake because, despite all these books and documents, millions of children are languishing in slavery in various sectors of the economy. The gravity of this issue should worry us.

In the developing countries, poverty and child labour are two inseparable things. They are akin to the age-old question: which came first, the chicken or the egg. Child labour continues to perpetuate because of perceived advantages to employers of being the cheapest input for the extraction of maximum work, utter obedience, with no threat of unions or the Labour Court, and above all, exploiting the physical and mental vulnerability of children.

In conclusion, I feel that child servitude thrives due to six conspicuous reasons: The prevalence of myths to justify child servitude/labour, the lack of social awareness and sensitisation, the lack of political will, ineffective legal instruments, large-scale ignorance amongst children in servitude and their parents, and finally, anti-childhood developmental policies and programmes. Let us examine them one by one.

Almost all sections of the society contend that unemployment, poverty, illiteracy and the demographic explosion are four prime reasons for child servitude or labour. A closer analysis of these so-called contributory factors would dispel these misconceptions.

Child Labour and Unemployment

In South Asia alone, there are about 80 million child labourers, whereas the number of unemployed adults is much higher. In India, as per the latest figures, there are about 55 million child labourers. Interestingly, this figure is almost equal to the level of unemployed adults. More convincingly, the figures for children in labour and unemployed adults were the same (around 10 million) in 1947. It is evident from this that the eradication of child labour in India will instantly open up job opportunities for more than 55 million adults. Now think about this for a while: Will the end of child labour spur unemployment or would it create employment avenues for adults? Several in-depth studies have revealed that child labour is rampant in those communities where parents remain unemployed for around 100 days in a year and during employment are paid wages lower than the statutory minimum wage. It can be easily inferred that the removal of child labour would benefit the parents and adult family members of these children.

Another misconception lies in the thought that poverty is the main cause behind child labour. Poverty has a direct bearing on the unemployment situation of the parents and the child's other legal guardians, apart from widening the gulf between the rich and poor because of skewed incomes. Profit hardly ever percolates down to the lowest rung of society. Today, in India, 55 million child labourers earn about ₹ 150 million a day which translates to less than ₹ 3 per child. According to the Asia Labour Monitor's report, children in India contribute more than one-fifth to the total GNP of the country. But they do not get even one-fifth of what they produce.

How then can poverty be removed? With the abolition of child labour, adults will, by necessity, have to be employed, earning at least 5-6 times what the children were getting. Also, the adult workers will collectively have bargaining power as the employer would no longer have recourse to cheap labour in the form of children. Secondly, the replacement of children by adults in the labour market would also enhance the purchasing power of individual families, thereby raising their socio-economic status as a whole.

Child Labour Spurs Black Money

An oft-observed fact is that child labour is a paramount factor in the growth of black money. Children earn between one-fifth and one-tenth of what an adult labour gets as per statutory minimum wage rate. However, the company accounts reflect the payments to only adult labourers. This amounts to direct savings of billions of rupees in the case of big industries, such as carpet, diamond cutting and polishing, the manufacturing of matches and fireworks, handlooms and much more.

Child Labour and Public Health

On health, it has been observed that among the general category of patients in public hospitals, about 70 percent were once child labourers. This percentage increase hiked to 80 percent in the case of tuberculosis. Constant exposure to smoke, dust, noxious gases, chemicals and high temperatures affects the lungs, eyes, kidneys, liver and other vital organs of children. Continuously sitting in a cramped posture for long hours in vocations, such as carpet weaving, affects the spinal cord, resulting in cerebral damage. Working in dim light, poorly ventilated and unhygienic conditions adversely affects their growth, vision, and more.

What does this indicate? By letting manufacturers exploit children as inexpensive labour, the government is inheriting an army of sick and invalid persons in the years to come. The working children of today are virtually the liabilities of tomorrow. Is this a far-sighted strategy? A lion's share of the government's budgetary allocation for health care will have to be spent on millions of crippled adults and invalids in the foreseeable future. The average yearly addition to the sick population would be between 5 and 6 million adults. Is this what you call poverty alleviation? What does it say about the so-called economic leap of India, as claimed by those at the top?

Child Labour and Poverty

Another prevailing misconception is that child labour, at the very least, takes care of the immediate needs of the child's poor family and/or supplements the family income. For instance, let's examine the carpet industry. When we launched our campaign against child labour more than a decade ago, we also considered the impact on the poor families if child labour were to be abolished. But the reports by the Commission of Enquiry set up by the Supreme Court of India, *Gandhi Vidya Sansthan* (Varanasi), coupled with our own experience with ground reality, set all doubts to rest.

In this industry, out of the total 3,00,000 child workforce, 70 percent are migrants and engaged in bonded labour, hailing from the states of Bihar and Madha Pradesh in India, and Nepal. They subsist on scanty and unhealthy food given by their employers, are paid no wages or given merely a pittance. Our enquiries with various post offices in rural areas of the aforementioned states reveal that no money orders had been delivered to any of the parents whose children were working in various carpet looms for years altogether. In most of the cases, the only amount which the parents received was the advance ranging from ₹ 500 to ₹ 1000, given by the agents of the carpet manufacturers at the time of procuring the children. In our hundreds of rescues, we have never seen even a fifty-paisa coin in the pocket of a rescued child.

It is also not fair to generalise that all child labourers hail from very poor families. A team from the National Labour Institute recently found the other side of reality in the pottery industry of Khurja in the state of Uttar Pradesh, India. The parents, by and large, squander away most of the money they earned, drinking and smoking, whilst their children toil all day. A similar trend also exists in many other industries, such as brassware in Moradabad, lock-making in Aligarh, brick kilns and stone quarries.

Child Labour and Population

A phenomenon worth noting is the trend of the high number of children per couple which prevails in those sections of society where the environment is conducive to child labour. The general convictions amongst these people are: The more the children, the more pairs of working hands, and, therefore, the higher the income. Could this probably be an inducement to these parents to have more children? To them, children are instruments of economic stability, whereas the middle-class families only have children when they are economically stable. Reports have noted that in the past decade, there was a 23 percent population growth. This rate goes up to 30 percent in child labour-prone areas. The reason is evident. The government's population control programmes cannot bear fruit unless all employment avenues for children are closed. A conscious approach to educate these same sections of society will have to be adopted.

Child Labour and Illiteracy

In truth, child labour is the cause of illiteracy and not vice versa. Millions of child workers remain illiterate throughout their life, and the nation inherits this malady.

The average dropout rate from primary school is 40 percent in our country, whilst in areas where there is a high prevalence of child labour, the rate increases to 85 percent. This clearly demonstrates that there is a causal link between illiteracy and where child labour predominates. The distressing feature is that in most of the schools in these localities, the teachers remain absent for weeks altogether. The parents are lured by industrialists and their middlemen to send the children to factories. The abolition of child labour, and free and compulsory primary education for all children is the only panacea for this malady. Our approach can be further substantiated by intensive research, in-depth studies and investigations.

The Lack of Political Will

The fourth paramount cause for the perpetuation of child servitude is the utter absence of political will. Today, there is no dearth of legal instruments and international conventions to protect the rights of children. It is an irony then that although all the political parties agree that child labour is a blot on our society and that it should be wiped out, this issue has yet to figure in their political agenda or in their election manifestoes.

Here I will refer to an incident from my childhood when, like any other school-goer, I used to participate in the Children's Day celebrations held on the birthday of the first Prime Minister of India, Pandit Jawaharlal Nehru. I became morose when I could not find any traces of a smile on the face of the cobbler's son. As old as I was, he worked tirelessly in front of my school gate the whole day. Since the era of Pandit Jawaharlal Nehru, no Congress Government had accorded any priority towards the elimination of child labour. It baffles me still as to what the affectionate term for Nehru viz. '*Chacha* (Uncle) Nehru' stands for. Was he the *chacha* only of those children who were fortunate enough to attend schools and wear tidy clothes? These children do not constitute even one-fifth of the total child population of the country.

Let us reflect on the history of the Bharatiya Janata Party, which has emerged as the second largest political force in the country. During the Ayodhya dispute, they coined an enchanting slogan, "Every child belongs to Lord Ram and so should work for His birthplace." If Ramesh, the boy working in the *dhaba* (roadside stall), or Tasleem, the rag-picker child, or Kesav, the carpet-weaving child, are children of God, then they should be given freedom, education, food, medicine and other basic facilities for their proper development instead of commissioning them to wage a war for *Ram Janmabhoomi* (the birthplace of Lord Rama).

The slogans to protect the Indian culture and Hinduism are deceptive strategies. For this, they leverage a wide network of *branches* belonging to the Rashtriya Swayamsevak Sangh (widely regarded as the ideological parent organisation of the BJP) and *Saraswati Sisu Mandirs*. These self-proclaimed custodians of Indian culture would do well to answer this question: How is it that only 20 percent of middle-class children are the offsprings of Bharat Mata (Mother India). To whom do the unfortunate 5.5 million child labourers belong? Without concrete action for the welfare of these children, any talk of the Mother Land and Holy Land has no meaning at all and smacks of hypocrisy.

Likewise, the Janata Dal and several other political parties tried to project Mandal Commission report on the reservation for Other Backward Classes, as a panacea for the prevailing social injustice, ignoring the stark fact that jobs in the Union Government do not exceed 125,000 per annum. Similarly, other parties such as the Bahujan Samaj Party relentlessly demand the removal of 'Brahminical dominance over backward communities' to bring about the just social order. It is worth noting that 75 to 80 percent of child labourers belong to Harijans, tribals, minorities whilst the rest belong to other backward castes. Is it not an irony that the parties who orchestrate catchy slogans of social justice have hardly anything to offer for the abolition of child servitude in their agenda?

As far as the Left parties are concerned, such 'programmes of reforms' do not fall within the ambit of their political doctrines. Our leftist friends believe that as long as the proletariat and farmers are unable to wield political power, these problems would persist. Strangely enough, despite the long and successive rule of communist governments in West Bengal, the magnitude of child servitude has multiplied. We can wait out even 20 to 25 years to realise a radical social order, but in the case of children, we cannot wait. Their childhood is just for today. Tomorrow is too far off. The shackles of labour need to be broken right now.

Generally, all the political parties have outfits to look after the interests of various strata of society in the form of women's cell, minority cell, *Harijan* (untouchables), tribal cell, and so on. But unfortunately, there is no cell for children in chains. To a discerning observer, it is clear that the new political culture sizes up the masses in terms of vote banks, and that children have no place in that spectrum. Under these unfortunate circumstances, who will lend their voice to these voiceless millions? Who will take up the cudgels for their cause?

It is a clear case of the absolute absence of political will that not a single employer of child labour has been brought to book till date, despite legal instruments, namely the Bonded Labour Abolition Act (1976) and the Child Labour (Prohibition & Regulation) Act (1986) being in existence. The tragedy is that many state governments have not even promulgated relevant legislation on the basis of federal legislation. Instead, they hide their failure to curb the growth of child labour. They shamelessly declare, even in Parliament, that as long as poverty exists, child labour cannot be wiped out.

It is pertinent to mention here that our Constitution adopted the guarantee 'to provide free and compulsory education to all children in this country' in 1950. Last year in 1993, the Supreme Court, in its epoch-making judgement on Capitation Fees, categorically emphasised that to be educated is the fundamental right of the child. Nevertheless, the political powers are still trying to sweep this under the carpet. Till date, nothing has been done to put in place this cardinal constitutional guarantee. The case is similar in almost all the developing countries. In addition, our annual budget allocation for primary-level education has been scaled down to a dismal three percent.

Hypocrisy under the Garb of Religion

Without throwing light on one or two concrete examples of the political game of hypocrisy in the name of religion, the narrative will be incomplete. Two years ago, in January 1992, we organised a raid in a village Jagdishpur, in the Varanasi district of Uttar Pradesh. The local tehsildar (district officer) and two policemen, along with the parents and guardians of the children to be rescued accompanied us. Among them was Sita Ram, from Jamua village of Garhwa district in Bihar.

His son was a child slave in a carpet manufacturer's mill in Varanasi for the last two years. It was this father who gave us the primary information about a broker, who had duped many poor parents by paying advance money of ₹ 5,001 each and painting a rosy picture about the bright future of their children in the carpet industry. Armed with this fraudulent story, he had managed to whisk away 13 children.

With no news of their children, aside from there being no remittance, even after several months, the parents had gone looking for their children in Jagdishpur village, ready to return the advance money to secure their children's release. Several of the parents had raised a small amount of cash from loans with exorbitant interest rates, just to cover the cost of travel and other incidental expenses. The parents and guardians had not only been unsuccessful in getting their children back but were also humiliated and assaulted by their children's employers.

As soon as we reached the village, the loom owners along with hundreds of local people gathered and launched physical attacks on our team, not even sparing the media people who were present. The escorting police officials watched the enfolding scene like mute spectators. Despite this, we successfully rescued the 13 children from a dark and dank room nearby.

Unfortunately, when the time came to record statements, to our surprise, Sita Ram refused to recognise his own child, probably due to fear of a future attack from the goons of the loom owner. Even little Shanker did not identify his father. We were able to present all the rescued children at the District Magistrate's office only after herculean efforts on our part.

There the very same children and parents, who had been afraid to recognise one another in front of the loom owners, broke down in each other's arms. Sita Ram saw the hands of little Shankar and found that his fingers were burnt and deformed. The boy explained that while cutting the knots of the carpets using sharp and heavy knives, his fingers often got cut. The utterly inhumane employer used to dust the fingers with match powder and set them alight so that the blood, skin and flesh would stick together. This shocking and pre-medieval method demonstrates the sheer cruelty with which these children were treated.

Shanker is the name of the Supreme God of Hindus. He was even worshipped by Lord Rama. The house from where our little boy Shanker was rescued belonged to a local leader of the Bajrang Dal, an outfit of Hindu fundamentalists. There were big and bold writings on the walls of his house, repeating the slogan "Every child belongs to Rama and he is born for Rama's work". I ask you who are these hypocrites deceiving: the Gods or themselves?

Another incident etched in my memory took place in May 1993. We had conducted a raid in Ausanpur Village in the Allahabad District in Uttar Pradesh and liberated around 150 children from the faraway villages of Garwah, Palamau and Darbhanga in Bihar. These children were rescued after breaking open stuffy and poorly ventilated underground rooms. In the process, the police even confiscated a loaded gun from the mill owner.

Among these children was Tasleem, a boy of barely 6 or 7 years. I observed that after the rescue, he appeared to be numb to all human feelings. There was no trace of happiness nor sorrow on his visage. However, underneath his expressionless face, I could sense the agony of his little heart. I pulled him into my arms, hugged, and cajoled him to talk, and he eventually broke down. He recalled that one time, he had missed his mother and called out, weeping for her. The ruthless, irritated owner hit young Tasleem with a rod. After that incident, Tasleem no longer displayed his emotions.

After a three-day ordeal of producing the paperwork to legally free the children, we finally reached Tasleem's village. It was Eid, the Muslim celebration after the fasting month of Ramadan. His mother had stopped celebrating any festivals after she found out her kidnapped son was being kept as a slave for three years in a carpet factory. As if this misery was not enough, she lost her vision too. Ironically, Tasleem had been rescued from the hold of an influential Muslim religious leader. We were told that he had been actively involved in the Babri Masjid movement. I am haunted by the question of how long we can remain passive when humanity keeps getting sacrificed at the altar of religion?

The Blunt State of Laws

The fourth biggest hurdle in the way of the abolition of child labour is the ineffectiveness of the laws because they are fraught with loopholes and anomalies. For instance, in 1986, a separate law was enacted to prohibit child labour, with certain industries being classified as 'hazardous'. Twelve such industries were listed in this category. It is amply clear that anyone could employ any child in these industries by declaring him or her a brother, a sister, a son or a daughter.

In umpteen instances during our raids, employers have said that the children working there were their kith and kin. Even the children endorsed this statement out of fear. The carpet industry which has enslaved thousands of children continues to thrive on child labour even now, under the dubious garb of family businesses. The children have been given the seemingly official status of *Kishore Shilpi* (child artisans).

To circumvent the Indian Factory Laws, the employers conveniently scatter their units in villages instead of having them under one roof. How can work which is classified as 'hazardous', and hence forbidden for children, be permissible for one's own kith and kin? Is this not a mockery of the constitutional guarantee? The reality is that any form of child labour is against the ethos of humanity as this is a direct exploitation of children's physical and mental vulnerability, crushing all avenues for their growth and development.

The Bonded Labour (Abolition) Act (1976) provides that an officer of the rank of Sub-Divisional Magistrate is empowered to deal with the problems of bonded labour in his area. It is an open secret that very often, local politicians, industrialists and other bigwigs dictate the rules to these officers. The result is that the offences that ought to have been treated under the category of Child Bonded Labour are instead registered as a milder child labour case. The offender is let off the hook, despite his persistent abuse of the law. This is why offenders of child labour law or bonded labour law carry on their business freely, and fearlessly. Unfortunately, there is no law to book a negligent officer in whose jurisdiction this horrendous system is rampant. How can we seek protection for working children on the basis of weak and toothless laws?

Ignorance of Parents

One of the most immediate and obvious causes of child servitude is the stark ignorance of children and their parents. They have minimal awareness of the complex vicious circle of economic exploitation. The tragic part is that they are clueless about the impact and effects of child labour and the host of fatal diseases that often accompany it. This ignorance is perpetuated through an unfounded and well-contrived media plan, especially through government-controlled audio and Doordarshan (TV) that are distressingly mouthpieces of multinational companies and the ruling elite.

These two most popular electronic media go to any lengths to earn revenues to advertise for the sale and promotion of products, transcending all barriers of decency and decorum, and affecting, irreparably, cultural norms.

The issue of child labour does not figure in their scheme of things. Apart from the odd slogans of UNICEF, one can hardly come across any programme relevant to child rights in these media, although they have the universal reach to every nook and corner of the country. It is evidence of the deliberate denial of educating the unfortunate parents of disadvantaged children about the disastrous effects of child labour.

The Anti-Childhood Development

In the list of contributory factors that perpetuate child labour, lopsided development plans and government policies of developing countries take a prominent role. The first and prime casualties of thoughtless development projects are children. Their parents are compelled to migrate in search of employment, leaving their homes, fields and forests. Is it really development when migrating people are forced to survive on scum, with the security of the family disrupted?

An example of this catastrophe can be observed in Palamu in the state of Bihar, where Koyal Karo Dam stands as a monumental testimony to this. Due to the construction of this dam, a whopping 17,000 to 20,000 children were pushed into work as their parents were virtually uprooted lock, stock and barrel. In the case of Sardar Sarovar Dam, which includes the Narmada Dam, this figure is approximately a staggering 40,000.

Who are these countless children leading subhuman lives in the slums of the metropolis, picking up rags from the stinking garbage early in the morning, selling newspapers in the evening, cleaning the windscreens of the cars at road crossings and begging on the roadside? They are none but the victims of thoughtless developmental schemes.

Today, the issue that rocks the conscience of any sensible person is how these children cope with the challenge of the changing development priorities in the wake of the loan from the World Bank and IMF, which drives millions to flee and lose themselves in the wilderness of the cities, while pushing their children into the labour market. The first casualty in the race for capital generation and profit-oriented ultramodern technologies invariably will be the poor. These policies also open up avenues for cheap and risky employment to extract maximum profit with minimum input. Who is it that fits this mould? It is, of course, the children of the poor. It would be a sound prophetic declaration to say that only social sciences based on humanitarian values can guarantee the security of our children's childhood, and not the economic dogma of the free market.

Our Struggle Against Slavery

It would be worthwhile to briefly enumerate our accomplishments through our strategies and methodologies. In the 1980s, when we launched a crusade against bonded labour and child labour, not only were the government and non-government organisations (NGOs) not willing to hear our voices, but even our friends and families were in deep doubt. Against these odds, we were able to free a large number of bonded labourers, including child slaves, with the help of the Supreme Court of India.

With the passage of time, our movement gained momentum. Our strategies were unionising the disorganised labour in various industries, involving the news media for mass awareness and pressurising the enforcement agencies to take speedy action, among others. This approach is followed even now.

In those days, we became active in stone quarries, brick-kilns, the agricultural sector, construction, carpet, glass and bangle industries, etc. We succeeded in the rescue and release of over 25,000 child labourers and 20,000 adults from debt bondage. With persistent follow-up, we forced the sluggish and indifferent government machinery in various states to rehabilitate many of the released children under the central government-sponsored schemes. We created a model for the rehabilitation of the freed child labourers and adults, and gave them where relevant the necessary vocational and social skills training at Mukti Ashram. During this eventful time, many of our activists and I became victims of brutal physical attacks. Two of our senior colleagues were killed.

Our experience showed that children are the worst affected by the perpetuation of the gruesome system of bonded labour. Because of this finding, we recognised the urgent need to pursue the issue of child bondage, rampant in many industry sectors. We learnt that the conditions of children in labour were similar in most South Asian countries. This prompted us to hold the First Seminar on Child Labour in 1989 in Delhi involving South Asian NGOs, human rights organisations and trade unions to combat this menace jointly in the South Asian region. Thus, the South Asian Coalition on Child Servitude (SACCS) came into being with the initial strength of 60 organisations. It has now increased to 200 to date.

Consumer Awareness Campaign

During the early years of my work, I found out that thousands of people and children were employed in regularised as well as non-regularised carpet-making units in India. The magnitude of child labour increased proportionately with the rising demand for carpets abroad. We realised the urgent need to raise awareness amongst foreign consumers about the connection between child slavery and carpets.

As Germany held a major share of the European market for carpets, we used the country as a launch-pad. In 1990, we initiated a vigorous consumer campaign with the vociferous support of certain like-minded organisations. This soon spread to the United Kingdom, Sweden, France and the United States. Right from its inception, we had made it clear to the consumers, importers and exporters that we are not rooting for the decline of carpet exports. Our approach was to educate buyers not to buy products made by children and to guarantee that child labour is not involved. They should insist on a stipulated 'label' on the carpet that certifies the same before purchasing.

Here in India, a rare achievement of this campaign was the resolve of a group of 50 carpet manufacturers to come together and produce carpets without child labour. They formed the Carpet Manufacturers Association without Child Labour with several industry captains showing the inclination to join this group. Our sincere efforts, supported by the cooperation of carpet manufacturers, international organisations and experts helped in the formulation of a system with the label "Rugmark" to monitor and issue of labels indicative of child labour-free carpets.

A similar action plan is being attempted in the carpet industry of Nepal and the garment industry of Bangladesh where child labour is rampant.

The campaign won support from international leaders. Both in the Senate and Congress of United States, Senator Tom Harkin, Congressman George Brown and his colleagues introduced an epoch-making bill seeking a ban on the import of all products made by children. They also endorsed and stood in solidarity with our efforts. This became a shot in the arm for our movement.

We further arrived at the conclusion that the prerogative to certify whether an imported product is free of child labour should not just be limited to the importers and the government of that country. Instead, an independent professional body comprising various stakeholders, including NGOs from exporting countries should be empowered to do this certification. I held meetings with Senator Tom Harkin and colleagues of Congressman George Brown besides other legal luminaries, trade unions, human rights organisations, senior officials from the United States Department of Labour, to convince them to amend the Bill.

The pathbreaking achievement of SACCS lies in the worldwide attention it managed to garner on the issue of child labour, generating consumers' concern on the issue of child labour, and for the first time, having this issue acknowledged in the import-export business.

Mass Awareness

To educate the masses on the magnitude of the child labour problem and to pressurise the government to implement legal provisions granting rights to children, we took to sit-ins, rallies, meetings, protest marches, and street plays along with availing the help of the press and electronic media. One such rally was our 2,000-km-long march from Bihar to Delhi organised last year. This march passed through the most child labour-infested belts of Uttar Pradesh and touched millions of people from all walks of life. It was inspirational and its impact strengthened our future strategy.

Political Campaign

During this time, we realised the urgent need to bring the political parties over to our cause. We established contacts with scores of Members of Parliament (MPs) of both Houses in India and arranged meetings and debates on the issue. We urged them to take up the cause of these voiceless millions and apprised them of relevant facts and figures on which they could raise the question in the Parliament.

The 1993 Budget session was unique for the precise fact that, for the first time, the Parliament was rocked by questions on child labour. The subsequent sessions were also tense with questions on the callousness of the government in tackling child labour. Inspired by the response, we mooted the idea of forming a Parliamentary Forum on Children. Around 50 MPs, hailing from the different political parties agreed to be members of this Forum. The first meeting was held in April 1993 with 13 MPs, chaired by the erstwhile President of India, Gyani Zail Singh, where we formally established the Forum. The Forum is an ongoing process and its last meeting was held recently in May 1995.

In November 1993, after consultation with our associates, we resolved to launch a political campaign introducing the eradication of child labour as an electoral issue during the Assembly elections in Uttar Pradesh. We named this movement *Bachpan Bachao Andolan* (BBA – 'Save the Childhood Movement' in Hindi) and decided that similar campaigns should be launched in all parts of the country with complete vigour. The impact of the campaign was mammoth, with response from hundreds of NGOs and volunteer organisations, thousands of village chiefs and volunteers, etc., that helped reach millions of people directly.

For the campaign, we engaged about two thousand volunteers. These volunteers contacted the candidates contesting in the elections and gathered their opinion on the eradication of child labour and child slavery, and the provision of free and compulsory education to all children, among other issues. Their opinions were recorded and a signed pledge obtained from those who answered positively. Those who supported our cause were called 'Pro Childhood' and those who did not were categorised as 'Anti-Childhood' candidates. Their names were published in the local newspaper. Our volunteers contacted about 2,000 candidates from the political parties as well as independents, winning the attention of the masses through media, which highlighted this necessary but novel aspect. We now have 47 Members of the Legislative Assembly who are "pro childhood" out of 422 elected members. Thus, the BBA with its roots in our 14-year-old struggle emerged as a strong mass movement.

We call upon you to share the story of our movement, BBA, to whomever you can. You may be a labourer, an activist, a trade union member, a founder of a human rights outfit, an environmentalist or a writer, an intellectual, a lawyer, or a teacher, a doctor or a government official but if a child's rights are in any way usurped, it will have a direct bearing on his or her childhood. If we do not bother to restore the rights of children, our struggle would just be an economic and selfish endeavour, nothing more.

During our crusade, we felt that the trade unions that stood for the rights and privileges of the adult labour force could play a vital role in eradicating child labour. The prevalence of child labour reduces the bargaining power of adult labour, which, in turn, affects the entire trade union movement. We initiated steps to bring various trade unions under one platform to tackle this scourge of child labour. We convened a meeting in January 1994, wherein all the prominent trade union members actively participated and resolved to take up the issue of child labour jointly. Thus, a trade union forum against child labour was formed and the trade union members themselves also launched several projects on this.

Religious Forum

Religious leaders command immense respect among members of their faith. This influence, instead of being channelised for the good of mankind – which is the essence of every religion – gets misused to provoke communal frenzy. Children are believed to be images of divinity by every religion and we thought it imperative to mobilise the support of religious leaders and holy men in this crusade. A multi-religious congregation was organised in October 1994, attended by men of major faiths, with the result that a Multi-Religious Forum Against Child Labour was resolved to be formed.

Linkage with Other Movements

BBA as a movement is indirectly linked with all other movements against injustice, undemocratic systems, anti-human rights policies and human rights violations all over the world. We join in all these movements and endeavour to showcase, through them, the issue of child labour.

Let us take the case of the issue of minimum wage. As cheap child labour is still easily available, adult workers will not be able to get reasonable wages. Where parents do receive reasonable wages, we have to ensure that this money is not squandered away by gambling, smoking, drinking and other vices. So, our slogan became: 'Give minimum wages to adults. Wipe out child labour'.

It is obvious that the removal of child labour means the automatic opening of employment avenues for adults. Therefore, wherever there is any movement to agitate for employment guarantee and the right to work, our slogan became: 'Employment for every adult and education to every child'.

Let us discuss the problem of housing. We have seen that the majority of families, who do not have a roof over their heads, are those who have child labourers. In the developing countries, it is commonplace to see children born to poor parents in cities and those who migrated from villages due to anti-human rights policies or other calamities and spend their childhood on footpaths, in bus stations, and on railway platforms, etc. They are compelled to fulfil the demands of goons and police out of the little earnings they could manage. They also become victims of sexual exploitation, drug-pushing and trafficking and other anti-social elements. Our slogan here became: "Let there be a roof over each head, education for each child."

The denudation of jungles, and the submersion of agricultural land as a result of the construction of gigantic dams are also a cause for concern. Our point is that the green movement against the indiscriminate felling of trees, the protection of water sources, etc. are aimed at (indirectly) saving children from becoming helpless migrants, destitutes and children in bonded labour. We also support movements against disproportionate regional development and for giving more powers to the states. It is a tragedy that the natural and mineral resources of one region are being systematically exploited (neglecting the area's overall development) and pumped into the already developed region. In the process, children are sold and bought like domestic animals.

Many examples are visible, with the children of Chhattisgarh, Uttarakhand, Bundelkhand and so on, working in the palatial bungalows of the rich as domestic servants. This philosophy has been echoed in our slogan: 'Save Chhattisgarh – Save Childhood'.

Any sensible person would agree that a mother's role is cardinal in the upbringing of a child. It is impossible to ensure the protection of children's rights in a society where women are not treated on par with men and with respect. We have extended our support to feminist organisations, particularly for saving the girl child labourer from sexual abuse.

Our 'Save the Childhood' Movement has links with movements against unethical and lewd fashion shows, consumerism, and the promotion of tourism at the cost of culture and the environment, etc. It is crystal clear that the worst victims of these vicious activities are children. The cases of violence, rape, drug addiction, etc. are all mounting day after day. Another dreaded killer, AIDS, is a result of unprotected sex and unsafe sexual habits, with many children being born with this life-threatening disease. Countries like the Philippines, Thailand, Indonesia, Sri Lanka, and cities like Hong Kong among others, run sex industries to promote tourism, and pushing young boys and girls into the whirlpool of child sexual exploitation. It is not an exaggeration to say that of the total GNP of these countries, 10 to 15 percent arise from this source alone. In South Asian countries like India, Pakistan, Nepal and Bangladesh, this trend is catching up. Here our slogan is: 'Save childhood, stop violence and regressive cultural practices' and 'Stop sexual abuse to promote tourism – Save childhood'.

We have also joined the struggle against alcoholism and drug consumption because the ultimate victims of these vices are children. Hence, we proclaim: 'Quit drinking: Save childhood', 'Stop drug consumption: Save childhood'.

Sometimes countries with agro-based economies formulate schemes detrimental to children. The exorbitant prices of essential commodities, the deprivation of avenues of traditional employment, the migration from villages to cities and metros are some of the impacts of anti-poor and anti-agricultural schemes of the governments. We strongly advocate for just prices for agro-products, the proper and immediate implementation of land reforms, including the effective distribution of land to landless. Often, children and their childhood get trampled in the process of internal colonisation of villages by the urban elite. Our 'Save the Childhood' Movement will incorporate all these different facets.

The unfortunate nexus between casteism and communalism and the bondage of adults and children should also be mentioned here. We have seen that a majority of bonded labourers belong to Harijans and Other Backward Classes. Children are direct victims of untouchability, social backwardness and communal clashes. Before wisdom dawns on the realities of these caste-oriented problems, too many children are crushed.

How many children are orphaned by terrorists or communal fanatics everyday? Is it not a fact that these children grow in frustration and to wreak vengeance on the perpetrators of violence? Hence, we raise the slogan: 'Wipe out casteism and untouchability: Save Childhood', 'These children are offsprings of Ram and Rahim, Liberate them and bring good to the nation' and 'Of what use is the issue of temple or a mosque when the offsprings of both Ram and Rahim are slaves'.

We are convinced that the step-motherly treatment of government towards education is a prime reason behind the snail pace's progress in learning in Hindi-medium schools. The children of the ruling elite, industrial barons and businessmen send their children to ultra-modern, English-medium public schools by paying skyrocketing fees. On the other hand, children from backward sections in villages and cities learn under the open sky or in tents with broken and inferior furniture. There are no daily checks on the attendance of teachers. The dominance of English is still there in all spheres of growth and development, and students qualifying from Hindi-medium schools are mostly at a disadvantage. This is the result of deliberate negligence on the part of the government to instil the importance of English in the curriculum. Hence, we support the movements against this dual-faced educational policy.

The last thing that I would categorically emphasise is that we always have to ensure a yardstick for every movement and its achievements. Our assessment of the movement's impact lies in assessing whether the benefits have percolated down to the children of various deprived and backward sections of society. If the answer is 'no', we posit that the whole exercise was myopic and selfish, or even self-annihilating. We hereby ensure that only a righteous and judicious movement will have a link with the 'Save the Childhood Movement'.

□

Children and Democracy

The life-philosophy of Kailash Satyarthiji is the philosophy of creating a child-friendly society. In his opinion, childhood is not merely about age, but a value integral to life that keeps us simple, spontaneous and transparent. Many people either take pity on children or use them for their own benefit. To creating a developed, safe and better world, Shri Satyarthi emphasises the creation of a child-friendly society, a successful experiment of his which is transforming hundreds of villages across the country into Bal Mitra Grams (child-friendly villages). The mission to create more and more Bal Mitra Grams is ongoing. In these villages, basic but effective changes have been introduced: inclusive of democracy, the involvement and leadership of children, child-centric development programme, the end of child exploitation, ensuring education for all children and equality of boys and girls, among others. He had written this extensive article on the ideological background and practical processes involved. Originally published in January 2011, it is published here with some edits.

—Editor

This is an incident from the year 2001. We were having a meeting with villagers at Navrangpura village in Jaipur District in Rajasthan. Almost all children, women and men of the village were present. Perhaps it was the first time that a meeting like this had taken place there. *Bachpan Bachao*

Andolan initiated the *Bal Mitra Gram* programme in this village as an experiment, the year before. Both the common folks along with the local *Gram Panchayat* and *Bal Panchayat*, had come together after the successful election of the *Bal Panchayat*. A 12-year-old girl, Hemlata, was present at the meeting as a representative of the *Bal Panchayat*. I asked her what differences she has noticed in the village as a result of the *Bal Mitra Gram*. After thinking for a few minutes, she replied, somewhat sheepishly, "First and foremost, a change can be seen in that a girl like me is speaking on the mic and such a large number of women are sitting here without the *Ghoonghat* (veil)." The village elderly also took part in this meeting and yet women were sitting on the dais. I probed further, "Tell us if you had experienced some changes in your own life too?" Hemlata was thoughtful for a while and then answered, "These days, when my mother asks my father what vegetables she should cook for lunch, my father says that she can decide for herself or to ask me."

This was not an everyday incident for me. I am aware that in this remote village of Rajasthan and in millions of villages and cities in our country, even the simplest thing such as the menu of the day is decided by the men of the house. Since Hemlata was speaking on the microphone, I asked the same question to the audience present there. I was taken by surprise and an overwhelming sense of pleasure when most of the people said, "Even children have opinions of their own. So, we have started involving them in decision-making." So far I had not seen or known of a village where children had the right to speak their mind. It was a blessing to see our philosophy take a concrete shape.

In India, 50 to 60 million children are engaged in child labour. Almost the same number of children or probably even the same children are deprived of education, thus doomed to be stuck in the vicious circle of poverty. More than 70 percent of such children live in villages. Gandhi*ji* used to say, "The soul of India dwells in the villages." In my opinion, this soul actually dwells in children of those villages, especially in girls of underprivileged, oppressed, deprived and minority groups, who are labouring in the fields instead of going to school. For me, Hemlata's freedom is definitely a benign attempt to awaken the soul of India.

We had an unplanned encounter with Hemlata again after a little more them a year. This time, when I met her, she was protecting against her *dada-dadi* (grandparents), *mama* (maternal uncle) and *bua-fufa* (aunty-uncle) because they were trying to marry her off at the tender age of 13 or 14. Her parents were not in favour, but Hemlata's marriage was fixed with a boy in her extended family at the early age of 5 or 6, and now her parents were scared because calling off this marriage would be perceived socially as breaking a promise.

This village had the incidents of child marriages. This illegal, anti-human and anti-women practice is an esteemed norm in Indian society. Amidst all this, Hemlata's rebellion was a distinctly extraordinary incident. Our *Bal Mitra Gram* workers helped Hemlata with the support of local people. Other girls of the village, teachers and youths got involved in this campaign. At last Hemlata defeated the age-old rotten custom: Her marriage was called off. This became one of the rarest of the rare incidents when a girl child in a village protested against her elders, and refused to get married.

Children: An Eternal Source of Energy

Zainab, Anand, Raziya, Pooja, Sajida, Gayatri, Rajkumari, Premlata, Rajni, Prem Pratap, Priyanka and Lali: dozens of such names and faces come to my mind, who might dwarf many activists like me. They are the children who fought their own battle against the traditions of an orthodox society and feudal system. With their work, they have demonstrated that the adage "Children are the future of a nation," is an incomplete one. The truth is that children are also the present of a country.

Several of these children struggled and got child labourers in their area freed, and also sought admission for them in schools. Others raised the issues of the lack of teachers in schools, to have separate toilets for female students, highlighted irregularities in the mid-day meal scheme, the lack of clean drinking water, library, boundary walls, lack of proper classrooms and the matter of asking for more funds under the pretext of school fees from students. They were successful in their advocacy work. These children are the most valued partners of the *Bal Mitra Gram Nirman* campaign run by BBA. A programme to convert 317 villages to the *Bal Mitra Gram* model is currently on. Most of them have already been converted, 80 are in the process. Credit for this goes to our rural workers, who made this idea a reality by empowering the rural community and children of the village.

Fifteen-year-old *Bal Panchayat* leader Santosh, who belongs to Jagatpura in Jaipur, set an incredible example. Until the age of 11 or 12, Santosh was a child labourer, cleaning and mopping nearby homes. When Jagatpura was chosen to be converted into a *Bal Mitra Gram*, not even a single girl from that village used to attend school. Our workers spread social awareness against the evil of child labour in the villages. Santosh listened keenly to this call to action. She told her parents that she will not go to work from tomorrow and was adamant about it. Her parents tried to persuade and tricked her by saying that she was answerable to her employers, but she did not give in. At last, the rebellious child won.

The biggest challenge Santosh now had was to get enrolled in a school because she neither had a birth certificate nor any other official document. After a long struggle and with the help of workers from our movement, she gained admission into a school. Better late than never; a new Santosh had been born. It was akin to the incarnation of Goddess Durga to end the exploitation and illiteracy of children. No one can say when or how she decided that none of the girls in the entire Jangpura will labour and each one will go to school. Now Santosh is a leader and our activists are following her lead. No house in the slum, no hut, no street or bylane was out of her reach now. Santosh untiringly tried to convince children and their parents to stop sending them to work and to let them attend school. She has devoted all her time to it, she starts before her parents wake up and works till late when her parents have already slept. She used to visit those households who hired child labour and warned them that if they would not free the child, they will end up in jail.

Santosh was very clever. During her campaign, she always carried pamphlets and leaflets of BBA in which the provisions of punishments were mentioned in bold letters. Although it took Santosh two to three years, finally her hard work reaped success. She had removed 161 girls and boys from child labour, mainly rag-picking work, and got them enrolled in a school. In 2005, during the World Congress on Child Labour and Education, Santosh narrated her story of struggle and success in front of the then Union Education Minister of India and various representatives of different countries and they all had goosebumps listening to her.

It goes back to 2009. At the Gandhi Darshan Bhawan, Rajghat in New Delhi, the *Rashtriya Bal Mahapanchayat* of *Bal Mitra Gram* was being held. Almost 150 representatives of *Bal Panchayat*s were present. The Chief Guest for that event was a Supreme Court Justice, Dr. A.K. Sharma. Excited children were telling the stories of their struggles, successes and achievements. We were all surprised along with Justice Dr. A.K. Sharma. It was taking a long while to listen to their stories individually. I requested the children to raise their hands to respond to stories as a group. Among the children leaders, 45 of them raised their hands when asked how many had got more than 300 children to leave their jobs as child labourers and enrolled in school in the last one year. It is worth mentioning here that during this period, more than 4,000 children were removed from child labour and enrolled in schools. Eighty-one children were successful in getting new toilets constructed in their schools, out of which most were used by girls. Forty-nine children managed to make clean drinking water available in their schools, and there were three brave students who were successful in calling off the child marriage custom in their villages.

The story of the 2010 *Bal Mahapanchayat* is no less inspiring. When I asked children to raise their hands to account for different accomplishments during our *Mahapanchayat* at Rajasthan and, later on, asked them to narrate their stories, one by one. It was like the whole auditorium was brimming with a strange excitement. It was just an unforgettable experience to me to witness the enthusiasm in those kids to tell me their story before their friends. Be it the children from Jharkhand, tribals from remote areas or children from Muslim villages of Meerut, from backward and underprivileged population of Bihar, or from the hilly villages of Rajasthan, no one was ready to fall behind the others. Especially the younger girls. They appeared innocent and shy, but inside each of them was a little dynamo. No matter if their individual stories would not earn them a place in history, but these are such indelible footprints in the history for the protection of children's right that will facilitate the journey ahead for our country, and the world at large.

The 66 children present there had pulled another 600 children out of child labour and enrolled them in schools. Fifteen of those children struggled with their school administration to get the toilets installed in school premises, 18 were successful in making the clean drinking water available in their schools. Another 15 were there whose efforts helped in the construction of new school buildings or in the addition of new classrooms in the schools.

Out of these children, six were successful in upgrading their primary schools to the intermediate and high-school level. Two child leaders took action to get extra teachers appointed in their schools and three children were successful in persuading the authorities to distribute free books to children under a government scheme. Two of the children not only stopped the illegal collection of undue fees from students but also managed to get all such forcibly accumulated fees returned to the parents. One of them also stopped a child marriage taking place in his/her village. All these achievements were earned by our children in the span of a single year, between 2009 and 2010.

The Need for the Creation of Bal Mitra Gram

All said and done, what is this *Bal Mitra Gram* all about? Why was there a need to create them? How are they being created? And what is BBA's vision for it? It is very important for all the activists and leaders of our movement to know the answers to these questions. First of all, we will discuss why BBA needed to create the *Bal Mitra Gram* and when this need arose.

Quest for New Strategies; Guerrilla Actions for Freedom

Our campaign against bonded labour and child labour started in 1980. Today we are exercising many strategies. The very first strategy, which was the need of the hour, was conducting raids or guerrilla action. Wasal Khan, father of a 14- or15-year-old girl Sabo, along with several other families were taken to Punjab from Uttar Pradesh by some brokers, around 17 years ago. These families were sold to several families who owned brick-making plants. For 17 long years, the poor families worked as bonded labour just for the need of daily food. Many other children along with Sabo were born there and absorbed into the work of brick-making. But this was not an end to their tyranny. One day, Wasal

Khan learnt about his master's plan to sell his daughter to a brothel. Somehow he managed to escape from the plant. During those days, we were publishing a magazine *Sangharsh Jaari Rahega* to give a voice to the underdogs and the unprivileged sections of society. By chance, an anonymous reader of that magazine helped Wasal reach us. Understanding the gravity of the situation, we decided that mere documentation would not help him. We planned a raid to get Sabo and the other bonded labourers freed. In the first instance, it was unsuccessful. We came back beaten and defeated. But somehow, at the end, we got them all freed. This is where our movement started. There was no organisation in place then. This incident and several other similar incidents pointed to the need for an organisation for this purpose.

Initially, our organisation was named *'Bandhua Mukti Abhiyan Samiti'*. Several other names were given and then withdrawn. With growing work and fame of the organisation, the ambitions of several senior allies started rising. The political parties also used such ambitious people which resulted in many ups and downs, and splits within the organisation. Despite all this, BBA never compromised with its ideology and character. We used to get complaints and leads from parents and other sources, and based on this information, we used to raid places or plan guerrilla actions. Since India has a proper law to prevent bonded labour since 1976, we try in all cases, that the children can be removed from bonded labour under that law. This law has provisions for punishment of the plant owners, as well as rehabilitation for the children. Raiding a plant or factory has other advantages too. This spreads the message among other business owners and home owners in that area who put children into bonded labour. It also leverages the media well which helps in spreading awareness about bonded child labour and child labour, in general. Third, the children who are liberated, return to their villages and tell their stories to other villagers, and thus the community becomes alert to the threat of brokers and child traffickers to protect their children.

The only successful way to attain freedom for those children who become the victim of child-trafficking and bonded labour is the raiding strategy. Since 1981, a total of 78,000 children have been freed by employing this strategy.

Creation of Unions

In the beginning, most of the men, women and their children were rescued from brick plants and quarries. Brokers used to take a large number of families and later sold them to the owners of quarries and brick plants as bonded labourers. The lack of information and awareness in society, the complicity of government officers with these plant owners, the laxity of the judiciary, there being no rehabilitation facilities for children who escape or get rescued, and above all, due to our own limitations, it was not possible for us to get hundreds of families freed by raiding. These conditions led us to a new idea: the formation of labour unions in quarries and brick-making plants. All child and bonded labour came from the unorganised sector where no labour law was applied. Labourers do not even know about their rights. Even the law on minimum wages was unknown to them.

The problem of child labour and bonded labour is not usually prevalent in the organised sector. In 1982, we created the first quarry labour union in Faridabad, which was later given a national structure. In the same year, we started labour unions in brick-making plants. We faced serious resistance and violent attacks from criminal owners. Among our old friends, perhaps there is no one who did not have scars on their bodies from that period. Our office was set on fire. Our colleagues Dhoomdas and Aadarsh Kishore attained martyrdom during such struggles.

The impact of both these unions was very favourable. Labourers became aware of their rights, and with that, started demanding education and healthcare for their children too. Sit-down strikes, protests, processions, strikes: everything was done. As a result, for the first time in the country, a minimum wage rate was set for quarry workers and labourers working in brick-making plants. Prior to this, everything was done as per the will of the owners. Once the minimum wages and other legal provisions were implemented, the foremost priority of the labourers was to get school education for their children. The union itself started twelve schools. Later, the government started allocating budgets for these schools. In Faridabad, Gurgaon (now Gurugram) in the state of Haryana, and Ramganj Mandi in Rajasthan, almost all children were enrolled in schools.

Support of the Judiciary

All this time, we felt that the courts of justice in the country and the numerous legal processes have not proved helpful to the interests of the poor, especially in the case of labourers from the unorganised sectors. We learned two lessons from this, which gradually turned into future strategies. First, generate sensitivity at the highest level, meaning at the level of the Supreme Court and High Court and ensure that the system is active. Second, raise a movement against child labour and bonded labour. We are one of the pioneers of the Public Interest Litigation (PIL). We were the first to introduce this approach to obtain justice for bonded and child labour. We sought the intercession of the Supreme Court in various cases from brick-making plants, placement agencies, quarries, the slate-pencil industry of Mandsaur, the carpet industry of Uttar Pradesh to the matchbox industry of Tamil Nadu, and bagged some landmark decisions in legal history. Even today, BBA is a trailblazer in leveraging the judiciary in various cases.

In 2010, the Chief Justice of the Supreme Court took an important step. For the first time in the country, the National Legal Services Authority (NALSA) and BBA together opened a children's cell, which is governed by the National Headquarters of BBA.

Need for a Movement

Our organisation has always been committed towards the movement. Our priority has been to enable the children, who have been victims of child labour, to handle their own leadership. We believe that the organisation should help them to cope with their pain, angst and shape their creativity, but the children and parents should go ahead and grab their rights at every stage. Our movement initiated many campaigns to attract the lay public, apart from the victims, and these campaigns are still running, both in villages and in the cities.

In 1994 from Palamu in Bihar (now Jharkhand) to Delhi, in 1995 from Kanyakumari to Delhi, in 1996 from Kolkata to Kathmandu, we marched to protest against child labour and this created waves throughout the country. Due to this, child labour emerged as a burning issue on the political horizon. In 1998, a global march against child labour, and in 2001, a march to campaign for education also proved successful, and with this, we attempted to give this issue a high-level signature such that the scourge of child labour cannot just be wiped away. This is a social evil, legally a crime, an obstacle to development and a mental bondage which certainly calls for an extensive movement.

BBA has been doing various innovative things, apart from strengthening its movement, by marching thousands of miles for the cause. We have always known that Shankaracharyas, Mahanths, imams, churchmen, saints, Jatthedars, monks, religious preachers have greater access to, and a hold on common people than voluntary organisations. The movement made various efforts to attract them to our cause. In 1994, a conference of major religious leaders against child labour was held in Delhi. It was a very successful event. All the religious leaders collectively signed a manifesto against child labour. Such events were organised at the local level as well in various locations.

It is remarkable that BBA had initiated efforts to attract all the national labour unions to stand together against child labour. In 1994 and 1995, we played our role in sensitising these trade unions against child labour and made them active by organising numerous successful conferences. In the same way, we initiated activities towards a common platform of non-government organisations, as a result of which, firstly, the South Asian Organisation Against Child Labour was formed and then the grand alliance called Global March Against Child Labour was created.

Consumer Awareness Campaign and Responsibility of the Corporate Sector

We discovered another strategy during the creation and development of our movement. We saw that national and international consumers extensively used items made by children, like firecrackers by Sivakasi or carpets from Mirzapur-Bhadohi. Many consumers are actually filled with human compassion but they are not aware that the shoes, clothes or edible items they are consuming have been made from the blood and sweat of an innocent child. Neither do they know any alternatives to these utilitarian items. On the other hand, there is a long chain of local contractors, brokers, supply producers, national companies, agents, foreign importers and sellers, which is difficult to break.

Every single link in this supply chain is not only getting richer with free or cheap child labour, but also getting stronger financially by accumulating black money. It needs a stick from both the demand and supply sides. On the supply side, legal proceedings should be initiated against such companies, and on the demand side, consumers should be made aware of and sensitive to the issue of child labour, and to take action so that pressure can be built on the corporate sector to increase accountability. To achieve this, BBA started a consumer awareness movement in the 1990s. This spread pretty fast and gave way to a new discussion on the 'social responsibility of the corporate sector'. It also created a sense of moral responsibility in consumers.

This strategy was most successful in the carpet-manufacturing industry at the international level, whereas on the national level, it was equally effective vis-à-vis the firecracker industry. More than two-thirds of total carpet-manufacturing is done in India, Pakistan and Nepal, which is mostly exported to Western countries. An awareness campaign for child labour-free carpets was started in 1990. Soon there began a storm of demand for such carpets, which guaranteed that its manufacture did not involve any child labour. It was a big challenge that we faced. Sometime in 1995, along with many national and international organisations, we were successful in discovering a method that could guarantee it. A label named 'Rugmark' was started. The organisation behind 'Rugmark' was given the authority to monitor every aspect of carpet manufacture, to issue licenses to such manufacturers who were committed to manufacturing carpets that did not involve any form of child labour, and after the certification of such carpets, a 'Rugmark' seal was placed on each carpet. It was the first label in the world of this kind, viz. certifying that a product was child labour free. With this example, many countries of the world came to learn new ideas for the labelling of ethical production of goods. It would be remarkable to quote here that all these strategies, especially the strategy to raise awareness and put pressure on consumers impacted the carpet industry of South Asia, wherein the number of child labourers decreased from 1 million to about 200,000. Thus, tens of thousands of children were freed from labour and bondage, with a similar number of adults getting jobs.

In India, children have been working in the firecracker industry from Sivakasi and Virudnagar to Sattoor in the state of Tamil Nadu. As a result of our movement, the number of child labourers in these places has also been reduced to an insignificant number. Our movement had successfully run a campaign in the 1990s to boycott fireworks on Diwali, the Hindu festival of lights, and other occasions in more than 10,000 schools in India. Tens of thousands of students boycotted fireworks by following the slogan "Light the *diyas* (candles) to celebrate Diwali, don't burn childhood." Consequently, even giant companies had to disengage from using child labour in factories and had to advertise extensively that they were not in favour of child labour.

Even today, BBA is playing its pioneering role in this direction. Be it in the textile industry, the mining of mica, the carpets industry or any other industry, we are active everywhere.

Initiative of Rehabilitation

The rehabilitation of children who were removed by direct action or by other efforts remained the biggest challenge. And rehabilitation of such a kind was needed that could connect these children to the mainstream in society and education. At the same time, we also had to ensure that these children did not get caught again in the cycle of child labour, poverty and illiteracy. To take on these challenges, we persuaded the government to take responsibility for the process of rehabilitation of these freed child labourers. Non-governmental organisations could also provide some support or set an example, but at the end, it is mainly the responsibility of the government. As a result of our efforts, the Central and State Governments started many rehabilitation programmes for bonded labourers. These programmes had been successful to an extent in the case of bonded labour, but the government had yet to come up with a solid rehabilitation scheme for child labourers in general.

The movement has taken efforts to provide immediate protection and partial rehabilitation by establishing *Swayam Mukti Ashram*, *Balika Ashram* (Girls' Home) and *Bal Ashram* (Children's Home). During the last two years, tens of thousands of students have benefitted from this. BBA has always sought to ensure that government aid should reach the right persons. This even includes reaching out to the judiciary time and again. Only then have we been able to distribute the benefits of the millions of rupees under government schemes to the tens of thousands of children rescued from child labour.

Child Labour and Villages

We in the movement have always felt that whether it is the areas fraught with child labour, or sources of child trafficking, or the challenges of rehabilitating these children, we mostly have to deal with rural areas. The vicious cycle of illiteracy, poverty and child labour is also crystal-clear if seen in the light of this. This is like a chicken-and-egg situation, that is, a relationship of cause-and-effect. In villages, people still believe that if children of poor people would not work, then they will either famish or become a thief. In a nutshell, they believe that child labour is their destiny. On the other hand, centuries-old casteism and fatalism have strengthened the roots of mental bondage. Many of the poor believe that it is the sin of their previous life or their ill-fortune that has made them poor or the reason why they have been born into a lower caste. Thus, it is not at all something out of the ordinary for them if their children get into child labour. This is not torture to them. And this mentality is even more shameful in the case of girls.

Altogether, it is very common for poor children to work in fields, and take the cattle, buffaloes and goats to graze. Due to the government's efforts in recent years, children have been enrolled in schools, for sure. But the same children either work in fields or at home, or work as bonded labour in a factory or mine as a victim of child-trafficking. In many cases, the names enrolled in schools are found to be fake. It is noteworthy that infrastructure for schools is spreading with great speed in villages. But the lack of teachers, the absence of school buildings and/or the decrepit conditions of the school buildings, the casteist, narrow-minded or feudal mentality of the teachers, the lack of good pedagogy, the lack of the feelings of respect and friendliness towards children, especially the girl-child and many other related issues are the reason that estrange the children of poor families from government schools. For richer children and even for the children of teachers, there is a mushrooming of expensive shops of education in the form of private English-medium schools. We have accepted all such issues as challenges and have begun to think about ways to nevertheless, reach the lowest units of society.

Four Kinds of Relationships with Children

Usually, not only humans but even animals take care of their offspring and give them affection. For their progeny, parents do not leave any stones unturned. But in most cases, it is limited to our own biological children. Right from one's lifestyle, psychology, sense of responsibility, parents' hard-earned money, to corruption and scams, many cases are linked to children. Amongst the wealthy, especially the nouveau riche, this affection, if unbridled, creates serious problems, such as a distorted consumerist mentality, unhealthy competition, carelessness, revenge and feelings of violence or excessive mental pressure and frustration. We see ever-increasing cases of road accidents by youngsters, habit of intoxication, violence and even rape. On the other hand, children get increasingly frustrated from not excelling in examinations, in singing or dancing competitions or in sports. Several children even commit suicide. All this is a result of improper and excessive affection, and the unreasonable expectations of children.

Now let us look at another kind of relationship. Across the world, good and noble people practise kindness towards children. They give them alms and feel satisfied, whilst others provide them with medicine, clothes or food and think they have done their bit for these children's welfare. Others open schools or orphanages or donate to such institutions, or help them in material kind. In contrast, a third category of people never fail to exploit the tenderness of a child's heart and body. Especially in the case of poor children, the mentality of these people can be said to have been negative right from their childhood. They treat children as a means of exploitation. The outcome is in front of us: Thousands of children disappear like inanimate objects; hundreds and thousands of girls go through the traumatic experience of rape and sexual harassment. Numerous children are bought and sold at a price lower than cattle. Millions of children are pushed into child labour and bonded labour. The organs of child-trafficking victims, are sold domestically or abroad at very high prices. Whether in the hot summer months of May to June or the chilly nights of December to January, criminal gangs force these children to beg at traffic signals, religious places and railway stations. Many children are mutilated so that they may arouse compassion in people and procure more money.

What could be more shameful than this that young children are engaged in manufacturing football, cricket and other sports gear. While making footballs, not a day passes when their tender, little fingers do not bleed from stitching these balls constantly for 12 to 14 hours. In Meerut and Jalandhar, I have met many such young children whose most cherished dream was to kick a football someday and play with it. In Mandsaur and Markapur, many kids who were engaged in manufacturing slate dreamt about learning to how to write the letters "A, B, C, D" and so on a slate board with chalk. Hundreds of thousands of children are involved in carpet-manufacturing. They do magnificent *zardozi* ('gold filigree' in Hindi) embroidery on cloth. They make various things like bags, purses, shoes, belts, caps and what not. These things are sold in the fashion houses of New York and London at prices one cannot even imagine. But these children and their families do not get enough clothes to cover their bodies, let alone shelter from rain and heat.

Like the stones and pebbles that are used in the construction of roads and bridges, the childhood and future of many children are shattered into pieces. These children never get to ride even a bicycle on these roads and bridges. Making bricks in the brick-making kiln, their blood turns black already in childhood, where the strength of each brick incinerates the nervous system of a child. These children do not live in a house like ours, made of bricks and mortar. While celebrating the festivals of Diwali and Dussehra, marriages, birthdays, the electoral wins of politicians, etc., we enjoy colourful fireworks. But we forget that even a small careless mistake whilst making these incendiary devices turns a child's body into flying pieces of explosives. The lives of these children are pushed into the dark, who ironically manufacture the bulbs we light in our homes as their little bodies are ruined by the fumes of molten lead.

This is happening all around us and we are looking away despite witnessing it with our naked eyes, much less be bothered by their plight. Most of us come under this fourth category of insensitive people, devoid of concerns and hypocritical. A category which has the greatest number of people in it. Those filled with incompetence, selfishness and false ego.

A Friendly Relationship with Children

In general, it is evident that adults have not been able to develop a healthy relationship towards children. A sense of fairness towards children seems a far cry. In an environment where there are unreasonable expectations, over-affection, kindness and charity, but mixed in with the exploitation, insensitiveness and apathy towards children, it seems strange to talk about friendliness with children. However, friendship means faith in one another and mutual respect, will power to learn from one another, the courage to talk openly, a feeling of happiness in helping each other, etc. Just think how many of us are out there who not just love or dote on children, but respect them too. Not only show them off but actually have faith in their abilities. Think honestly: How many times have you shown courage to learn something from them? What kind of relationship do you have with them?

In our society today, childhood is considered a synonym for folly and foolishness. When elders make any mistakes, in refined language, instead of calling them foolish, we call their behaviour 'childish' or we say that the 'person has still not gained his maturity'. When an elderly person has achieved something outstanding, we do not hear people complimenting the person saying,"Bravo! What a childish thing you did." Our mentality is shaped from the thought that children are ignorant, foolish or silly or naughty, while all the elders are learned or wise. We are made to learn this from our childhood to our deaths. These are the values we inherit.

Our mental journey starts with a full stop, not a question mark. It starts from agreeing, not learning or knowing. For millennia, we have imbibed that what our religion or the sciences teach is the only truth. We forget that religion and the sciences both seem different, with both based on facts or statements collected to support hypotheses and values. This means that what someone else has created in his or her mind, or what someone else has discovered, we take it to be the truth without any investigations from our end. Our knowledge does not inspire us to know more but is satisfied by teaching others. We want to pour our readymade ideas into others' heads what we believe to be true. Whether we have agreed to it because it has been said by a *pandit*

(Hindu Priest) or by Christ. Whether we agree to it because of Darwin's experiments or because of our teachers' chastisement, at last, we have to agree.

With the so-called information, knowledge and the pouring of others' beliefs into our minds, we are filled with a false vanity. Under such conditions, how are we to develop a friendly relationship with kids whose minds have not been abused by any *pujari* or *mullah* (Muslim cleric) or by those who in the name of science are promoting the commercial consumerism of technology.

We have developed such a relationship with children as if they have just started learning to walk up the stairs to the first floor as if their learning has just begun, while we think of ourselves to already be on the 10th or 12th floor of a 25-floor-storeyed building. How can our hands clap with such distance between us? How can we walk together? I do realise that I might sound rather strange but please look inside yourselves for once, for the truth. How can we then approach children with a message of friendship?

In the Indian society, we exemplify the friendship between Krishna and Sudama. Krishna was a king and Sudama was a very poor fellow who was not able to make both ends meet. Sudama was persuaded by his wife to meet Krishna. When he did so, Krishna treated him as his equal. He made his friend Sudama sit on his throne, washed his feet and applied ointment on his cracked feet. Without saying anything, he did some magic and Sudama's house was changed into a palace. If Krishna's wife had not stopped him, then perhaps Krishna would have become Sudama and Sudama would have become Krishna. This friendship was not based on charity but respect. There was no place for vanity; rather a deep sense of equality. In this story, Krishna rose from his throne and rushed to the gate to welcome his friend, whilst we sit on our chairs and children sit on the ground below us. Degrees of status we hold: the chairs of offices we are holding, our seating plans which symbolise our relations. There are such numerous layers that take us away from our children. How many of us can actually gather the courage to get down from these chairs while meeting children and stand on the same ground where they are standing? If we cannot do this, then what kind of friendship can we have with them?

This is very difficult to practise. It is not easy to discard all accumulated knowledge, wisdom, customs, faith, etc. from one's mind, especially when one meets those who we might regard as ignorant and silly.

Where are Children's Rights?

Now I will discuss another issue that has already been mentioned previously – children's rights. The understanding of rights is preserved in the law. This means a system which can bring justice to those who are deprived of it. Social institutions, governments and international organisations have provided many solutions to bring about harmony and equality in society. One of these solutions is human rights and, another, the formulation of children's rights. The manifesto of human rights was prepared to take on the challenges that were brought about due to the political and human discordance after the Second World War and it was recognised in all countries. It encompassed the right of all men, women and children across the world. After forty years, a separate document on children's rights came into being. It was named the Convention on the Rights of the Child (CRC).

Actually, the formulation of rights and their promulgation into law is a very difficult work. It is a delphic task of settling the contradictions of thousand-year-old traditions, beliefs, dogmas, mentalities, political systems, economic pressures and greed, etc. and in the process, give shape to a just and equal philosophy and provisioning for its legal status. That is why, it is very difficult to create national or international laws for the interests of children, women, and the poor. To implement them is a bigger challenge, especially when they are related to legal rights.

This is the reason there is always a gap between society and human rights. Those whose rights are taken away, they are not empowered to leverage the law, whilst the exploiters are, in contrast, proficient enough to deal with the law and judiciary as per their interests.

This is what happened to children's rights. It is useless to expect from ordinary children to be aware of their rights but to carry this message to their parents and numerous poverty-stricken people was an even greater challenge. The children's rights recipe was served with many tweaks and flavours in the 1990s. Intellectuals, researchers, analysts, sociology departments of universities, child welfare departments of governments and NGOs have suddenly revitalised, making fortunes. Many national and international seminars and conferences were organised. Many new organisations came into existence. Millions of pages were written on the subject matter of children's rights. But the basic issue was there in its basic shape. Where was 12-year-old carpet-maker Nageshwar amongst all this hoopla, who was burnt with crackers on the day of the Hindu festival of lights, Diwali? When I took Nageshwar to the hospital, he had burns on 70 percent of his body. Even the doctors cursed the legal and constitutional system of our country. Nageshwar's only fault was that he was trying to escape from a carpet manufacturer who was busy celebrating Diwali. Where were these documents of children's rights when 14-year-old Gulabo died in my arms crying for help? She was just a child who worked at a quarry and had severe tuberculosis. Seminars, conferences and trainings were still going on, and on. But, in the midst of all this, at Bilaspur of the state of the then Madhya Pradesh, houses of *satnamis* were set on fire by upper caste mobs, just because they dared to send their children to the same schools where children of upper castes were studying.

I am not negating the efforts made for children's rights, nor do I want to ignore or disrespect them. But I am talking about conscience, and the hollowness of the idea of translating these into the affected children's lives, by all those who purport to help them. Rights and laws are not only limited to books. It is important to translate them into our lifestyle, our civilisation and culture. It is one thing to talk about the rights of children but quite another to live it each moment in our communication, lives and daily routines. First, we will all need to take a deep look at ourselves and realise that we either only just talk about children's rights or we try to live that way.

The Concept of Children's Rights and the Real Face of Villages

The discussion over children's rights in the context of Indian villages is an unsolved riddle. Parents, teachers, neighbours, relatives, employers of child labour, doctors in hospitals, bus drivers, conductors, etc. are a few of those people who come in close contact with children. Hardly anyone among them possesses formal knowledge of children's rights. People seldom employ a friendly, dignified approach when dealing with children. Growth opportunities, education and health benefits to every child, letting children have a say in matters related to them, ensuring their participation in development, and children having a right to lead a respectable life, etc. are a few things that are not considered their rights *per se*. Some of these points are deemed to be the prerogative of the ruling government and the concept of children participating and voicing their own rights are regarded as paradoxical to social mindset and traditions. The matters related to education, health, etc. are like legacies or playthings of government officials, *panchayat*s (Village council), headmasters, doctors, etc. Again, children's participation in decision-making and referenda are a few of those ideas that do not have any place in our traditions and mindsets.

Girls are still considered a burden in our society. Therefore, some of them are killed before they are even born, whilst some are killed after their births. The birth of a boy is announced by beating plates and *dhols* while the arrival of a girl child is declared by breaking a clay pot outside the house. For those alien to Hindu culture, clay pots are also broken when in mourning. Food is served to the men and boys first, and the girls and women survive on leftovers. Girls do not enjoy the freedom of hanging around and playing like the boys do. But yes, it is definitely their responsibility to walk miles and bring drinking water, fodder for animals and wood for fuel, carrying vessels on their heads. Instead of encouraging them to study, the girls are groomed from an early age for marriage and life in their in-laws' home. The teenaged girls, who fail to get married fast, are forced to live a life of stigma. These girls are deprived of education and freedom, and hence they are left with no choice but to spend their cursed lives in the daily grind of domestic chores.

Alcohol addiction in poor fathers has an impact on children's lives. The fathers, who borrow money for satisfying their addiction or for spending on wedding celebrations, funerals or festivals, push their children into working as bonded labourers. Overall, the welfare of these children does not figure as a priority for the family.

Here, it would be proper to share another very important point. As a consequence of *Panchayati Raj*, laws framed in India in 1992, vis-à-vis the developmental budget related to villages, decision-making regarding rural schemes, the responsibility of implementing them and their maintenance, all these matters now fall under the jurisdiction of *gram panchayat*s. It was certainly a highly revolutionary measure. However, a greater revolutionary step has been the introduction of special reservations in the

Panchayati Raj for women and for those communities who have been regarded as untouchables for centuries. The good and bad outcomes of the *Panchayati Raj* system are now coming to the fore.

The decentralisation of the power of governance and, perhaps, also the decentralisation of corruption has been gathering pace. The positive result of this development is that it has now become more difficult to conceal or gloss over when the *panch sarpanch* (Village Council Chief), district officials, civil servants and officers indulge in corrupt activities at the rural level. Someone or other will certainly get wind of such activities, because a large number of people now participate in the rural governance, and not all of them are corrupt. Women and younger *panchayati* leaders, in particular, lean towards learning and doing something innovative. They are also not involved in most of the corruption scandals. Hence, in the given scenario, the protection of children's rights cannot be ensured unless the current system in the villages is taken into account. Moreover, it is a matter that concerns 70 percent of children in this country.

The Right to Information as promulgated under Indian law is a very potent weapon in the hands of the common people, provided they use it to its fullest potential. It is simply impossible to sincerely implement social welfare and security schemes and programmes without the participation of the people. The Mahatma Gandhi *Grameen Rozgaar* Guarantee, *Sarva Shiksha Abhiyan* ('Education for All' programme), mid-day meals, the Right to Education, etc. require the leadership and participation of the people. Some of these laws and programmes are new while some of them have been in existence for many years.

The BBA acquired a thorough understanding of all these issues and concluded that we require new practices and initiatives.

The Changing Priorities and Ethos of Non-governmental Organisations

Here I would like to highlight the challenges, rapidly changing ethos and priorities of non-governmental interventions. I would not talk about matters too old. Merely thirty years ago, several of my friends and I started the Bachpan Bachao Andolan. Let us begin there. Until the 1980s, the term 'NGO' had not been invented or imported into our country. Generally, the efforts made by the non-governmental organisations used to be Gandhian, *Sarvodayi* or voluntary in nature. The cultural, social and religious organisations used to run human welfare, women emancipation, and Dalit emancipation programmes on a grand scale, which, in fact, has been the tradition of our country for centuries. For instance, features like *dharmashalas* and *sarais* (inns) spread all over the country, where people can stay briefly for free can be found only in our indigenous set-up. No emperor or government has been able to provide as many drinking wells, fruit and shade-giving trees, free medical locations, *pyau, langar,* and *sadavrat*, etc. that has been made possible by our society alone. Human welfare has been a part and parcel of our society, and it has also made a deep impact vis-à-vis the Gandhian efforts.

During the 1970s, the indignation of the youth against the dictatorial approach of the immediate government took a democratic and creative shape. Hundreds of thousands of young men and women joined the movement with the re-establishment of the republic as their guiding aim. The movement brought about a change in the government. In 1977, a few people left to form the government but thousands of other young men and women, equipped with the consciousness and resolve of social change, never went back to their universities or their careers. Some of them formed small groups and moved to rural areas, where they set out to enhance social awareness for equality and justice. A few others, having been disillusioned with the political system, became Naxalites and left for the mountains and forests. During the 1980s, the debates on women's rights, environment, adequate rural development, public-oriented economic policies, and the rights of Dalits, unorganised bonded labourers and children became more intense. Gradually, new kinds of organisations came into being.

The 1990s saw a tremendous change in the ethos of this field, the inception of which had already taken place some time ago – it was the impact of foreign money, foreign ideas and foreign ways.

In the west, noteworthy work was being done on matters related to human rights, development, the environment, the welfare of women and children, etc. New definitions and terminologies were created. Over there, subscriptions, donations and governmental funding were organised on a grand scale for accomplishing these activities. The quick impact of these developments became evident in the developing countries including India. Equipped with imported terminologies, mode of operation and money, soon a new NGO culture emerged. This decade saw greater emphasis on rooting out problems, analysing their reasons and exposing them. It also led to a change in the ethos of the media. New trends, such as human rights journalism, development and environment journalism, etc. evolved.

Exposing the problems in the NGO field is still an ongoing process, and it is significant in many ways. Media and foreign charity organisations have also played a great role and helped in this matter. However, one finds a paradox here. It is not possible to determine time limits for solving problems, especially when they are connected to cultural or systemic causes. Moreover, new problems keep cropping up every now and then, with abundant donations made solely for these fresh problems.

Well, that is another issue. We were talking about the phase that came in the wake of problems being exposed. In the final years of the 1990s and the beginning of the new millennium, greater emphasis was placed on traditional ways of solving problems, such as enacting laws, implementing them, pressurising the government via organisations and movements to implement welfare schemes, like schools, hospitals, employment, housing, etc. However, a fresh requirement was felt in the final years of the previous decade – the requirement for seeking original and innovative solutions, their collation, analysis and exchange of solutions based on conclusions and testimonies. People are engaged in seeking alternative solutions all over the world, not just in our country – be it on developmental, market or energy related, environment protection, climate change or human rights issues. The search for alternative solutions is going on in full swing, everywhere. Emphasis is being put on looking for new ways of advocacy. In the wake of these developments, the non-governmental organisations today are increasingly making their presence felt in policy and decision-making processes in governments, international organisations and the corporate world. Encouragement is being given to social entrepreneurship in the NGO world.

And, here, another thing should be kept in mind. On one hand, a lot of emphasis is placed on content-related expertise and skills, but on the other, the philosophy of the totality of problems and solutions is also being upheld.

Science and technology have provided greater encouragement to this totality – be it in the sphere of life-centred scientific philosophy, therapeutics or information technology. The demand for mutual complementarity and totality is on the rise.

Bachpan Bachao Andolan **Initiative**

Now, let us throw a glance at the fundamental philosophy and aim of our movement. We have not deviated at all from our dreams and aims of ending child labour and offering every child all their rights, including the right to education. Our penchant of continuously learning from our efforts has been one of our greatest internal strengths, and it has led to the growth of new practices and strategies. We have already discussed these points.

We have never regarded child labour as a one-sided problem. It has been the greatest cause and consequence of upholding the unequal, unjust system. Therefore, our fight is directed against all those causes and consequences that are related to child labour and child slavery. We consider all those measures, strategies and efforts with the holistic perspective that can directly or indirectly help us realise our dream of eradicating child slavery and make it a reality.

For the last 30 years, we have been making efforts to establish and promote the principle of the triangular relationship of child development at national and international levels. Initially, we relied on our experiences to build this concept that later on was proven valid through different surveys and research work. The eradication of child labour, proper education for everyone and the abolition of poverty are the base for holistic child development. Child labour is the greatest factor that deprives children of education and subjects them to poverty for generations, not just for a lifetime. We just cannot compromise with child labour in any of its forms.

Learning new skills at home or helping out parents during leisure time is a different matter altogether. Until good schools are provided and sincere efforts made to eradicate unemployment, inequality and poverty, the abolishment of child labour will remain a difficult task. Thirdly, it is not possible to achieve permanent success in poverty eradication until every child is rescued from labour and is engaged in qualitative education.

The Development of Rights-centric Thinking is a Must

The vision of a child-friendly village was one of turning a new philosophy into reality. It was founded on the dream of starting with a small unit and then transforming the entire society and, finally, the entire globe into a child-friendly world. We were aware that the concepts of brotherhood, friendship, respect, assistance, love, and philanthropy are merely words loaded with cumbersome moral values that, broadly speaking, do not have any definite form. When a moral value is given definite form, it implies implementing a social process that is continuous, long-lasting and self-sustaining.

A few conditions were critical to the establishment of a child-friendly village. Firstly, children, parents, villagers, *panchayat*s, school teachers, etc. had to be made aware that the responsibility of creating children's present and their future should be shared by the entire village. The second condition involved the participation of every person in the village in fulfilling this responsibility. The third condition included increasing awareness in the family and villagers about the knowledge, usefulness and respect concerning children's natural, constitutional, legal, social and cultural rights.

These rights have emerged after years of continuous brainstorming and lessons from experience. Fourthly, it was necessary to change the trend of commonly ignoring the perspectives and opinions of those who do not enjoy high status within the society. In other words, an environment was to be created that would encourage and accommodate the views and opinions of the people, who are not elites, at least with respect to issues, such as education and its quality, the provision of toilets and drinking water, the availability of teachers, security in schools, etc.

The fifth condition was to convince the parents and factory owners about pulling out children from work. Apart from creating awareness, it required involving the rural community, teachers and *panchayat* representatives. And the next step was to enrol the children in schools. The school principal plays the major role in this step because children come from different backgrounds and belong to various age groups.

Currently, a new kind of polarisation is rapidly thriving in our society. It can be referred to as the modern-age caste system. You are well aware that among the four castes in India, the first one has always kept a hold over education, the second one on governance, and the third one on production and the market. The group that failed to have any control over education, governance and property was ousted from the social mainstream. This group became employees and slaves, and formed the fourth caste.

In today's world, this triad comprising the governance, the market and education has succeeded in keeping out from the mainstream millions of people. One out of every six persons is forced to sleep without having a meal. They are also among the poorest ones. One out of every three persons has no access to clean drinking water. One out of every six persons has neither been to school nor received any basic education at home.

A small section of the population in a few of the rich and poor countries of the world have monopolised education, governance and the market. Quality education is the only tool that can break this triad and help establish equality within society.

Four Phases of Building Child-Friendly Villages

Liberation from Child Labour

The whole process has been developed in a holistic fashion and divided into four phases. First, every child should be freed from child labour. Traditionally, most child labourers work in agricultural fields or take cattle for grazing, etc. Their owners are landowners belonging to the higher castes or are wealthy people. In the cities, we take legal action or conduct raids for rescuing bonded child labourers from factories, brick furnaces and mines.

But, in rural areas, legal action is used only as a last resort. In most cases, strategies like social pressure and persuasion are sufficient for getting the desired outcome.

The question that could be raised here is how the family would make both ends meet if parents were to pull their children out of labour. There would be a sudden decrease in their income. This argument is not only unethical but also illegal, and it tends to promote social crimes and poverty. The children in most of the families who work on agricultural land are not employed on daily wages. Not only the adult labourer, but his entire family is also destined to lead a life of ceaseless hard labour. The children are also forced to work in the farms along with their labourer parents or sent for cattle-grazing. Some children are made to do cleaning jobs in the owners' homes. When these children are pulled out of labour, it does not cause any loss of daily wages for the family; rather, they get freedom from invisible slavery.

Another point: Children are tempted by money and made to work, while their parents and other adults are deprived of full-time employment. Why would any land-owner employ adults and pay higher wages when he has easy access to free or cheap child labour? This vicious cycle not only makes a mockery of the minimum wage law and other pieces of legislation, but also ends up depriving the children of their rights to education and normal development.

Nowadays, parents have slowly begun to realise the significance of education. However, more efforts should be made in this regard. The children, who engage in hard labour, suffer continuous damage to their delicate organs. It is possible to convince every class in society about the concerns related to children's health and the resulting expenses on their treatment and, consequently, build an environment that opposes child labour. It is certainly possible to free children from every such work that may act as a stumbling block to his or her comprehensive education, health, entertainment and development. Awareness in parents and the rural community can certainly be brought about in this way.

All these developments are taking place in the development of child-friendly villages. A few years ago, a sociologist friend of mine visited Thanagaji block in Alwar, Rajasthan to appraise an organisation. He got the opportunity to visit several villages. He became curious when he saw notice-boards with the words "child-friendly village" written on them, and so, checked out a couple of them. It did not take him long to realise the difference between an ordinary village and a child-friendly village. He did not find any child working in the fields or grazing cattle and he noticed that among the children going to the primary school, a large number of them were girls. Children's faces were shining with self-confidence.

Five years after building the child-friendly village, I got the opportunity to visit Pohli village in Meerut along with my co-workers. We were sitting in a school auditorium. I asked all those children to raise their hands who earlier had been child labourers. More than half the children told me that they used to do work, stitching footballs. Courtesy of the child-friendly village, they were receiving education in the school at the time.

Fourteen-year-old Vyomkesh, a member of the child *panchayat*, said, "I aspire to become a social worker when I grow up so that I can free other villages from child labour, and transform them into child-friendly villages."

All Children to be sent to Schools

The second important phase towards the creation of a child-friendly village is to get all the children enrolled in schools. It is necessary to realise that the centres of power and might are consistently shifting. In earlier times, one who owned more land wielded more might. Later on, those who acquired guns or weapons became all the more powerful. With the advent of new technology, the class that started using tractors, agricultural machinery, and means of transport, such as motorcycles, jeeps, etc. became more influential in the village. Then, the child of one of the villagers managed to study in the city, returning as an officer, and it led to a sudden increase in his respectability and status in society.

The determining factor here was the power of the administrative system or law. However, we are in a period that has seen the development of computers, information technology and fresh sources of knowledge. In this scenario, the more one has access to modern knowledge, information and technology, the more he or she earns money and respectability. As a whole, it is obvious that previously the centre of might shifted from land to the gun, and then it went to the pen and today it rests on the fingers that run computers. This development can be attributed to the mushrooming of English-oriented schools and centres teaching information knowledge in the villages and suburbs respectively.

Hence, it implies that the significance of modern education is rapidly taking root in society. While building a child-friendly village, we try getting every child in the village enrolled in school. It is a necessary step, particularly, in the case of girls belonging to the backward castes, tribal communities and minorities. I have always maintained that social justice cannot simply be established through major governmental schemes. Social justice is born right at the moment when the daughter of a Muslim or a Dalit (untouchable) sweeper shares the jute mat with a child from a Thakur or Brahmin (The second highest and highest of the four castes, respectively) family, and learns the alphabet or shares drinking water from the same clay pot.

With respect to education, the thought behind the movement has always been clear-cut. We consider it different from the work done by the voluntary organisations and endowment institutions. Access to education is every child's birthright, and it is also his other legal right. The state has the responsibility of providing this right, and it is the duty of the citizens to seize it for themselves.

We believe in four-pronged approach to the educational system. Its first leg dictates that education should be completely free till the age of 18 years. Apart from fees, the government should also bear all the expenses for uniforms, books, day meals, commuting, etc. Secondly, education should be made totally compulsory. It should be mandatory for the municipality, *panchayat*s, educational department, schools and guardians to make sure that every child receives full-time education. The third leg consists of useful, quality education. It broadly implies that the level of education should be upgraded, education should be conducive to fulfilling social and financial needs and furthermore, it should strengthen human values and human dignity. The fourth leg stands for uniform education. There should not be any differences in the kind of education received by the children of elites, officers, and rich people, and the children of farmers, labourers and peons. The endeavour of quality education in government schools would remain a distant dream as long as the dual education system prevails.

Education implies more than merely attending school. Education should be instrumental in exploring and developing the underlying faculties of every child and that of the entire society, delivering them from the shackles of inequity and injustice, protecting and enhancing respect for people and the environment, and finally, making our beautiful world all the more beautiful.

Creating Child Panchayats

The third phase of this process includes the creation of child *panchayat* by all the children of the village. It is a very interesting process. The concept of child *panchayats* rests on how children can develop collective leadership by working together, and how they can imbibe the concept of the democratic electoral process.

It is common knowledge that during elections, the rapidly expanding middle class and the educated lot do not visit polling booths and stand in long queues. Nearly half of this population does not exercise its voting right. Most of the voting takes place in villages, suburbs and by the city's poor. It is well-known that communalism, casteism, alcohol, and the purchase of votes in return for money and gifts of saris play havoc with our electoral process. Children grow up watching these practices and gradually, either they become disillusioned with the electoral process and politics or they also learn these corrupt practices and, later, follow them.

This process involves every child in the village. Girls and boys rescued from child labour, and children belonging to different castes and communities fight elections in the child *panchayat* and cast their votes. They file nominations for the posts of the child *panchayat* president (*pradhan*), *panchayat* ministers and *panchayat* members. They prepare their respective issues and manifestos. Based on these issues, the candidates and their supporters try convincing the child voters. The secret ballot process is accomplished with the help of teachers, child-friendly village workers, and youth and women's associations. The children cast their votes into locked ballot boxes. Later on, these boxes are opened in front of everyone and the votes are counted. The children elect their leaders in this manner.

However, it is easier said than done. In many places, it has come to light that the coalition of guardians, casteism and political clout tend to have a hold over the child *panchayat* elections. Parents also get involved in the electoral campaigns of their children. It is only with the help of local teachers and conscientious people that the movement workers are successful in putting a stop to these interventions.

Coordination between Village Panchayats and Child Panchayats

The fourth most important step is to establish coordination between the *panchayat* elected by the children and the local village *panchayat*. To achieve this coordination, it is important that leadership qualities, the understanding about rights, and the skills of effectively presenting one's ideas and the proper identification of concerns and issues are developed in the children.

It is also necessary to sensitise the village *panchayat* representatives to the issue of children's rights and make them aware. Our movement's workers have made intensive efforts to spread knowledge about children's concerns among the village *pradhans*, and *sarpanch*, and ensure the children's participation. The result of this coordination is evident when the *panchayat* representatives begin to take part in the child *panchayat* meetings. At the same time, the child *panchayat* representatives are given the opportunity to express themselves in the village and to veto *panchayat* meetings.

It is indeed a very tough job. If strong assistance to the child leaders elected by the village children is not available, hardly any social worker would be able to link the village *pradhans* and *panch* with the children's concerns. What is unfortunate here is that either the *pradhans* are unaware about it or a large number of *pradhans* use up the funds from the government meant for the children for their own benefit. The whole world knows about the mid-day meals scam openly taking place in schools. Appropriating money in the name of school building construction is very common.

Under these circumstances, it is not easy for them to face the moral might of the children, and coordinate with them for making plans and taking decisions.

The transformation of an ordinary village into a child-friendly village takes place only when these four phases are completed. The movement neither makes any donations nor runs any projects in the creation of child-friendly villages. This initiative is solely based on the awareness in favour of children's rights and public participation. The truth is that the *panchayat*s have access to a large amount in child education and development. This amount should be bona fide spent for the welfare of children. Youth associations, women's associations, and other supportive groups are formed at the rural level for maintaining continuity and sustainability so that two to three years later, these groups may shoulder the responsibility of retaining the village as a child-friendly one.

After a definite period, the movement ceremonially hands over the responsibility of the child-friendly village to the *panchayat* and such other groups, and distances itself. It does not imply that the movement workers sever their connection with the village for good. It simply means that they free themselves of the daily responsibilities and maintain only general contact with the village.

The Role of Activists: Most Important

Here I want to stress the fact that the success of this campaign depends on the dynamism of our activists. In fact, it is absolutely important for every active member to align with the role and culture of *Bal Mitra* ('Child-friendly') viz. to have an uncompromising attitude against child labour and illiteracy, and to be ideological, sound, and committed to achieve the goal and possess the art of presenting his or her view in a proficient manner. Those people who are associated with the *Bal Mitra Gram* merely for service or employment are neither doing justice with themselves nor to this noble dream. A service mentality cannot bring societal change. We know that everyone needs money for meeting his own and his family's needs. At the same time, to move forward in life or to improve the world, we have to set dreams and to achieve them, we have to strive incessantly. The second option is to associate ourselves with a big dream and nourish and nurture it with our soul and blood. Wherever *Bal Mitra Gram* experiments have been successful, workers there have been exemplary in their abilities and efficiency. The youth wing, women's wing and representatives of their *panchayat*s have done commendable work. They stand as able helping hands along this long journey. But our real heroes are the leaders of the *Bal Panchayat*. Innumerable success stories are associated with their commendable achievements. There are no parallels to their courage, patience, constant efforts, and their determination to reject defeat, find clarity of goal, whilst demonstrating honesty and leadership quality. Whenever I interact with these children or listen to them in *Bal Panchayat*s or other programs, I am delighted with pride.

Six Basic Foundations and Their Lasting Results

To begin with, I will first discuss the major and permanent outcomes of the formation of the *Bal Mitra Gram*, which form the theoretical and ideological foundation of this initiative. First is empowerment from the ground to the top. Second is integrated and inclusive growth. Third is participatory democracy. Fourth, a children-oriented or a child-centric decision-making process. Fifth, to end the age-old mentality of discrimination, and sixth, is to collectively meet the challenges of environmental problems. To me, the collective outcome of these six points can bring about revolutionary changes in any society.

Empowerment from Top to Bottom

Let us take the first point – empowerment from the ground up. The daughter of an exploited labourer, who works in the field or as a servant in the master's house is probably at the bottom end of the social strata in that village, socially and financially, perhaps the weakest one. The ideological base of the *Bal Mitra Gram* aims to empower her in such a way that she can narrate her problem to the *Gram Pradhan* and if need be, without fear, puts her point before the Prime Minister of the country. In this, everyone, whether from the upper caste, teachers, youth, women and every villager should take part. When all children of the village together participate in the activities of one another, under such conditions, it becomes difficult for their masters or parents to force them to do labour by preventing them from going to schools. In those villages that have transformed into *Bal Mitra gram* ones – this dream has turned into reality. These are very rare examples in the history of this country or in the history of the world where an oppressed group has courageously faced and compelled the political and administrative forces, capable of solving those problems, to use the state machinery in favour of the oppressed and deprived group.

In many instances, it was also revealed that the moral power and determined voices of these children has motivated the women, people from marginalised sections, guardians and even the teachers. They have broken the age-old silence, using their much needed voices. This work on children's rights has immediate effects but the far-reaching consequences are more critical. Those children who are blessed with education without suffering any exploitation and have become a source of strength to one another in the *Bal Panchayat* can no longer be pushed back. In future, they will prove to be responsible, strong and active citizens.

This incident relates to Kukara village in Lakhimpur. In one corner of the school premises, there was a police post. The entire day, criminals and people with doubtful credentials were brought in here and beaten. The police post was the centre of sad and pitiable complainants and accident victims. All this adversely affected the concentration and study of the school children in the same compound. After the formation of the *Bal Panchayat*, the child leaders – Adil, Aafareen, Alka, Anees, Ishrat and Parveen, etc. made the removal of the police post from the school premises their first priority. First, they met the Head Master who did nothing. Then they met the officer-in-charge of the police post. He refused to remove the post from school premises. All this did not discourage the children. They collected funds among themselves, formed a group and went ahead to the police headquarters to meet the police superintendent with a written complaint. The police superintendent could not ignore their genuine demand and ordered an immediate inquiry. The villagers extended full support to the children's brave efforts.

Integrated Development

Different definitions and concepts (hypotheses) of development keep evolving from time to time. However, the fundamental point is that any development, for the benefit of a few people or a few sections of people, at the cost of culture, environment and habitat ultimately leads to disaster. Market and consumer culture has pushed us to the brink of ruin. This can be understood by the simple fact that the looming danger of climate change may wipe out mankind and nature. In the name of development, one-sixth of the world's population has monopolised half of the resources of the planet. Today, the main thrust is on sustainable and integrated development. With this view in mind, the conservation of nature and development by all and for all must be ensured. What can and should be done for the world may be a good topic for debate and seminars but at the local level, we have addressed these towering problems through the initiative of *Bal Mitra Gram* villages. Our child leaders of *Bal Mitra Gram* are aware of their rights, and at the same time, are equally alert to the need for environmental conservation, the eradication of the caste system, bridging the gender gap and combating the monster of communalism.

To ensure that all girls and boys are enrolled in schools and complete their studies is an important mission of an integrated child development programme. Activists of the movement have also endeavoured to ensure that the benefits of government schemes reach those families whose sons and daughters have been deprived from being a part of the mainstream.

Razia Sultan of Janikhurd village in Meerut district is testimony to dynamic leadership quality at the tender age of only eleven. Earlier, she worked in a factory where sports items were manufactured. She was engaged in the sewing of footballs. At the behest of Razia, all the boys and girls were enrolled in schools. Thereafter, she took the lead for the construction of a girls' toilet, a boundary wall and kitchen within the school compound. But she was not satisfied with these small achievements.

She was aware that in ten villages nearby, the work of village transformation was going on. She had met with these *Bal Sarpanch*s (Child mayors) during a session of the National *Bal Mahapanchayat*. There she learnt that school children were being robbed by having to pay for school fees or on some other pretext. She learnt that education was officially completely free in these schools and to charge any fees was illegal. She assembled ten *Bal Sarpanch*s and together they marched to the offices of the District Magistrate, the District Education Officer of Meerut district and also knocked on the doors of the editors of *Dainik Jagran* and *Amar Ujala*. Both newspapers highlighted this episode with full vigour. The bureaucrats came under tremendous pressure to take immediate action. As a result of this operation, not only the practice of charging school fees stopped but the guardians of these students got a refund of what they had paid. The

Bal Panchayat proved very successful in the implementation of government schemes for the poor.

Participatory Democracy

The third is participatory democracy. In the guise of democracy, influential sections of society misuse government machinery. Years ago, nepotism in democratic institutions and in politics was perceived as an evil, but now it does not attract any serious attention. In the oldest democracy of the world, America, the dominance of only a few families can be seen. The largest democracy of the world, India, not only suffers from the Gandhi-Nehru family syndrome, it also suffers from nepotism at the central and provincial level of politics. Today, there are hundreds of Members of Parliament, Members of the Legislative Assembly, ministers who have become torch bearers of democracy only because they are simply the successors of their well-known fathers, husbands, uncles, or brothers. Similarly, there was a time when the participation of criminals in politics was severely detested. Today, it is routine, at any cost, and no more than a mere news item. From every political party, hundreds of criminals, even convicts of rape and murder cases, contest elections from prison and win. We have already discussed above the factors that affect democratic elections. In such a situation for transparent and effective democracy, we will have to start from somewhere. Why not start this process from the children in our villages? Rich or poor, upper caste vs. lower caste, girls, boys, Hindus, Muslims all together can give shape to our concerns and help in forming the democratic shape and structure. This is what happens in *Bal Mitra Gram* villages.

In the initial phase, the children are not totally immune to the maladies of the vicious political atmosphere. But very quickly, they understand the importance of honesty and integrity. They have a clear vision and goals, and are eager to do something new and wonderful. They soon learn how to work together as a team by forgetting the differences how to reach the common goal of asserting their rights and how to learn from one another. This is the responsibility of the active members of *Bal Mitra gram* villages to inculcate good feelings among the children of elite families of the village towards the other children, and encourage the children of downtrodden groups to develop leadership qualities and to work together. In the formation of *Bal Panchayat*s, children do learn about healthy competition but here efforts are also made to teach them to rise above simply winning or losing. The child who gets the maximum votes becomes the *pradhan* but the child who comes second is honoured as U.P. *pradhan*. The same rule applies to the minister and junior ministers posts. Together as a team, they form a council of ministers. Education, sports, health, rural development, environment, etc. portfolios are allotted to different office bearers. All the posts are divided among the competing candidates. And this is how the foundation of participatory democracy is laid down in a small village.

Child-Centric Decision Making

The fourth is a child-centric decision-making process. For the creation of a child-friendly society, it is necessary to change the thinking and mentality of the people who are at the helm of family, social and village affairs. But this is the hardest nut to crack. Generally, priorities of village *panchayat*s are dictated and guided by political considerations. Whether it is road construction, the installation of hand pumps, providing employment or electrification – all these are decided on the basis of caste, vote bank or future elections. Apart from exceptional instances, no consideration is given to the concerns of children by *panchayats*. The fundamental reason behind this is the habit of not giving any priority to children's needs. But another reason is that there is no one to raise the children's voices, either directly or on their behalf in the *panchayat*s. The same happens in schools and in homes. In classrooms, teachers do not pay attention to children's questions. At home, he or she is treated as incapable and their opinion is never sought.

In *Bal Mitra Gram* villages, one does not try to change this mentality through just preaching. It is necessary to enlighten the society about the needs of children but equally important is to create an atmosphere and the necessary conditions so that people in power give priority to children's needs. It is not for the *panchayat* to bypass the demands raised by *Bal Panchayat* – a duly elected body, which is formed with the concurrence and participation of villagers. Parents cannot dare to stop their children from going to schools by engaging them in labour. A huge group of village students stand by those children who do not want to do labour, and are eager to attend schools.

Gradually, it becomes very difficult for parents to ignore the wishes and demands of the children. In all crucial decisions, the children's voices start getting priority. In many villages, the roads are constructed to connect the schools instead of leading towards the *pradhan*'s residence. Water tanks are constructed in schools, not at the bus depot. Toilets for girls have been given priority over the construction of *goshala*. In this way, in *Bal Mitra Gram* villages, a culture is developing which accords top priority to children's needs.

In Amarola village of Saharsa district in Bihar, the formation of a *Bal Mitra Gram* village was taking the desired shape. But there, the school had no building of its own. A *Bal Panchayat* was formed. Deepak Kumar, Hira Kumar, Khushbu, Kanchan and Lakshmi were representatives of the *Bal Panchayat*. For a school building, the *Bal Panchayat* started correspondence with government offices, and at the same time, they started lobbying the *Gram Samaj* to render help for a school building. After some time, the government acceded to their demands and granted funds for a *khaprail* building. But the biggest problem was of getting land for the school building. Taking notice of the children's effort for a social cause, the entire village came in to help and support. Respecting the sentiments of the children, a villager donated a piece of his land to the school. Today, a hundred students are being educated in that school. The education department has now appointed two full-time teachers in the school.

Similarly, in Ramchandra Nagar, in the state of Bihar, a liquor shop was opened on the route to the local school with the connivance of the local police. The children would often see drunkards sprawled on the road or lying in drains, brawling and fighting with one another. At times, they would reach dangerously close to the school gate. Ajay Kumar, the child *panchayat* leader, got together with other members and launched a protest against it.

He cautioned the villagers that the liquor shop owner was a criminal and if he was allowed to operate, it might prove detrimental not only for the children, but also for their families. It took some time for the child *panchayat* to expand its support base. Eventually, all children in the village agreed to take a stand against the liquor shop. Their mothers turned out to be their greatest supporters. Men would drink alcohol and then, under its influence, they would beat the women and would often sell off household items. The protests began with the children and women taking out a procession in the village against the shop. Subsequently, they convinced the village *pradhan* and approached the higher authorities. It led to the liquor shop being shut down within a few days.

Doing Away with Discrimination

Human history bears testimony to the innumerable kinds of discrimination that have always existed amongst people all over the world. The inherent human desire to prove oneself better than the other, or the tendency to exploit others for one's own interests has been at the root of a variety of commandments, superstitions and also the framing of the code of conduct. Such developments have led to far-reaching and profound consequences. How did the mindset behind apartheid come about? Why has been society segregated, based on communities, and why are they made to fight with one another? Undoubtedly, these trends are backed by the vested interests of a handful of people, but at the same time, the roots of mental acceptance of these phenomena run very deep. Hardly anyone would stand up against the caste system and dare to mingle with the lowest of the castes and form marital relationships with them. It is not possible for any leader or political party to come to power without playing the caste card, whether it is in the remotest of the villages or the capital, Delhi. Even today, Dalit families are forbidden to draw water from wells belonging to the Thakurs and Brahmins. It is still a dream for the Dalits to gain into the temples that have been monopolised by the upper castes for centuries. Despotic rulings are passed in the name of *gotra* and *khap*. Inter-caste marriages do not stand any chance at all when young men and women are killed for merely marrying in the same *gotra*. Most villages have designated residential areas for upper castes, Dalits, and Muslims. Brahmins, priests, *moulvis* (Muslim clerics) and *tantrics* have such a hold on the popular psyche that people do not have any qualms about killing their children in the name of beliefs. Astrology, belief in auspicious timing, and fatalism is an integral part of life. Children are not affected much by all this during their initial years. However, as they grow older, their impressionable minds become contaminated with the concepts of discrimination, orthodox ideas and superstitions. Children's participation, mutual interaction, coordination with one another, the courage to speak up in front of elders, and elections and responsibilities of the child *panchayat* are efforts made in the child-friendly villages that succeed in bringing about a revolutionary change in the discriminatory mindsets.

Chhitouli village in Alwar, Rajasthan is famous for its idol stone making. The youth, elderly and children are engaged in making idols. There is also a school in the village. A few years ago, the movement selected this village for transforming into a child-friendly one. A child *panchayat* was formed as a part of this process. Twelve-year-old Anand was chosen as the child *sarpanch*. Just a few days after his election, it was found that a child marriage was to take place shortly in the village. Child marriages are very common in this area. It is a rare occurrence here that boys and girls are married off after 25 years and 18 years of age, respectively. Most boys and girls are married off while they are quite young. People do not bother about these things. However, it is true that 10- to 12-year-olds are married off in a hush-hush manner.

Anand and Pushpraj immediately called a child *panchayat* meeting when they got to know about it. As they narrated later to us, half of the children were scared to protest against the marriage but Anand did not give up. He gathered all those people who were ready to support him and approached his Master*ji*. He, too, could not muster any courage. Eventually, these child *panchayat* leaders barged into the house where the marriage was about to take place. Obviously, nobody listened to them and drove them away. But it did not lessen Anand's and his companions' resolve. They went to the *panchayat* chief, who tried to convince them that child marriage was a good concept and if the marriage was called off on the day of the wedding, it would ruin the lives of the two would-be child bride and groom. However, the chief could not convince the children that child marriage did not ruin lives, rather postponing it might be more harmful. The children remained restless till the evening. They called up the *Bachpan Bachao Andolan* workers. Then all of them decided that the father of the girl and relatives would be given a final warning. They would be told that if they did not call off the wedding, the child *panchayat* would inform the police. The confidence and courage of the children scared these people. By night, a larger number of youths and conscientious people had joined the children. Finally, the child marriage was called off. Later on, we learnt that this incident became known in the surrounding villages and, consequently, many child marriages that were about to take place during those days were also called off.

Zenab is a little girl, who lives in Muslim-dominated Chandoura village in Meerut. Most of the girls in this village are not sent to school. A handful of little girls do receive education in *madrasas*. Since the time Zenab fought elections in the local child *panchayat*, her personality has undergone a miraculous transformation. She perceived early that in spite of the elders' opposition, it was very important for her to get an education and not just that, other girls should also be provided with mainstream education. Zenab was threatened. She was reminded of the traditions and norms, and efforts were made to convince her that girls should not cross their limits as decided by custom. It was not easy for Zenab and her many friends from the Muslim community to stand in defiance to the orthodox voices. However, the self-confidence in these girls was unshakeable. They were armed with rock-solid arguments and an unrelenting mind. Finally, the parents and the rural community had to give in. Every girl and boy in the village was enrolled in school. At present, Zenab is an inter-college student. The village school has classes till the eighth standard. Zenab and other children had to go to the neighbouring school to finish the ninth and tenth standards. Now, she cycles eight kilometres everyday to the inter-college located in the suburb. Today, Zenab, the first daughter of Chandoura, is a source of pride for the whole village. She is also a role model for children in the neighbouring villages. Child *panchayat* worker, Sher Khan, has also played a very important role in these villages.

Activism of the Child Panchayat on Environmental Issues

In child-friendly villages, the issue of environment preservation is given higher priority vis-à-vis the ones that concern public consciousness. Children put it into practice too. In many villages, trees are planted at the initiative of the child *panchayat*s. Arrangement is made with regard to water maintenance and cleanliness. Voices are raised against pollution in mines and from furnaces. Under the cleanliness drive, children take the initiative to clean ditches, drains, etc. They pressurise the *panchayat* that cleanliness should be maintained in the village, and that proper conservation of rain water and trees is necessary.

An incident once took place in the Wazeernagar village in Khiry district of Uttar Pradesh. There were no arrangements made for the drainage of dirty water in the whole village, including the area surrounding the school. The drains were damaged and would always be filled with muck, and mosquito breeding was rampant. The child *panchayat* raised its voice against this situation during the process of establishing a child-friendly village. On their own accord, the children took this up, sending the message of cleanliness to the *panchayat* and villagers. They believed that it would shame the village *panchayat* and, consequently, would ensure cleanliness in the village. A few weeks passed with great anticipation but nothing happened. One day, the children from the child *panchayat*, namely Gayatri, Alok, Anuradha and Prempratap took a unique step. They set out again with brooms but instead of cleaning the drains this time, they went to the village *panchayat*'s house and handed her a broom. The children told her, "You are our leader and the village chief. Today, you will be the first one to clean the dirty drains and then, we will follow suit." The poor *pradhan* had no choice but to accompany these children. It was the first time in her life that she had to clean the drains. The whole village watched the enfolding drama.

The followers of the *pradhan* also got down to cleaning with great enthusiasm. They too wanted to show their worth. This went on for a few hours. The next day, nobody was surprised to see the village sweeper finally doing his job. The *Pradhan* also allocated funds towards maintaining cleanliness and clean drinking water.

Another interesting incident in the context of the environment occurred in the Narhat and Bavanbaans Chougan villages in the Alwar district of Rajasthan. Both these villages share boundaries with a forest. There were hardly any useful trees but wild trees were aplenty. During the process of transforming the village into a child-friendly one, concern was raised in the child *panchayat* that the number of trees was rapidly decreasing in the surrounding area. This issue was raised in the combined meeting of the youth associations and child *panchayat*s of both villages. Several members of the youth association thought that outside contractors were cutting the trees in the dead of the night to take them away with the connivance of the forest department employees. Hence, a group of youth association members was formed so that accurate information and evidence could be collected. Within a few days, information was gathered and based on this, the child *panchayat*s and youth associations wrote a letter of complaint to the senior officers. However, no action was taken for weeks. Finally, a covert group was formed, and at night, with each member having his or her face covered, they hid in the bushes outside the village. A little while later, the tree cutters began to arrive. Among them were two employees of the forest department as well, who arrived on a scooter and stood waiting at a little distance. At an opportune moment, the youths hiding in the bushes started making calls of wild animals. The tree cutters got scared and began to run helter-skelter. Four of them were apprehended right there and then, and were handed over to the police the same night. This action not only helped in saving the forest but also acted as a source of inspiration for other people in the vicinity.

I would like to clarify here that awareness of one's rights, respect for others, handing over leadership to the marginalised classes, creating a conducive environment in which the upper and the lower castes could communicate directly and seek relief from socio-economic inequities and feudal ideas, and develop a democratic culture are some of the ideas that are difficult to suppress once they have found a foothold in the popular psyche. When these ideas find a place in the popular mindset, instead of getting eliminated in the face of opposition, they instead flourish in leaps and bounds.

When the level of social consciousness rises and the perspectives towards priorities and development change, even if it happens through children's initiative, they generate far-reaching and profound results. All these are evident today in the child-friendly villages.

Identifying the Five-faceted Power Within

I would like to try out an analytical tool here. Let us use it to analyse the experiences of the child-friendly villages because this technique allows us to move ahead. It is known as SWOT. This abbreviation stands for S – strength, W – weakness, O – opportunity and T – threats. It refers to moving ahead by identifying and evaluating one's strengths, weaknesses, opportunities and threats.

Our first strength comprises children's natural honesty, their clarity in understanding the issues of child labour, education and children's rights, their enthusiasm, idealism and determination, replete with moral values. These strengths are generally not visible much in adults. Many difficult issues become simpler to handle when children learn something together and develop the concept of collective leadership. Every worker in child-friendly villages should make sure that this strength is utilised optimally and wrong aspirations do not develop in the children's impressionable minds. Creative activities and innovative ideas should be encouraged that children find interesting so that they can get inspired to go ahead and do something commendable in life. Our second strength is that the ethos of the constitution and laws are in our favour. Child exploitation is unconstitutional and illegal. The Indian Government has signed many international treaties with the aim of preventing harm to children. India is one of the signatories of the international efforts to ensure the provision of education to all children by 2015. If this strength is to be used appropriately, the workers should have optimum knowledge about child labour, children's rights, the laws regarding child welfare, and various governmental schemes and how to leverage them. Our third strength consists of being a part of an established, famous and influential national organisation like the *Bachpan Bachao Andolan* movement of child-friendly villages. The workers should have accurate knowledge about the history, aims and programmes of the movement. It will provide them with inspiration and self-confidence. They would also be able to impress officials and put pressure on them on behalf of the organisation. The children are our fourth strength, those who have been rescued from bonded labour or child labour, and have been provided with education and training in our rehabilitation homes, viz. *Mukti Ashram* and *Bal Ashram*.

These children can play a very important role in the child-friendly village development process, and, in fact, they are performing that role currently. The ideological base of the child-friendly village is so complete that it indeed figures as our fifth strength. We do possess various other strengths but we will not discuss them here. You can point them out yourself. For instance, having a *Bal Ashram* in Rajasthan is a strength in itself. Our campaigning for forests and the environment in Karnataka can be a source of additional strength for the child-friendly village located there.

Lessons Learnt from Weaknesses

Let us now examine our weaknesses. Leaving aside the workers engaged in the child-friendly village movement, many senior officers have not yet been able to embrace the concept and the ideological basis of the movement in its true essence. Often, when I interact with them, I am aghast to find out that they spend more time chatting with the youth and their friends, and less time among the children and child *panchayat*s. In many cases, it has come to light that the election of a child *panchayat* is considered the mark of success of a child-friendly village. In all those places where child *panchayat*s have been formed, people believe that the whole village has now become a child-friendly village. And then there are places where many workers believe that success achieved in getting the children enrolled in schools is the only parameter of a child-friendly village. All these developments are definitely very good, and they should happen. However, the real child-friendly village comes into being only when the teachers, *panchayat*s, and parents succeed in establishing a friendly relationship with the children, a relationship which allows them to take decisions together. Therefore, I believe that our greatest drawback lies in our lack of efforts in trying to change the rural mindset.

Broadly speaking, in today's NGO culture, there is a serious lack of struggle to bring about social change. There is hue and cry about national, international, governmental or non-governmental funds. Villages, where such volunteer organisations are working, their activists or workers' life-style, approach towards life, ways to entice villagers or the execution of some small-time welfare programme, can practically impress anyone. Many *Bal Mitra Gram* activists started comparing themselves with these workers. While doing so, they tend to forget that they are craftsmen in a new society and warriors fighting against centuries-old tradition of a social, economic and political system that is against children. Then why demonstrate any inner weakness?

There is another shortcoming – when the fully structured and ready *Bal Mitra Gram* is handed over to the villagers, then our workers' connection with their contacts in the village gets weaker with time. Now and then, meetings with the youth wing, women's wing, teachers and/or the *panchayat* members take place but there are no frequent meetings as such with the child leaders. It is good that every year, a new *Bal Panchayat* is formed smoothly and that communication with representatives of the *Bal Panchayat* remains sound, but it is of utmost importance to remain in contact with the previous leaders of the *Bal Panchayat*. This is the responsibility of local activists and officers of our movement that these children remain in contact with us in a planned manner.

We have another shortcoming. It is the problem of considering the *Bal Mitra Gram* as only a project. Activists who try to fit themselves in it inconventional fashion can make the reports at the end of the work day but they would not return from work filled with a sense of self-pride. It is important to follow some basic principles, ways and programmes. But in order to transform a thought into a movement, we do not need a closed mind, but passion and enthusiasm. It is this enthusiasm that lets you learn new ways to get more effective results in less time and with fewer resources. For this, it is necessary that we form an active unit of BBA in every village with the support of villagers.

Search for Opportunities and Potential

Let us discuss the opportunities that are helpful in creating a *Bal Mitra Gram*. Programmes by the central and state governments in this direction provide us with such opportunities. When mid-day meals, scholarships and facilities are provided and distributed well, it strengthens the speed of the *Bal Mitra Gram* campaign. Proper information regarding these plans, their budget, and information regarding officers and the related departments is of utmost importance. The second opportunity lies in the importance of education in the present political scenario. Over the last several years, it has been observed that civil service and political organisations advocating for the welfare of backward castes are realising the importance of education. They cannot avoid the issues of women and backward classes because there is reservation for these groups under the *Panchayati Raj* system. The election of women, tribals and underprivileged representatives is inevitable. The politics of these newly emerging players is not as nasty as that of the old ones. At all schools where workers of the *Bal Mitra Gram* were able to sensitise the school children, the results have been extraordinary.

Villages are no longer ignorant about information technology, computers, the Internet and mobile phones. Unfortunately, these are being used in the growth of markets, business and consumerism. But its positive side is also very important. The movement's activists should have a hold on these technologies. There is no better resource for new experiments and sharing achievement stories and thus attracting people to the cause.

There are many other opportunities. Finding them depends upon your insight and energy and how quickly you identify them.

Confrontation with External Challenges

We also cannot overlook the challenges surrounding us. The first major danger is the lack of concern towards children's rights, and the mentality to protest against that on the basis of customs, religion and culture. We all have to struggle with it. Another danger is political cliques and caste-ism. The third is the extinction of traditional employment in villages due to national and international policies, which are against the masses. Climate change and the depravation of the ecosystem is also a cause for the uprooting of the poor.

Due to these conditions, whole families are forced to migrate. Children and women are brought to cities via trafficking. Brokers take away children by enticing them or by giving loans to their parents, taking these children to very faraway places. The rural communities in the *Bal Mitra Gram* have certainly achieved great success in addressing these situations with local solutions. But these are dangers that can happen in a single instance of carelessness.

Here I would like to quote a successful example. In 2008, the state of Bihar witnessed an enormous flood. *Bal Mitra Gram* areas were highly affected. Hundreds and thousands of people were forced to leave their homes and find shelter in villages and islands located at higher levels. By setting up emergency camps, government, NGOs, and international organisations were focussed on relief operations. Such operations usually show their impact in the medium-term and, in many cases, these efforts alone are insufficient. This presents a golden chance for child smugglers to exploit relief operations. Like in previous occasions, they started hovering around relief camps. At that time, the BBA started campaigning vigorously at these camps, railway stations and bus stations. The smugglers were trying to lure the children to take them to big cities like Mumbai and Delhi, by putting on the mask of relief workers. The movement distributed tens and thousands of pamphlets, pasted thousands of pictures and installed loudspeakers to alert the population to the danger of such people. Despite this, some smugglers were successful in taking away children. When we got an inkling of it, we raided railway stations, bus stations, etc. and freed dozens of children from the grip of these traffickers. In almost all the sensitive areas, our movement deployed small raid squads with the help of people living in the neighbourhood and other helpful organisations. It must be mentioned that none of the children from a *Bal Mitra Gram* fell prey to traffickers, because in these villages, the inhabitants were aware about children's rights and accorded it priority.

Crisis of Faith

Villagers nowadays regard volunteer organisations in the same manner as they do to government officers, police and politicians. When officers and activists of a volunteer organisation visit a village, they are not trusted. Our *Bal Mitra Gram* programme was started a few years ago in Samastipur district in the state of Bihar in a village called Dineshpur Tola. When movement activist Neelumala started meeting villagers, children and other classes of society, then none other but the *Gram Pradhan* of that village was the first person to protest. The *Pradhan* said to Neelumala, "You and your organisation must be selfish in wanting to remove children from labour and enrolling them in schools." Neelu tried her best to make him understand that the organisation is not concerned with governmental funds. At this, the *Pradhan* retorted that if the movement was getting a lot of money to work in villages, then why do we not get a school building constructed and also install hand-pumps? Neelumala tried again and again to clarify the situation but it was no good. Finally, the matter was resolved with the help of several learned villagers and it was decided that she could only enter the village if she presented the budget of the *Bal Mitra Gram* to the *Pradhan* and other eminent personalities in the village.

Neelu immediately reached out to the Delhi office of the movement. In the same week, a programme coordinator was sent to Dineshpur Tola as a matter of priority. The *Gram Pradhan* was taken aback to see an educated officer coming all the way from Delhi. Our officer asked the *Pradhan* first of all whether he could show him the budget to all his *Panchayat* members? Several villagers were also present. Our officer further persuaded that it was not a big deal if he could not show the budget to him. But he should at least inform the villagers how much funding he has received from the government for the welfare and development of the village and where that money had gone. The *Pradhan* was taken aback. People started whispering that the Delhi officer had a point. The *Pradhan* had never made his accounts public. Seeing the pale face of the *Pradhan*, our officer took out the budget of the *Bal Mitra Gram* and placed it on the table. It had nothing except the meagre expenditures of Neelumala's travelling costs. The *Pradhan* apologised and the people present gave us a round of applause and welcomed our activist back into the village to proceed with her work.

The Commercialisation of Education

The rapidly growing commercialisation of education is a big challenge ahead of us. Due to the central and state governments' policies and the flaws inherent in the current Right to Education law, private schools are proliferating like never before. In the *Bal Mitra Gram*, teachers in government schools play a huge role. If they were not able to extend interesting and quality education to the children by being present at the school everyday, then the children would be forced to leave the school. Even families with somewhat modest resources would start sending children to private schools. Here we must highlight that when the educational system becomes the root of inequality, it would be impossible to stop this inequality from spreading to the economic and social spheres. Today, we can see this everywhere in our country. Equal and quality education for all should never fade from our priorities.

The goal of this analysis is that organisations and activists should work constantly to change their inner weaknesses in their power, and convert external dangers into opportunities. Whatever has been learnt in the past ten years from both our successes and failures, can be helpful in devising new ways. For example, the *Panchayat*s and government departments must be made ready to view different development plans in a holistic manner. Families who have benefitted from the Mahatma Gandhi National Rural Employment Guarantee Act (MNREGA) must send their children to school at any cost, instead of work. Likewise, more efforts should be made to connect villages with an income growth plan, and volunteer groups on the issue of education. Many new programmes to spread awareness about climate change and preserving our ecology could be devised and launched.

Lastly, I would like to reiterate that our goal of uprooting child labour, free and equal education of all, along with children rights cannot be achieved by a one-dimensional process or approach. Furthermore, I do not think that whatever the BBA has achieved in the last 30 years, or whatever experiments it has done, are final. The day when our workers and leaders would start believing that they know it all, or that they are the only ones to have the most valid opinion on issues, the fall of our movement will start from that very moment. The drive to learn and the will power to get going with new experiments can be the only inspirational force for a permanent solution to a problem. And we can learn most from those who consider us their rival or competitor.

□

Child Labour Explained

In the last 35 years, I have been asked hundreds of questions about child labour. Those asking these questions are not the ones who support working children or those who perpetrate atrocities on children. But too many people are ignorant about the links between child labour, illiteracy, poverty and other social parameters and factors. The oft-repeated question is: if children in poverty-stricken families are not allowed to work, how would they survive? Who would look after and raise the children, whose parents are old, ailing or handicapped?

I wish to address these issues in detail. One must understand that if poor children continue to work as child labourers, then they would always remain poor, illiterate and deprived of all opportunities for their development and growth. Most often, child labourers grow up to become weak and hapless individuals, completely trapped in the vicious circle of illiteracy, unemployment, poverty and physical ailments. Their future generations would not be any different either.

Secondly, parents of child labourers are usually jobless or underemployed. India has the dubious distinction of being home to around 60 million child labourers and 65 million unemployed adults. Employers prefer children over adults because they are docile and the cheapest source of labour. It is important to take cognisance of the fact that a child normally works in place of an adult. This fact has been brought to the fore in various studies, time and again. The

Indian scenario is not very different from other countries across the globe. There are 215 million child labourers in the world whilst 200 million adults continue to remain unemployed. In view of these statistics, there is no merit in employing children and making their parents run from pillar to post in search of a job.

Adult employment rate plummets drastically in regions where child labour is rampant, because employers find it lucrative to employ children in place of adults, as children do not command high wages and often agree to work for free in lieu of food and shelter. In these situations, the parents of these children are unable to find suitable employment and enter the vicious circle of poverty. It is important to debunk yet another myth that a child works to send money back home for supplementing the household income. Under abject exploitation, often the child is barely able to meet his or her own ends, let alone extend any help to his or her parents whatsoever.

It is equally important to know that only three out of 1000 child labourers are orphans, therefore one cannot generalise that children work primarily because their parents are not alive. As far as these few orphans are concerned, does it not become the responsibility and obligation of the state, civil society, religious institutions and corporates to take care of their education and well-being? If even this minimal support cannot be extended to such children, what is the use of having so many charitable organisations and governments in the first place?

Such children must be guaranteed their basic needs of survival, coupled with all the opportunities and constitutional rights that they are entitled to. It should be noted that there are several welfare schemes available for the disabled, the old and those who fall below the poverty line. Would it not be more appropriate to work for the implementation of such schemes rather than justifying child labour? I am yet to see a 70-year-old father who has a

10-year-old child. It is very unlikely that very young children have very old parents. Therefore, we cannot assume that too many adults are incapable of taking care of their children.

People also tend to think that it is absolutely normal for poor children to work to beat being hungry at home. A common perception prevalent among the illiterate and poor communities is that more children are tantamount to having more pairs of working hands. This perception fuels the innate desire to have more children that further exacerbates poverty, hunger and child labour.

It has been established through demographic analysis that the population growth rate is much higher in child labour-prone areas and potential source areas of child-trafficking as compared to other areas.

I would like to draw your attention towards the perils that child labourers are exposed to. Children are more prone to injuries and occupational hazards than adults. Prolonged exposure to dust, chemicals, pesticides and heat makes them vulnerable to incorrigible diseases. Children working in stone quarries and mines are often injured carrying heavy loads, while the ones working on the agriculture fields suffer from respiratory disorders from inhaling toxic fumes while spraying pesticides and insecticides.

I have come across several cases where children are crippled by the sharp tools that they use, without the required supervision or necessary safety measures. I have rescued children from claustrophobic workshops and, therefore, from my experience, I can tell you that working under unregulated conditions for almost 12 to 14 hours in a day formidably affects their eyes, livers, kidneys, lungs and tender limbs.

Ailing child labourers more often than not end up spending a fortune on their healthcare for the rest of their lives. Many children who fall ill owing to occupational hazards are mercilessly turned out by their employers who find them of very little or no use. Hence, it is clear that a child who is used as an asset for reaping profits suddenly turns into a liability for the rest of his or her life.

I would like to apprise you of the fact that there are several child and bonded labour rehabilitation schemes run by the Central and State Governments. In addition, various landmark judgments have been delivered by the Honourable Supreme Court of India and other High Courts against child labour. The families of bonded child labourers who are rescued under the Bonded Labour System (Abolition) Act, 1976 are entitled to a statutory compensation of ₹ 20,000 sponsored in equal proportion by the Central and State Governments.

Besides the aforesaid benefits, the parents of these former child labourers are given preference during the allocation of government jobs and welfare housing schemes as well. The Child Labour (Prohibition and Regulation) Act stipulates for a recovery of ₹ 20,000 from the employers for every child that is rescued by the Labour Department. This fine is deposited in a Child Welfare Fund that caters to the expenses incurred over education expenses and other costs accrued to the rehabilitation of rescued children. A proactive civil society can ensure that child welfare laws are appropriately enforced in the best interests of children.

In reality, poverty and child labour share a chicken-and-egg relationship. It is extremely difficult to pin-point which precedes the other. Child labour fosters a vicious circle of poverty because such children remain uneducated and keep performing unskilled repetitive tasks that erode their employability in the future. Here, I am not suggesting that we stop working towards poverty alleviation. What I am saying is that it is equally important to target both the issues simultaneously. Poverty cannot be eliminated until child labour is eradicated. Similarly, it is not possible to end child labour completely without addressing the poverty suffered by the parents.

An adult in place of a child could possibly earn nearly eight times as much. An employed adult, therefore, can easily foot the cost of his daily household expenditure and, at the same time, provide education to his or her child. This would not only curb the rising unemployment and associated poverty but would also ensure a brighter future for our children.

Additionally, it would foster a sense of social justice and equality in the society. In a larger context, the inter-related issue of child labour and education could be best understood by considering the examples of Kerala and Uttar Pradesh – two states with almost similar incidences of poverty in the past. While Kerala has a nearly 100 percent literacy rate, Uttar Pradesh languishes way behind with almost one-third of its population unable to read or write.

A recent study conducted by the International Labour Organization (ILO), a specialised United Nations agency, suggests that every single rupee invested towards the eradication of child labour today would reap seven rupees as profit over the next 20 years.

I am often asked the main reasons behind child labour. In my opinion, apathy and the lack of respect towards preserving one's childhood are the biggest drivers of child labour. This attitude is manifested inter alia, in the low level of social responsiveness emanating from the lack of concern towards poor and neglected children. The second reason is the lack of political will – a clear fall out of the inadequate implementation of social welfare protection schemes and the weak enforcement of the existing labour laws.

Our governments do not allocate the necessary funds towards education, healthcare and the eradication of child labour at the time of formulating the annual budget. Thirdly, the lax enforcement of rural development and poverty alleviation schemes, no assurances of minimum wages for adult workers, farmers not getting a fair price for their produce, and the absence of free and quality education also exacerbate child labour. Social aberrations like gender inequality and caste biases further foster this crime.

Not mindful of the harm that child labour causes to children, society continues to employ them. Children can be seen working on ancestral lands in the villages to support themselves. Children are preferred over adults for more reasons than one. Besides being the cheapest source of labour, they keep working under inhumane conditions without a whimper. Unlike adults, children do not form unions to exert pressure on the employers. It is easy to coerce children to work for long hours or even during the night for little or no pay at all. It has been often observed that child labourers are treated as inanimate objects and are forced to live in the very workshops where they work.

It has also been noted that areas affected by natural calamities, such as floods, famine, earthquakes and conflicts turn out to be hotbeds for child-traffickers to operate in. Children from these areas often land up in prostitution and/or forced into begging by gangs involved in child-trafficking.

Readers might think that if the causes of child labour are so difficult to ascertain, it must also be impossible to eradicate. Many forget that about a century ago, child labour was a serious problem in almost all countries including the industrialised ones such as the United Kingdom, Norway, Sweden, France, Germany and Japan. These countries realised that child labour was detrimental to enforcing social justice, ensuring education for all, enhancing productivity and accentuating economic stability. Therefore, they systematically worked towards its eradication.

High awareness, an effective social security and welfare system, stringent laws and quality education have steered these countries towards a child labour-free society. Countries such as Turkey, Brazil, China, South Africa and Sri Lanka have also made exemplary progress towards eradicating child labour.

Let us take the example of the state of Kerala in India, where almost all children attend school. This remarkable achievement is the fruit of strong political will, social awareness, and the drive towards free and quality education by the government. States like Uttarakhand, Himachal Pradesh, Tamil Nadu and Gujarat are also making steady progress towards the elimination of child labour. Bihar is also making substantive efforts in this direction.

It is interesting to observe that the incidence of child labour is comparatively lower in states where schemes like the Mahatma Gandhi National Rural Employment Guarantee Act (MNREGA), *Sarva Shiksha Abhiyaan* (Education for all), mid-day meals and those related to rural development are being efficiently implemented. Active trade unionism has been able to contain child labour to a fairly large extent. From a global perspective, it is important to note that the unorganised sector and informal economy are key breeding grounds for child labour. If honest, collective and progressive efforts are made towards tackling the issue of child labour, it would not be impossible to uproot this crime.

I would like to cite a few examples to explain. A few years ago, the Government of Brazil had introduced a welfare scheme called *Bolsa Escola* ('school bag' in Portugese), which was further expanded in its scope and outcomes to be renamed *Bolsa Familia* ('family bag' in Portugese). The *Bolsa Familia* has three main pillars – cash transfer, the associated terms and conditions and complementary actions. The cash transfer provides immediate relief to the country's poor population on account of income inequalities. The associated terms and conditions reinforce the population's access to their basic social rights like education, health and social security, whilst the complementary programmes' objectives are to assist families' development with positive incentives to send and keep their children in school, whilst making sure they have appropriate healthcare as a way to mitigate the risk of future poverty. The overall aim is to break the pattern that if you belong to a poor family, you will necessarily be poor as well.

As a direct outcome, nearly six million children have already been withdrawn from work and enrolled in schools. The efforts to eradicate child labour have been extremely successful in Mexico, Peru, Tanzania and Sri Lanka. By making education free and improving its quality, countries like Kenya, Tanzania and Malawi have also been able to significantly reduce the incidence of child labour.

The distribution of food grains to poor children in Bangladesh's schools, mid-day meal schemes at government-aided schools in India and encouraging the girl child by conferring scholarships and providing incentives like bicycles, have yielded significant results.

I would also like to highlight the impact of consumers' awareness and action vis-à-vis goods produced by child labourers. Consumers are more aware than ever and do not hesitate in boycotting goods produced by children in the developing world. Similarly, the media has played a significant role in exposing the tyrannical conditions under which children under certain global supply chains work.

As a result of enhanced consumer awareness and active media intervention, the corporate sector was forced to acknowledge the violation of human rights in its supply chains and, in turn, in some cases, enforced codes of compliance in the premises of their international suppliers. Although a large number of corporate houses do not take the initiative of ensuring that the code of compliance is adhered to up to the last node in their supply chains, it is a fact that segments of the supply chains that are well monitored, are less likely to perpetrate human rights' violations.

For instance, a decade and a half ago, about 300,000 children were working in the carpet manufacturing belt of Banaras, Bhadoi and Mirzapur in the state of Uttar Pradesh, with most of them trafficked from Bihar and the adjoining areas of Nepal.

These children used to work as bonded labourers in the carpet weaving units. BBA spearheaded a consumer awareness campaign across the globe and invented a social labelling mechanism called 'Rugmark' (now known as 'Goodweave').

Under this initiative, every rug that was produced was accredited with a child labour-free label. This endeavour coupled with other actions like raid and rescue, and social mobilisation, resulted in the reduction of child labour in this belt by nearly 80 percent. This scheme of labelling was rolled out in South Asia where about one million children were working in the carpet-manufacturing industry in India, Nepal and Pakistan. As a result of the interventions under Rugmark, the number of child labourers in South Asia was reduced by almost 70 percent.

On another occasion, BBA, with the help of school children, ran a nationwide campaign against child labourers employed in the fireworks industry. Many children were known to be working under extremely inhumane conditions in the fireworks factories in Sivakasi in Virudunagar district in the state of Tamil Nadu. This intervention significantly reduced the number of child labourers in the fireworks sector. Similarly, non-governmental organisations and trade unions across the world are engaged in the eradication of child labour and are actively working towards the cause in building knowledge, and developing policy and best practices.

I am often asked why children from poor families should attain education at all when they can choose to work early and earn money to beat hunger. This fallacy actually stems from a deep-rooted social bias, which is one of the biggest reasons behind injustice in our society. We conveniently develop different perspectives and adopt double standards for different sections of our society.

We apply them in a way that further fuels inequality and discrimination. We fail to understand that in all fairness, the norms that apply to children belonging to poor sections of society must be no different from the ones that apply to our own children. If you believe that education fosters unemployment, then why do you spend a fortune towards your own child's education? The rules of the game should not change drastically from one section of the society to the other.

This is an era of globalisation that thrives on information and technology. The notion of education has undergone a complete change over the last twenty-five years. Earlier, the mantra used to be 'Education for Employment'. Today it stands at 'Education for Empowerment'. In this age of knowledge economy and capitalism, education is the most important tool for sustaining one's identity and existence.

We must not forget that education is an internationally acknowledged human right. In fact, education is the key to all other rights. The denial of education is an outright denial of all human rights.

However, we cannot ignore that quality, social concerns, equality and human values are often ignored in our existing education system. I strongly recommend a four-pronged education system that is free, compulsory, equal and useful in terms of social responsiveness, quality and employability.

For instance, in India, I do not attribute economic prosperity completely to the government and political leadership. The credit also goes to the bright Indian youth who have excelled in the fields of medicine, software, information technology and many other fields of advanced knowledge, bringing pride to the country. Today, any discussions on the global economic landscape cannot be imagined without including countries such as India, China, Brazil, Turkey, South Africa and South Korea. This has been possible only on account of knowledge and education. There are a few important economic research work corroborating this.

A single year of primary school increases the wages people earn later in life by five to fifteen percent for boys, and even more so for girls. For each additional year of secondary school, an individual's wages increases by 15 to 25 percent. No country has ever achieved continuous and rapid economic growth without first having at least 40 percent of its adults able to read and write. A child born to a literate mother is 50 percent more likely to survive past the age of five years.

Another study has shown that seven million cases of HIV/AIDS could be prevented in the next decade if every child were to receive an education. Education is imperative for enhancing agricultural productivity, increasing transparency in governance, ensuring inclusive development, sustained growth and promoting active public participation towards an efficient democracy.

I am also asked about why religious leaders do not speak out against child labour if it is so wrong. Since time immemorial, holy men across all religions, temples, mosques, churches and *gurudwara*s (Sikh temples) have together spread the message of humanity, then why not eliminate child labour?

In my view, there is a peculiar relationship between religion and children. Babies are born without a religion. It is we, the adults, who give them distinct religious identity and further compartmentalise them by performing rituals like baptism (in Christianity), *khatna* (circumcision in Islam), tonsure, etc. (in Hinduism), etc. to connote affiliation of a child to a particular sect or religion. In my opinion, the moment a child is labelled or tagged with a religious identity, humanity loses out on yet another precious member.

There are around one billion poverty-stricken children across the globe. Almost 210 million children work at the cost of their health and education. Globally, ten children die from malnutrition every minute. Seventy million children have never seen a classroom. Nearly 150 million children are compelled to leave school before completing primary education.

Tens of thousands of children who are victims of trafficking, end up in the sex trade. Many are abducted and their organs sold in the market. Children work in bondage in the fields, factories, kilns and brothels. 500,000 children are either employed as soldiers against their wishes, or find themselves in armed conflict in one way or the other. At an age when they should be playing with toys, these children are left holding lethal weapons like the AK-47 and AK-56.

Despite sermons in churches, mosques, temples and other religious institutions the problem of child labour still exists in its worst forms. Although I fail to understand the apathy of religions in eliminating child labour, it may be an offshoot of the influence of the rich and elite who are essentially responsible for this age-old crime. Seldom do these institutions work for safeguarding the rights of children.

In Hinduism, a child is equated with God. Certain girl children are worshipped by Hindus. Hindu epics reveal that there was no gender inequality in the ancient times. The religious childhood tales of Lord Rama and Krishna are an integral part of Hindu culture. In *Gurukul*, Prince Krishna and poor Sudama stayed and studied together without any discrimination or prejudice. There was complete equity in education, irrespective of gender or economic background.

In Christianity, the Bible shows that children were very dear to Christ. Christ in this holy book says – "Let the children come to me and do not forbid them, for the Kingdom of Heaven belongs to such as these." One must understand that it is not just the baptised children that Jesus calls upon but he clearly beckons to all children irrespective of their caste, creed and religion. More importantly, he accords priority to those who believe in him by putting 'children on the centre stage'.

There are umpteen numbers of examples in Islam that prove that children are the most cherished possessions of mankind. Prophet Mohammad himself had only one child – a daughter. He said that daughters were a divine gift. Islam reiterates the importance and necessity of education for all.

The holy Quran teaches that the dignity of a child should be respected in every aspect, for example, children must have their identity and should be introduced in society with a deep sense of respect. My own encounter with Islam was through a cleric who used to live in a mosque, adjacent to my ancestral home. Since he was an innocent old man and friendly towards children, as a child I would be attracted to learn Urdu from him. He recited stories and teachings of Islam. One thing that I learned that I would never forget is that Allah, the God is incorporeal and assumes no shape or form, but one can feel his aura radiating from the smile of a child sitting in the lap of his mother.

Now let us look at the reality. There are people who worship a girl child and feel no shame in raping even a one-year-old. Statistics show that fifty-three percent of children in our country are victims of sexual exploitation in one form or the other. Female foeticide and infanticide are at an all-time high. Girls are sold and bought for prostitution and slavery. Young boys and girls are recruited in institutions like *madrasah*s (seminaries) in countries like Pakistan, Afghanistan, Sudan, etc. purportedly to learn religion, but they are instead brainwashed to become terrorists, and even human bombs, to massacre humanity and demolish the great teachings of Islam.

There are various instances of children being employed, and then physically and mentally abused mercilessly by those who are community leaders. I still remember rescuing a seven-year-old boy from a glass bangle factory in Firozabad, a small industrial town in Uttar Pradesh. He used to blow molten glass to make bangles. The child's skin had turned black from the unbearable smoke, heat and dust. He was a bonded child labourer who was working for a ruthless employer. The child was often beaten up for even small mistakes at work.

One day while the boy was at work, molten glass accidently dripped on his palms, grievously injuring him. The hot liquid pierced through his flesh and bone like a bullet. His employer, instead of taking him to the hospital, mercilessly started beating him. I was petrified upon hearing his woeful tale. When I asked him his name, he innocently replied, 'Mohammad'. His employer, a Muslim community leader did not once hesitate in torturing a child whose name coincided with that of the Holy Prophet.

I am reminded of yet another horrific incident that took place in Mirzapur in the state of Uttar Pradesh. We had raided a carpet factory unit to rescue twelve young girls, who were trafficked from Sarguja district of Chhattisgarh in then Madhya Pradesh, and brought to a village in Mirzapur district. They were held in bondage for about two years at this place. During the rescue operation, eleven girls rushed out in relief from the factory with our activists but one fourteen-year-old girl was still missing. Along with a lady magistrate, I walked up again into the small factory unit and was shocked to see that girl weeping incessantly, facing a wall.

We told her that she had been freed and that she would now be reunited with her parents. Hearing this, she started crying even louder. When we asked her why, she screamed in anguish, "I have lost all face to go home." Later we learnt that she had been raped by her employer and was carrying his child. She did not want to go back home. When we asked her name, she replied, "Sita." A pious name coinciding with that of Lord Ram's wife in the Hindu epic Ramayana.

More shockingly, her employer was a local Hindu leader, with slogans prominently inscribed on the door of his factory demanding the restoration of 'Ram' Temple at Ayodhya. Could there be a bigger paradox than this? How would you have felt, had you been in my place?

We have been facing huge problems in rescuing trafficked and enslaved children from certain Muslim-dominated localities of Delhi. Several of my colleagues and I were attacked by a communal mob in mid-2011 in East Delhi where we had organised a secret raid in a cluster of *zari* (Gold filigree) embroidery factories.

These factory owners had lured about three dozen young Muslim kids under the garb of *madrasa* education, in collusion with several clerics. These children were held in bondage. The employers created a mass frenzy by shouting and instigating others that a *madrasa* was being attacked.

It is quite evident that these incidences have no relation with any religion whatsoever, but should one ignore instances where some people exploit the poor and hapless in the garb of religion?

On various occasions, it has been revealed that the living conditions of children in many charitable institutions like seminaries, missionaries, orphanages, shelter homes run by various faith groups are astonishingly shocking. The children were found to have been sexually abused, physically tortured and exploited. They are bereft of all dignity and protection. Even incidents of rape and sodomy are not uncommon in some of these places.

Most of the social evils and vices prevalent in our society continue unabated in the name of religion. The heinous crime of child sacrifice has not been eradicated yet. Traditionally, with sons considered as the natural heirs, daughters are outrightly discriminated across families and societies. One manifestation of this mindset is rampant female foeticide.

Another reflection of this mentality surfaces in child marriages that are most commonly practised in rural India. It is indeed a disgrace that nearly 50 percent of girls are married off at an age when they should be enjoying their childhood and attaining an education for shaping their future.

In my opinion, socially responsive citizens should insist that all believers and, in particular, the holy men and clerics across all faiths, must condemn child abuse in all its forms and variants, and uphold the rights and dignity of the child. People from all religions and cultures must earnestly work towards protecting the rights of the children.

Our Constitution guarantees strong rights for all children, irrespective of gender, social standing, economic status etc. India has signed various international conventions and promulgated many laws against child labour, but, unfortunately, these laws are openly flouted.

According to the Constitution of India, no child below the age of 14 years should be employed to work in any factory or mine, or engaged in any other hazardous occupation. Our Constitution is against all forms of forced labour, human trafficking and exploitation. Additionally, the right to free and compulsory education for all children up to the age of 14 is also guaranteed. We have other strong laws like the Bonded Labour System (Abolition) Act, 1976, and Child Labour (Prohibition and Regulation) Act, 1986.

In addition to this, the Juvenile Justice (Care and Protection) of Children Act, 2000 stipulates that whoever ostensibly procures a juvenile or a child (an individual less than 18 years of age) for the purpose of any hazardous employment, keeps him in bondage, withholds his earnings and/or uses such earning for his own purposes shall be punishable with imprisonment for a term which may extend to three years and shall be liable to a fine. These laws are periodically amended as well. Any sort of victimisation or exploitation of children, putting a child into bonded labour or child labour (in listed occupations and processes) and child-trafficking are legally punishable offences.

The honourable Supreme Court of India and other High Courts have delivered landmark judgements for the eradication of child labour. These judgments stipulate the arrest of errant employers, the sealing of workplaces where children are found working and the recovery of back wages of ₹ 20,000 from the employer per rescued child. The judgements also accord for the rehabilitation of these children. The lack of legal awareness on part of the citizens, the unaccountability of government officials, political and administrative corruption, the shortage of able and trained labour inspectors, and the influence of black money often come in the way of law enforcement.

Black money and corruption breed child labour to a large extent. According to non-governmental estimates, there are nearly sixty million child labourers in our country. However, the official estimates claim that there are only 12.67 million child labourers (as per Census 2001).

According to the authorities, on an average, each child is paid about ₹ 15 (30 cents) per day. This means that all child labourers put together would earn ₹ 90 crores (US$ 18 million) in a day. If these 60 million children were to be replaced by an equal number of adult workers, and assuming an average wage rate of ₹ 115 (US$ 2.30) per worker (although this is less than the stipulated legal minimum wage), they would earn about ₹ 690 crores (US$ 138 million) in a single day.

Thus, it is clear that if employers were to employ adults in place of children, then they would have to cough up an additional ₹ 600 crores (US$ 120 million). Considering 200 days of work, employers on an average save ₹ 1,20,000 crores (US$ 24 billion) every year by employing child labour.

The employers conveniently fudge their account books showing ₹ 115 (US$ 2.30) spent towards the remuneration of every adult worker, and are able to save ₹ 100 (US$ 2) per worker. ₹ 1,20,000 crores (US$ 24 billion) thus generated is nothing but black money which is partially used to bribe police and politicians. This further augments the ever burgeoning shadow economy in our country.

People always want to know what they can do in their individual capacities to eradicate child labour. I tell them that it is time we collectively worked towards bringing about this transformation in the society. In your individual capacity, you must firmly resolve that you would never engage any child either at home or at work.

Please do not accept any kind of hospitality whatsoever, not even a glass of water at the homes of your friends and relatives who employ domestic child labourers. Be resolute for not availing the services of restaurants or commercial establishments that employ children. Do not buy from shops that employ child labourers. Boycott things that are made by children. Try inculcating these habits in your friends and relatives as well. Try persuading parents of child labourers to start sending their children to school and make them aware of their children's rights.

Warn those who employ children and if required, do not refrain from complaining about them to the police, labour department officials or the child helpline. This could be done by making a call, sending an SMS, writing an e-mail or filing a written complaint. As a socially responsible citizen, do not cast your vote in favour of a political candidate who does not condemn child labour or does not have a structured plan to eliminate child labour from his or her constituency if voted into power.

It is heartening to see that child labour has become a topic of discussion in the media. If you come across any incidences of child labour, please sit up and take notice. You must approach the media to spread your message to the masses in the shortest possible time; the impact could be manifold.

Use social networking sites like Facebook and Twitter to spread awareness about child labour, citing the importance of education, emphasising a sound federal budget for implementing anti-child labour programmes, advocating for the effective implementation of child labour laws, and spearheading anti-child labour campaigns targeted at consumers.

You could work with the volunteers of BBA or similar organisations to tackle child labour head on.

I would like to call upon everyone to do whatever one possibly could to end child labour. We cannot, and must not, wait for others to act before we do. Procrastination would only worsen the issue. As socially responsible citizens of India, we must do all that it takes to eradicate child labour; otherwise, we will not be able to justify our existence to generations to come.

□

CHILDHOOD FREEDOM

"Democracy is inseparable from freedom. And, freedom is inseparable from childhood. Childhood and freedom are incomplete without each other."

1. As per the 2011 Census of India, there are 11,720,724 child labourers in the country.
2. More than 50 million children are victims of child labour in India, according to non-governmental statistics.
3. According to a 2014 report of the National Crime Records Bureau, only 147 cases of child labour were registered.
4. The National Crime Records Bureau report reveals that 458 child labourers were freed in 2014.
5. Among all the cases registered with the police in 2014, employers in only 2 percent of cases were punished.

Domestic Child Labour: Slavery in Disguise

Finally, the global community has begun to notice the tens of millions of domestic workers in the world. Taking cognisance of these workers, the International Labour Organization (ILO), a key institution under the United Nations, has decided to mark June 12th as the World Day Against Child Labour. It is noteworthy that just last year, during its annual convention attended by governments from across the world, the ILO passed an international law to ensure the security, rights and conditions conducive to dignified work for domestic workers. This is known as Convention No. 189 (Decent Work for Domestic Workers), which was adopted by the International Labour Conference of the ILO. In June last year, the Parliament of India also passed a similar law. Before that, there was no law for the security of adult domestic workers. Even though India and many other countries banned domestic child labour a few years ago, the Parliament of India has yet to ratify it.

Domestic labour is a kind of invisible slavery: one in which, behind closed doors, men and women do bone-breaking work in the face of abuse, and atrocities. It is a modern form of feudal thinking and a system in which professional, well-educated and influential families keep a poor or helpless person enslaved for their own convenience. It would indeed be very hard for the law to reach such a place, where children and women are condemned to live and die in despicable misery.

Some of the incidents encountered during *Bachpan Bachao Andolan's* (BBA – Save the Childhood Movement's) campaign to free domestic child labourers in the past few years are so painful that one is horrified to the core. Once a couple of tribal folks from a village in Assam reached out to us in Delhi. They could not even speak Hindi. They explained that around six or seven years ago, a tout from a placement agency had lured their daughters to Delhi. There had been no news of the girls since. After an in-depth investigation, it emerged that the owner of that placement agency had closed the office and sold off the girls to another agency. At that time, the girls were hardly eight or ten years old. By cutting several deals, the agency owner had sold them at various places for amounts ranging from ₹ 25,000 to ₹ 35,000. And the police? The police were not only in cahoots with the placement agency, but also tried their best to protect the rich slave-owners. The owners did not pay even a single penny to the girls for enslaving them for so many years. One of the girls, Radha (name changed), did not even want to face her father after she was rescued. When she was sent to a juvenile home, it was discovered that the 15-year-old was pregnant. One can barely understand the agony of the poor father in such a situation.

Another incident is even more shameful. In the past year, a placement agency called 'Mariam Convent' had brought 12 adolescent girls from the Kokrajhar district of Assam to Delhi with the help of a local tout. After they reached here, the agents put the children in a room and asked them to take off their clothes completely, one by one. They were told that it was to check whether they were hiding a phone number, or an address, or a document or anything else that could be used to harm the future employers—but there were ulterior motives behind this. Most of the girls, feeling ashamed, did not utter a single word about their own treatment, but recounted how the agents subjected the other girls to unspeakable misdeeds before the girls were handed over to their employers.

Domestic child labour of all types has been illegal in India since 2006. In case of government officials, keeping domestic child servants has been prohibited since 1999. There is also a provision for one year's imprisonment for those engaged in child labour.

Besides being subjected to child labour, most girls also fall victim to human trafficking, slavery, bonded labour and many other crimes, each of which is punishable with several years of imprisonment. But the readers will be astonished to know that, in spite of all these provisions, not even a single criminal is serving time in jail for child or bonded labour in India!

How can this feudal system of slavery be allowed to continue under the garb of poverty? A shameful excuse often given in its defence is that if the poor girls are not given work, they will go astray, beg or die of hunger. Which implies that giving them a job is a kind gesture. A lot of people do not hesitate to offer the misplaced argument that the maidservant is just like their own daughter. But the reality is that they keep an innocent girl as a maid only because she is the cheapest worker available—who cannot raise her voice against an atrocity, who will neither insist nor does she need to return home, unlike an adult, in the evening. On the contrary, she readily accepts to spend her nights on a sack or torn mat in the dark and dingy garage, in a corner of the kitchen or even out on the balcony, crouching under a plastic sheet—come summer, cold or rain. Most employers believe they can rest assured that the girls would not steal and run away easily. Early morning, shivering in the cold, the girl would hold the heavy bag of the beloved son of their employer and walk him to the school bus, not uttering a single word of complaint. Is this being kind to them?

To keep up the pretext of child labour in the face of poverty is against the principles of justice. The first question to ask is this: Are the children guilty of poverty or are they victims of poverty? Is keeping these innocent children perpetually under the curse of poverty, helplessness, illiteracy, disease and slavery, the mark of morality in any civil society?

On the one hand, you have 60 million child labourers in the country and on the other, there are 65 million adults without jobs. Multiple studies have made it clear that a majority of these adults who are jobless or have only partial employment are none other than the elder brothers and sisters, or parents, of the unfortunate child labourers. If the children are taken off labour, it would be possible for the adult members of their family to get employment, thus alleviating them from poverty.

One must not forget that elementary school education is a fundamental right for all children in the age group of six to fourteen years. It is against the Constitution to make children work in homes, hotels, restaurants, etc. It is the responsibility of the Government to ensure strict enforcement of the law against child labour. In this endeavour, the Government should recruit a sufficient number of trained and sensitive labour inspectors and officials, besides involving, with due responsibility, the *Panchayat* system, voluntary organisations and resident welfare organisations in the cities. Perchance, if child labour continues in an area despite these efforts, then inspectors in the labour, industry and police departments should be held accountable and action should be taken against them. Volunteer citizen groups can also be constituted to conduct raids at different places. More important than all of these measures, however, is to socially boycott those families who employ child labourers—even if the families are our own friends and relatives.

□

(—June 2013)

Human Rights and Child Labour

Let me first applaud the leadership of Telephonica in the fight against child labour in the region. This conference is even more appropriate and timely to give a clarion call to the international community and all other stakeholders, just a few months before the Global Child Labour Conference in Brazil. I hope this conference will help in raising a sense of urgency and re-affirm the commitments we have made to children, time and again. Only two years remain for the deadline set to achieve the Millennium Development Goals, including the Dakar goals for attaining Education for All, and three years to eliminate the worst forms of child labour.

We have made significant progress in creating a child-friendly world, during the early years of the first decade of this millennium. The number of out-of-school children has decreased from 113 million to 61 million, as well as the number of child labourers from almost 250 million to 215 million. 161 countries have committed to eradicating the worst forms of child labour by ratifying Convention 182, and agreeing to eradicate all forms of child labour up to the age of 14 years by ratifying the minimum age convention, i.e. Convention 138. While no doubt there is headway, it is not enough as the number of child labour and out-of-school children have decreased, but at a lower rate than before.

One prime reason behind this is that the 215 million children now left in exploitative situations and the 61 million out-of-school children are the ones who are from a more difficult and harder to reach category, compared to before.

This clearly indicates that these children are most vulnerable, likely to be trapped under conditions which are hidden or invisible, afflicted by chronic poverty, discriminatory practices, socio-economic exclusion, slavery, trafficking, HIV/AIDS, conflicts, etc. and facing the worst human rights violations. These children need our urgent attention, beginning with addressing our knowledge gap of where and under what conditions these children are trapped.

Several human rights laid down under the Universal Declaration of Human Rights are violated when child labourers are employed or children are economically exploited. Article 3 of the Declaration (*Everyone has the right to life, liberty and security of person*) is violated when children are made to work under hazardous conditions as are found in the mining, construction and agricultural sectors, wherein the regular tasks allocated jeopardise their health. Article 4 (*No one shall be held in slavery or servitude; slavery and the slave trade shall be prohibited in all their forms*) is violated when children are made to work in bonded labour, forced labour and slave-like conditions, in supply chains of companies or at homes as domestic help.

Furthermore, one goes against the principle enshrined under Article 5 (*No one shall be subjected to torture or to cruel, inhuman or degrading treatment or punishment*) when child labourers are made to work under inhumane, unhealthy and dangerous conditions, and are physically and sexually abused by their employers. The right to freedom of movement conferred under Article 13(1) is violated often in cases of child trafficking for forced labour and work under slave-like conditions. Article 24 (*Everyone has the right to rest and leisure, including reasonable limitation of working hours and periodic holidays with pay*) is violated when children are made to work for long hours, without rest and many a time without a weekly day off. Lastly, the moment child labour occurs, the child's right to education as per Article 26(1) of the Declaration is denied.

Moreover, child labour and child trafficking, leads to the denial and violation of several child rights laid down under the United Nations Convention on the Rights of the Child (UNCRC). The survival and development rights enshrined in the Convention, viz. Article 6 on *Right to survival and development*, Article 28 on *Right to education*, and Article 31 on *Right to leisure, play and join cultural/recreational activities* are denied to children engaged in work at the cost of their education, health and education. Child labour also goes against the spirit of various legal instruments to protect the rights of children such as Article 19 on *Protection from all kinds of violence*, Article 32 for *Child labour*, Article 33 for *Protecting children from drug abuse and trafficking*, and Article 35 on *Protection from abduction, sale and trafficking*. Lastly, as per Article 15 of the Convention that deals with participatory rights, children have the freedom to form associations, but this right is denied when the child becomes a labourer.

Child labour also violates the principles laid down in various international treaties that are embedded under the human rights framework. These treaties include the UN Palermo Protocol on Trafficking and various ILO (International Labour Organization) instruments. Child labour is in violation of the four fundamental principles and rights at work laid down by the ILO, viz. freedom of association and the effective recognition of the right to collective bargaining, elimination of all forms of forced or compulsory labour, effective abolition of child labour, and the elimination of discrimination with respect to employment and occupation.

These principles and rights invoke the spirit of human rights – they uphold basic human values, which are fundamental to our lives. Child labour is in contravention to several ILO Conventions. In the case of Convention 29 and Convention 105 on *Forced Labour and its abolition*, many children are working under different forms of forced labour like debt bondage, trafficking and other slavery-like practices. With regard to Convention 87 on *Freedom of Association* and Convention 98 on *Right to organise and collective bargaining,* while children cannot unionise nor form organisations for their interests which encourages their economic exploitation, child labour weakens the collective bargaining by trade unions since children can be hired at lower than the minimum wage, and are made to work for longer hours, compared to adults. Convention 138 on *Minimum Age for Employment* states that children should not be employed until they have attained the minimum age for work or completed compulsory schooling, whichever is later. Further, Convention 182 on *Worst Forms of Child Labour* requires child labour in illegal activities, such as trafficking, armed conflicts, pornography, and hazardous work to be prohibited. Lastly, as per Convention 189 on *Decent Work for Domestic Workers,* children below the minimum age to work, or those labouring under hazardous conditions in domestic work should not be employed. Despite this, child labour exists and children as young as five years old are employed. 15.5 million children are engaged in domestic work globally.

There are several mechanisms for monitoring human rights and child rights as per the UNCRC, and the rights and privileges under ILO Conventions. The UN Human Rights Council is responsible for strengthening the promotion and protection of human rights around the globe and for addressing human rights violations and making policy recommendations. It assesses the human rights record of in all countries and conducts a universal periodic review of the same. Non-governmental organisations (NGOs) and national human rights institutions also contribute to the review process through written reports about the country under review. The UN Committee on the Rights of the Child monitors the implementation of the UNCRC by member states. All member states are obliged to submit regular reports to the committee on how the rights are being extended. Countries are required to report initially after the first two years after acceding to the convention, and consecutively, every five years.

For ILO Conventions, member states are required to report regularly to the ILO on the implementation of ratified conventions, indicating not only whether national laws are in conformity with the convention in question, but also informing the ILO regarding progress made to ensure the convention has had an impact at a practical level. Member states are required to report on measures taken to ensure the implementation of ratified conventions, and on any problems encountered in their implementation, at intervals of one to five years, depending on which convention is in question.

Child labourers are also denied various rights that are constitutionally guaranteed by the state to its children. For instance, in the case of India, specific provisions are laid down in the Constitution to protect children from economic exploitation and given the right to free and compulsory education to all children under the ages of 6 to 14 years, the prohibition of human trafficking and forced labour, and the prohibition of employment of children in factories, mines or in other hazardous occupations.

Not only does child labour entail a violation and denial of human rights on countless fronts, it also poses a hindrance to development. The links between child labour with poverty and education highlight the developmental challenge that child labour poses. Poverty has often been considered the key reason for the perpetuation of child labour. However, child labour is the primary cause of poverty, as it pushes children into premature labour, thereby denying children the opportunity to acquire the education and skills they need to obtain decent work and incomes as adults. The elimination of child labour is an essential prerequisite to the eradication of extreme poverty and hunger [Millenium Development Goal (MDG) 1]. The most common reason for decrying the scourge of child labour is that it comes at the cost of human development. Achieving universal primary education (MDG 2) is contingent upon freedom from labour to allow children to attend school and perform well. The UN Mid-term review of MDGs clearly identified child labour as a major obstacle to the achievement of universal primary education.

A survey of 120 countries from 1970 to 2000 provides compelling evidence that education consistently and significantly aids economic development and is a necessary precondition for long-term economic growth. A recently completed study of 50 countries established that every extra year of schooling provided to the whole population could increase average annual GDP growth by 0.37 per cent. This study shows that child labour holds back economic growth and countries' development.

To eliminate child labour, various gaps and deficits need to be addressed. These include overcoming cultural, financial, political, knowledge, and coordination and convergence gaps. There is still considerable acceptance of child labour across societies and cultures as child labour is seen as a natural recourse and the only available option for children from socio-economically disadvantaged families and backgrounds. Households employing child labourers often feel that they are helping children earn extra income to support their families, and not halting their growth and well-being as children. This is related to the problem of seeing child labour in the limited perspective of only an economic issue, and not as the violation of one's rights as human beings regardless of socio-economic backgrounds. Changing mindsets and attitude of people and overcoming this cultural gap is imperative to ending child labour.

Despite the gravity and the magnitude of the problem of child labour, the child labour portfolio is very small vis-á-vis HIV/AIDS, education, etc. and more funds and resources need to be mobilised. There is a lack of a dedicated global fund for child labour.

There are gaps too, at the political level, which need attention. The inadequate translation of international legal instruments and policy framework into national legislation, and their inadequate enforcement and implementation demonstrates the lack of political will of governments to end child labour. The civil society movement encompassing NGOs, child rights organisations, teachers' associations, trade unions, and the public need to urge governments to honour their commitments.

There is also a lack of adequate knowledge and data on various aspects and forms of child labour. For instance, there is a lack of disaggregated data on child labour, related activities, etc., in the various sub-sectors of the agriculture industry. Furthermore, there is also a lack of understanding on the issue of child slaves. Many child slaves have been reported in cocoa farming, cotton seed farming, domestic labour, and other sectors. According to ILO statistics, there are approximately 21 million victims of forced labour, out of which 5.5 million are children. There is a lack of clear definition, data and research on child slavery. When children, vulnerable and pliable, are made victims of forced labour and lose total freedom and choice (such as freedom of movement, rest at one's will, etc.) through deceptive means and/or false promises made to them/their families, it can be construed that such children are child slaves. Also, consent is not valid in the case of children. There is a need to clearly define child slavery so that such children can be identified and rescued and not remain hidden and invisible. The civil society needs to work and advocate for the inclusion of child slavery on the international policy agenda.

There is a need for greater coordination and convergence between international agencies dealing with the issue of protection of children from exploitation, to taking effective and concerted action for ending child labour. For instance, the ILO views child labour from a labour perspective and within the human rights framework; UNICEF views it specifically from the perspective of the violation of child rights, whereas the United Nations Office on Drugs and Crime (UNODC) views it from the perspective of crime of children being trafficked for forced labour. Furthermore, UNESCO only deals with the education of children. These different perspectives and compartmentalisation only lead to insufficient coordination and the lack of convergence in tackling the issue of child labour.

Along with addressing these gaps and deficits, there is a need to replicate and upscale practices, programmes, and schemes that work. There is no dearth of solutions for tackling child labour and relegating it to the pages of history. We have several examples which embody this. Firstly, various social protection and welfare schemes can be useful in tackling child labour by addressing not only children's vulnerabilities, but also that of the adult family members and the entire household. In India, it has been seen that the incidence of child labour is comparatively lower in states where welfare schemes like the Mahatma Gandhi National Rural Employment Guarantee Act (MGNREGA), which enhances livelihood security of people in rural areas, the *Sarva Shiksha Abhiyaan* (Education for All) scheme, mid-day meals in school to encourage enrollments, and those related to rural development, are being efficiently implemented.

There is also *Bolsa Familia*, a welfare scheme introduced in Brazil, in which cash transfers were given to poor families with the condition of sending their children to school. Abolishing school fees is another way. Education is a preventive measure in tackling child labour. If children are given access to education and are in school, they will not have to work. Making education free and improving its quality, like Kenya, Tanzania and Malawi have done has significantly reduced the incidence of child labour. We could also use social labelling mechanisms to prevent the engagement of children in exploitative work in supply chains.

To address child labour in the supply chains of weaved carpets and raise consumer awareness, BBA initiated a unique social label mechanism. Under this initiative, every rug that was produced was given a child labour free label. This endeavor, coupled with other actions like raid and rescue and social mobilisation, resulted in the reduction of child labour in the carpet industry by nearly 80 percent. Lastly, the certification of goods produced is another way of curbing child labour in supply chains. The purpose of the certification system or scheme is to verify and guarantee that the good has been made in compliance with certain specified standards, such as honouring the ILO Convention 182, and is child labour free. For instance, the Fairtrade Labeling Organizations International, Rainforest Alliance, and UTZ Certified are running certification schemes for cocoa production.

Although concrete results in the decrease of incidence of child labour is still awaited, multi-stakeholder initiatives and partnerships in the cocoa, tobacco, palm oil, cotton, garment and other industries at least have helped in raising awareness, enhancing accountability and generating knowledge. Some of them have also introduced product verification-certification systems.

To conclude, I reiterate that the total eradication of child labour is possible, affordable and achievable. What is needed is genuine political will demonstrated through the enactment and enforcement of appropriate legislation, backed by adequate resources, and instituting and strengthening accountability frameworks. Secondly, powerful and collective efforts and partnerships have to be built by civil society towards re-invigorating a strong worldwide movement against child labour. The creation of political will also depends on public demand and action. The international community and governments, in particular, must make honest effort at integrating and mainstreaming the issue of child labour into the human rights and development policies and programmes, particularly in dealing with all forms of discrimination and exclusion, ensuring education and alleviating poverty. Phrases such as – 'children first', 'children can't wait', 'children are the future', and 'urgency' must not remain rhetoric and superficial, but the spirit behind these words must be internalised and practised in reality to make the world free from child exploitation.

□

(—July 2013)

Child Labour and Millennium Development Goals: Connecting the Dots

June 12th is the World Day Against Child Labour. Today, all over the world, governments, non-governmental organisations (NGOs) and labour organisations are conducting myriad programmes to create awareness against child labour. This day is celebrated to highlight the various issues related to child labour. The theme this year, 'Go for the Goal: End Child Labour', has been chosen keeping in mind the World Cup being held in June to July in South Africa. The International Labour Organization (ILO) has also published a report recently on child labour.

According to the ILO report, 215 million children are still employed as labourers, of which 115 million are engaged under dangerous and worst forms of child labour. These children toil amidst dust and smoke in deep mines or chemical factories. There are millions who are bought and sold at rates lower than cattle's, who are enslaved or made to work as bonded labourers, who are exploited as child prostitutes and child soldiers, and/or who are made to commit criminal acts such as trading in drugs and narcotic substances.

Child labour is not an isolated problem, but is deeply connected with poverty and the lack of education. There is a deep cause-and-effect relationship among the three, that is, a chicken-and-egg situation. Child labour persists as a result of the lack of quality education as much as illiteracy thrives on child labour. Likewise, poverty perpetuates child labour which, in turn, perpetuates poverty. The year 2010 is very important from this perspective. Not only are international reports being published on these three issues, but the international community is coming together on future strategies, their implementation and monitoring at the top level.

An important high-level group of the United Nations held its meeting this January at the Ethiopian capital, Addis Ababa. Education ministers and senior labour officials from more than 40 countries participated in this meeting at which a report on the state of global education was tabled and widely discussed. According to the report, 75 million children in the age group of 6 to 14 years are out of school. Concern was raised in the report that the objective of providing 'Education for All' cannot be achieved by the year 2015. If the current situation persists, 27 countries could not achieve this objective. The report focusses on the lack of, and deterioration of, education for the economically and socially marginalised sections of the society.

Child labour has been cited as one of the biggest causes of illiteracy, dropouts from school in primary classes, and the erosion of quality in education. Governments have been advised that if they want to achieve the objective of 'Education for All', then they must pay more attention to the oppressed segments, the people and communities who are victims of social injustice and economic inequality, including child labourers. These communities have been listed under the difficult-to-reach section, which includes physically and mentally disabled children, victims of diseases such as HIV AIDS, orphans, Dalits, tribal groups, displaced, children in areas affected by war and violence, and bonded and child labourers, especially domestic child labourers and victims of child trafficking, among others. The children who are not in school today are not sitting idle at home. Special efforts will have to be made to extricate them from difficult circumstances and ensure their enrolment in schools.

At the high-level meeting, a joint declaration, called the Addis Ababa Declaration, was issued by United Nations institutions, governments and NGOs. Under the Declaration, the governments of developed countries committed to increasing the international aid grants allocated to education and the developing countries promised to spend at least 6 percent of their GDP on education. Most importantly, the Declaration emphasised eradicating child labour and doing everything possible to provide education to all. Until then, the issue of child labour had been confined, at an international level, only to labour ministries of the various governments and the ILO. The Addis Ababa Declaration strongly argues in favour of education departments working in tandem with other ministries and departments, which is a significant policy development. There is a great need to implement this at the national stage as well.

The other important event was the International Conference against Child Labour held last month. It was organised jointly by the ILO and the Government of Netherlands. The last conference on such a large scale was held in 1997. Representatives from around 70 countries, including India, participated in the event. At the conference, a roadmap to eradicate the worst forms of child labour by 2016 was prepared, which included several practical measures and commitments. The good thing is that there are many similarities between this roadmap and the Addis Ababa Declaration. For instance, the importance of quality education in the efforts to eradicate child labour, collaboration amongst the various United Nations organisations as well as coordination among different ministries and departments at the national level, increases in the allocation of donations and budgets to education, and the need to get buy in from all sections of society. The need to view 'Education for All' or 'Ending Child Labour' in conjunction with poverty eradication and Millennium Development Goals has been underlined in both the documents. All the same, in evaluating the success or failure of the Millennium Development Goals, the issues of education and child labour cannot be sidelined.

The third significant event for the world will take place in September this year in New York at the headquarters of the United Nations (UN). World leaders are meeting for a mid-term review of the Millennium Development Goals for the development and the eradication of extreme poverty. Heads of State of all the key countries of the world, including the Prime Minister of India, will attend this special UN summit.

In the run-up to the event, people are discussing a few progress indicators, but there are several grave concerns as well. In the year 2000, the global community sat together and ascertained eight goals, which included halving the poverty levels in the world, providing primary education to all children, and goals related to employment, environment and healthcare. For all, education is the second most important goal without which the other goals could not be achieved. Even though ending child labour is not included as a direct Millennium goal, we should not forget that without ending child labour, it would not be possible to achieve the other objectives related to education, poverty, employment and gender equality.

Today, the economic development of the world is dependent on the propagation of information and knowledge. It is not possible to decentralise business, markets and political power without quality education for all. On one hand, there are 215 million children engaged in full-time employment and, on the other, 185 million adults are unemployed. It is clear that the Millennium Development Goal of reducing unemployment is not possible without putting an end to child labour. Poverty eradication is also connected with this.

The Parliament of India has passed the 'Right to Education Law for All', which is a historic initiative. But the success of this law depends on how effective our society and government will be in connecting the dots between ending child labour and providing education. There is a need for the consolidation and reconciliation of the various different schemes being run in India such as the *Sarva Shiksha Abhiyana*, mid-day meals, scholarships for socially or economically backward children, *Rashtriya Bal Shram Pariyojana* and the Mahatma Gandhi National Rural Employment Guarantee Act (MGNREGA). Against the backdrop of a global economic downturn, if we want to ensure that the Indian economy grows between nine to ten percent, it becomes necessary that our country free those 50 to 60 million children from child labour—children who are not only our important human resources but also the foundation upon which the future of our economic development, social justice and harmony rests.

□

(—June 2009)

Need of the Hour: A Child-Friendly Mindset

In the world's largest democracy, India, 47 percent of children below the age of five are malnourished. UNICEF has recently revealed that, globally, out of the 9.7 million children who die before attaining the age of five, as many as 2.1 million are in India. Among the 155 million infants who are born underweight, 55 million are Indian. Every single day, 5,700 children die of malnutrition or diseases arising from it. Eighty percent of children are victims of physical or mental abuse of one kind or the other. Fifty-one out of 100 children are subjected to sexual exploitation of some kind. And two out of every three children are beaten up as a matter of routine.

Every year, 40,000 to 50,000 children disappear without a trace, in the manner of a mobile phone, wallet or toy. Around 50 to 60 million children are victims of child labour. Millions of children are bought and sold from one place to another., at prices below that of cattle In the Indian capital, Delhi alone, on average, six children are kidnapped daily. Notorious gangs making children beg on the streets after gouging out their eyes or amputating their hands and legs, is not just an imaginary scene from the movie *Slumdog Millionaire* but a stark everyday reality. On any given day, it is seldom possible to pick up the newspaper and not find a rape case of an innocent girl, or her murder. Two years ago, tough legal provisions were established in India to stop domestic child labour, and yet every other day, there occur despicable incidents of domestic maidservants being branded with hot irons or mercilessly beaten by their employer—be it an actress, a government official or the so-called educated middle-class professional. There is little hue and cry about it in the media. After every such incident, the 'sound bytes' of officials or leaders of voluntary organisations are played on news channels for a day or two. After that, it is back to square one.

We must look within ourselves: Personal, public and political honesty should be examined. People who do everything for the future of their own children—from working hard to indulging in bribery and corruption—are often the ones who do not desist from enslaving others' children. They go to great lengths to getting their children admitted to an expensive English-medium school, but they feel no shame in sipping tea made by a poor child at a roadside stall, or in asking him to polish their shoes. It does not occur to them that the future of India belongs not only to their beloved kids, but to other children as well. What other precedent of double standards in public life will you find than the fact that not only political leaders and government officials, not only the intellectuals who talk about child rights, but even social workers are guilty of espousing wrong assumptions? For example, they say that if the poor child will not work, she will die or become a prostitute—so child labour is a better alternative for them. Some people argue that India does not have enough resources to provide quality education to every child. Or, if poor children are forcibly admitted to expensive English-medium schools, the level of education will deteriorate. There are hundreds of other such fallacies.

A similar apathy prevails in the case of political will. There are around 260 million children below the age of 14 years in our country but it is incongruent that for their education, only a paltry 1.5 percent of the Gross Domestic Product (GDP) is spent; almost the same is the expenditure on their health. After a long wait of half a decade, education became a constitutional right, and it took another decade for this right to become a law. It is difficult to say how many decades it will take for the law to be effectively implemented on the ground. The legislation has several incongruities, but the biggest irony is that this law poses the danger of the privatisation of education or making it a consumer commodity, besides broadening the gap of educational inequality. Laws pertaining to the rights and welfare of children are routinely torn apart. Nevertheless, our leaders never shy away from giving elaborate speeches on Children's Day year after year.

Against this backdrop, it is also required to highlight the poor condition of the so-called juvenile justice homes meant for children in conflict with the law. According to a recent report, all children living in these homes consider it a 'jail for children'. Half of the youngsters will try to escape from it after falling prey to one or another act of violence by the adults in the facility. Eighty percent of the workers and officials employed at a juvenile home have no knowledge of the rights of children. One need not go far to see the dire consequences: in the past 10 months, at least 12 children have died in juvenile homes run by the government in Delhi, the capital of the country. Before that, in the two preceding years, 16 and 21 children, respectively, had lost their lives.

In our country, no training is given to labour inspectors and officials appointed for curbing child labour, to equip them to be sensitive towards children and mindful of their rights and dignity under interrogation. The situation with the police is even worse: their method of interrogating a child, who is possibly a victim of an atrocity, is absolutely crass, insulting and, often, anti-children. The police constable or superintendent receives no training to behave with children in a friendly manner. Unfortunately, even the courts fare no better.

Tens of millions of children are losing their childhood in the rough-and-tumble of globalisation, capitalism, and the scramble for a better career, more income and greater convenience. There is psychological pressure on children to get above 90 percent in marks even if they study in the most expensive schools. Likewise, unsafe schools that lack amenities, with no daily commute nor easy means of transport are constantly proving to be dangerous and perhaps even, murderous, for children. Indifference rather than friendliness is on the rise, not only for the children but also for their guardians and parents.

In fact, the tapestry of our society has been woven keeping in mind the comforts, needs, interests and rights of adults, especially men. Around this revolves our politics, law, our education and healthcare systems—along with the distribution of income and resources. As a matter of habit, we do not want to know about the rights of children, nor do we undertake enough initiatives for their safety and dignity. Yes, we do have pity or mercy for them because we consider them foolish, weak and helpless. Means of transport, vehicles, public toilets, restaurants, auditoriums, roads, railway stations, bus stops, even schools and hospitals are built or constructed with no consideration for the convenience and safety of children—because we do not take cognisance of children's existence.

We should indeed devise a new social mindset: the child-friendly mindset. To take pity on needy children is as flawed as it is to think of them as being helpless and exploiting them. Defending children's rights has remained limited to empty promises. Mere rhetoric, bookish deliberations and intellectual dalliance in seminars is not going to deepen our understanding of child rights, let alone defend them. Children's rights are not something that can be realised only with the help of law. It requires a sea change in our thinking, behaviour and lifestyle. In fact, there is a need to establish a culture that values children's rights. A beginning will have to be made, where people learn to respect childhood and to develop a friendly bond with children by winning their trust—at home, in schools and in our public life.

The need of the hour is to evoke in people a sensitivity towards childhood as well as to create awareness about children's rights and safety. The provision of quality education and training should be mandatory for all those who have to deal with children directly; whether these individuals are drivers or conductors of school buses, workers in educational institutes, teachers, principals, managers or employees of hospitals and health centres. This provision is even more necessary for workers and officials of juvenile homes, student hostels, police and labour departments and courts. An awareness of child safety also needs to be created among the common public.

Until our society and government make special arrangements for children based on their spoken and unspoken needs, keeping in mind their rights and physical or mental age, until they hold people appointed to implement the laws accountable and implement court injunctions and schemes related to children, until we develop a culture of friendly behaviour with children, and until we build a wide social and mental safety net for children—until then, serious crimes against childhood and children will continue to be treated as mere incidents.

After all, how long shall we continue the hypocrisy towards the present and future of our children? How long shall we continue to deceive them? It is true that most children today do not have the guts to question their masters, but be assured that the reality will be completely different in the times to come. Some children have started to challenge the age-old hypocrisy, habitual reneging and anti-child customs of the past, and it is a tide that cannot be turned back. Tomorrow, when every child takes her elders to task, will we have any answer to give her?

□

(—March 2009)

With the Nobel Peace Prize in Oslo, Norway (10 December 2014)

Addressing the International Labour Organisation (June 2015)

Receiving the Harvard Humanitarian of the Year Award (October 2015)

Dedicating the Nobel medal to the nation by presenting it to President Shri Pranab Mukherjee (7 January, 2015)

In discussion with Prime Minister Shri Narendra Modi for eradication of child labour in India (2015)

With the Hon'ble Chief Justice of India Mr T.S. Thakur (2015)

At an event organised by Bachpan Bachao Andolan with the then Vice-President Shri Bhairon Singh Shekhawat (2003)

Meeting with Leader of Opposition Ms Sonia Gandhi for the Child-friendly village programme (2015)

Meeting the then President Shri K.R.Narayanan to demand that education be made a fundamental right (2001)

Urging the then Prime Minister Shri Inder Kumar Gujral to take measures to protect children from violence (1998)

Calling for education to be made a fundamental right under the Constitution with the then Prime Minister Shri Atal Bihari Vajpayee (2000)

Leading a march against child trafficking in India with the then Hon'ble Chief Justice of India Mr. Altamas Kabir (8 December, 2012)

At a conference with the then Chief Justice of India Mr K.G. Balakrishnan (14 November, 2008)

Seeking support for the inclusion of child slavery, child labour and trafficking in the Sustainable Development Goals from fellow Nobel Laureate and President of the United States of America Mr Barack Obama, First Lady Michelle Obama, Wife Sumedha Kailash and some children (2015)

Walking with the then Prime Minister of the United Kingdom Mr Gordon Brown to participate at an event for child labour in Delhi (2008)

At the launch of 'Speak Truth to Power' in Washington DC with the then President of the United States of America Mr Bill Clinton, Ms Kerry Kennedy and freed child slave Kalu Kumar (1999)

During the Global March against Child Labour with the then President of France Mr Jacques Chirac (1998)

In deep conversation with American Senator Tom Harkin on issues of child slavery and human rights (1998)

Presenting a petition for the inclusion of child slavery, child labour and trafficking in Sustainable Development Goals signed by 550,000 people to the then United Nations Secretary General Ban ki Moon (2015)

Culmination of Global March at United Nations Palace, Geneva, when Mr Satyarthi along with some children was invited to address the International Labour Organisation convention in session (1998)

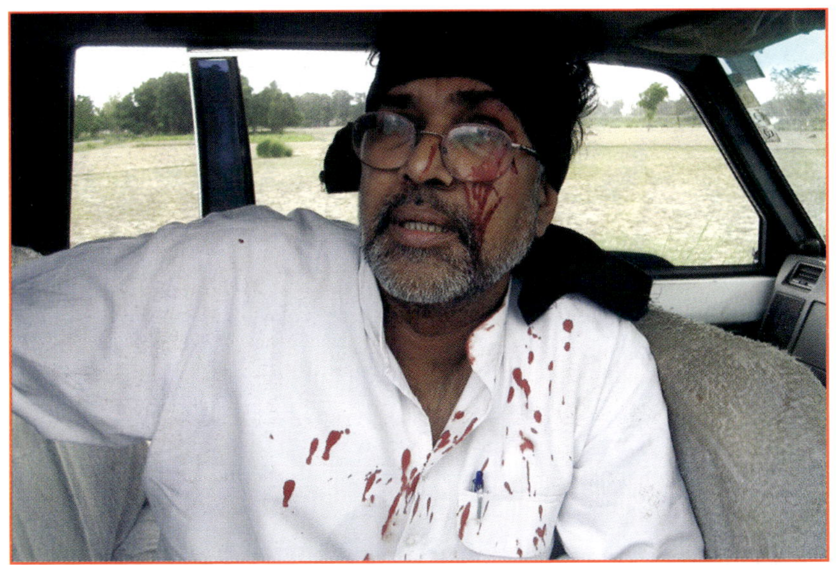

Attacked by circus mafia in a raid operation to rescue young Nepali girls who had been enslaved in Gonda district, Uttar Pradesh (2004)

In Pakistan during the Global March against Child Labour which traversed 80,000 kms across 103 countries (1998)

Global March against Child Labour in Costa Rica (1998)

Mr Satyarthi leading the South Asian March against Child Trafficking in Bangladesh. The march travelled 15,000 kms and witnessed participation of a million people (2007)

South Asian March against Child Trafficking in Nepal (2007)

Leading a protest march with parents of missing children in New Delhi (2007)

During the Bharat Yatra against Child Labour (1994). Under Kailash Satyarthi's guidance, the march went across the nation covering 5000 kms from Kanyakumari to New Delhi

Protest march against child labour in stone quarries of Faridabad region, Haryana (1981)

Taking part in a demonstration against child labour in Jaipur, Rajasthan (1982)

With child workers of cocoa bean farms in Ivory Coast, West Africa (2012)

At Bachpan Bachao Andolan's rehabilitation and education centre for freed child labourers, Bal Ashram in Virat Nagar, Rajasthan (2013)

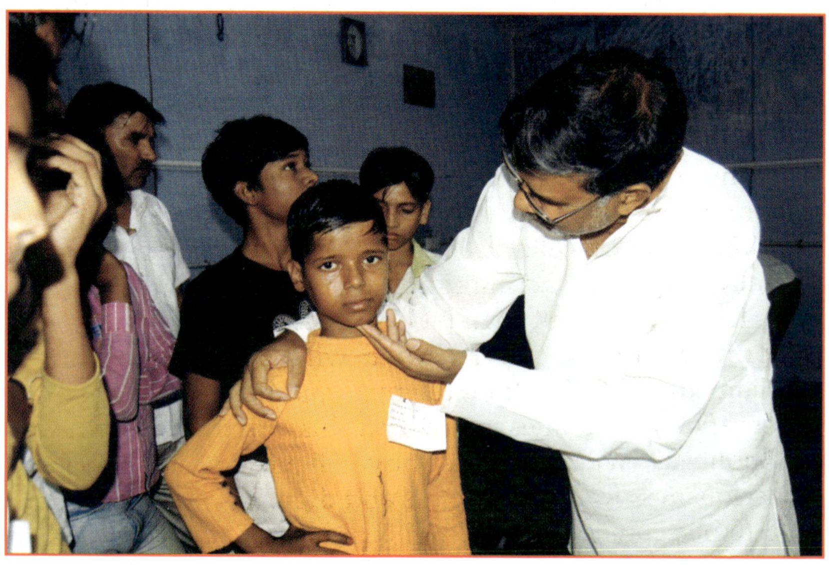

With a group of children, just after freeing them from bondage in 2010

Will Domestic Labourers Get Justice?

The world over, there are more than 100 million domestic labourers – mostly women and children. It might be astonishing that until a few days ago, there was no law to ensure safe and dignified working conditions for them. But an international convention has come into being at the annual convention of the International Labour Organization (ILO).

Hopes have risen with the new international law. Under the law, each member state will decide, after its respective Parliament's ratification, the method of translating the international standards into the domestic legal framework. Called Convention No. 189 (Decent Work for Domestic Workers), this convention is special in the sense that, rather than merely giving guidelines, it guarantees protection of all human rights of domestic workers. This law ensures that any coercion or discrimination at work, including child labour is completely abolished. It also guarantees regulated working hours, healthcare, weekly time off work, gender equality in labour and minimum wages.

The Government of India has agreed to the convention in principle. It is possible that it will be ratified by our parliament, but the fundamental question is: Can any international or domestic law end this evil in the absence of political will, administrative honesty, and social consciousness for human rights and dignity?

In our country about 5 million children up to 14 years of age are employed full-time as domestic labourers, out of which 90 percent are girls. Teenaged girls from 14 to 18 years comprise an even larger number.

I wish to recount a couple of incidents that took place in Delhi a few months ago. With the help of police, *Bachpan Bachao Andolan* rescued 14 girls from domestic slavery. It was found that a pair of twin sisters, Sita and Radha (names changed), were brought to Delhi from the West Singhbhum district of Jharkhand, three years ago by an agent. At that time, the girls were 10 years old. They had gone to a fair held outside their village when a lady, luring them with free entertainment shows, got them to board a local train. Coincidentally, their mother, who had come to gather twigs near the railway line, heard the cries of her wailing daughters through the coach windows. But the poor woman could do nothing for the lack of any evidence and in the face of police incompetence. Sudama, the lady agent, handed over the girls to one Anand Placement Agency in Delhi. After a few weeks, two separate masters took them to their homes to employ them as domestic labourers.

All this while, the girls did not even get a single penny. Their masters said that they had been paying salaries to the placement agency. But all that Sita and Radha got for the back-breaking 15 to16 hour-days, which included dusting and cleaning, cooking, washing and caring for the employers' children, were rebukes and abuses. After her rescue, Sita narrated how she would be slapped if she happened to play with her employer's children or look at the pictures in their books or sit on the bed with their dog. Her twin sister, Radha, was quite sharp. She faintly remembered the phone number of a relative from her village. After several failed attempts, she succeeded in reaching out to this relative and telling him about their abduction by Sudama, who lived near their village. This formed the beginning of their rescue. The owner of the placement agency was arrested, but the employers who had enslaved the girls for three years went scot-free.

For years, keeping maid servants has been an accepted norm in Indian society. Young or adolescent girls used to be part of the dowry of a daughter. Today, a large number of people like to keep village and small town girls as maids for their own comfort, convenience and security. Girl child labourers have been rescued from the homes of government officials, members of parliament, legislators, ministers and even judges from time to time. Not only that, one often witnesses incidents of torture on maids working in foreign embassies as well as in the homes of officials who are deputed abroad in United Nations institutions. These domestic servants are not paid on the pretext that the dues will be settled with their family folk back in India. Even their passports are taken away from them and kept by their employers.

The burgeoning middle class of an economically developing India finds a cheap child maid servant one among their sundry needs. This demand has engendered thousands of so-called placement agencies running illegally in the country. Delhi alone has around 2,200, of which nearly 2,000 forego registeration, or adherence to rules and regulations. There is an intricate web of child and women traffickers in several districts of states, like Jharkhand, Odisha, Chhattisgarh, West Bengal, Assam and others. As per a study conducted by a non-governmental organisation, 80 percent of homes prefer to keep children as servants, especially girls, below the age of 14, with the rest preferring adolescent girls. In about half of these cases, the maids are never paid any money. In the rare case that any salary is paid to them, it is usurped by the placement agents.

After being taken away from their homes, two-thirds of the children are left without any contact with their families. Adolescent girls suffer the most. It is a delicate age at which their bodies undergo rapid hormonal changes, an age when they need to be in emotional touch with their friends, mother, grandparents and other relatives, so that they can get some words of sincere advice. On the contrary, they face dire situations: they suffer from physical and mental frustration, and live in anguish.

This is something that needs to be addressed in the future.

□

(—July 2011)

Transforming Bihar into a Child-Friendly State

We recently rescued 62 children from bonded labour in the Bhajanpura area of Delhi. Aged 6 to 14 years, all these kids came from Sitamarhi and Siwan districts of the state of Bihar, in eastern India. They had been brought to Delhi by agents who had either lured them away or given monetary enticements to their parents.

Living bare-bodied in hot and humid stuffy rooms along narrow streets, these innocent children think nothing of the pain caused by needle pricks on their fingers while they create beautiful embroidery destined for the swanky stores of London or New York. The youngest of them, six-year-old Naushad, complained that Delhi was a harsh place because the employer used to scold him whenever he missed or mentioned his mother or father. His home or village in Sitamarhi was not prosperous. There were no arrangements made for children's education or their health. Besides, his parents were illiterate and unemployed. We spoke at length with these children and found that when asked about their country, they would take the name of their village, district of Bihar—they knew nothing about India or Hindustan.

Bihar is the largest hub of child trafficking in the country. One scarcely sees or hears of children being smuggled out of Mumbai, Delhi or remote Tamil Nadu into Bihar; but every year children from Saharsa, Darbhanga, Sitamarhi, Siwan, Madhubani, Madhepura and other districts of Bihar are taken away to corners of India as child labourers in various industries. Young girls from Bihar and Jharkhand are sold for child labour and as child prostitutes for prices below that of cattle. As per data from non-government organisations, 2.5 million children work as child labourers in Bihar, whilst official statistics put this number at 550,000. In this state, around 70 percent of the 25 million children are born malnourished. According to official data from the National Sample Survey, more than half of the children of school-going age, approximately 10 million, are not able to go to school. Out of them, 40 percent are those who were enrolled in school but they had either never attended school or dropped out of primary school. A UNICEF report revealed that 51 percent of girls had not even been enrolled.

Bihar is among the states that spend the least amount of money on children's health and education. According to the National Family Health Survey 2005 to 2006, in Bihar, 68.3 percent of women are anaemic. The infant mortality rate is 62 per 1000; 87.6 percent of children aged 6 to 35 months are suffering from anaemia, and only 30 percent of childbirths are in institutions. Only 32.8 percent of children between 12 and 23 months of age have undergone complete vaccination. The good news is that all these statistics have been taken very seriously by the Chief Minister and Deputy Chief Minister of Bihar. Whether it is the issue of ending child labour or the appointment of teachers that has been pending for years, the current government has certainly made an attempt to take the first positive step.

Besides the lack of education for children and the problem of malnutrition, other grave challenges in Bihar include child labour, child prostitution, the issue of street children, the poor conditions in juvenile justice homes and government-run homes for children, and child trade and trafficking from villages to the cities. These need immediate action, otherwise it will be impossible to remove the blemish of child exploitation and child slavery from this natural and human resource-rich land of Mahatma Buddha and Jayaprakash Narayan.

Social initiatives and government efforts must work in tandem. At the governmental level, strong steps need to be taken to provide free, quality and useful education to all children. For instance, the government can make provisions allowing for sufficient resources in the budget, appointment and training sufficient number of teachers, and make arrangements for the school building and educational material. Certain basic amenities must be arranged immediately: for instance, separate toilets for boys and girls, libraries, drinking water, sports grounds, electricity, furniture, coir mats, blackboards, etc. If children do not attend school regularly, then the accountability of principals and officials of *Panchayat*s, municipal corporations and education departments must be demanded.

Quality education is directly related to quality healthcare, the reduction in mortality rates of infants and mothers, and opportunities for better work and development. Within India, the state of Kerala is an example where almost all children attend school. This has been made possible by the joint efforts of social and religious institutions, political parties and the government. If states like Himachal Pradesh and Uttarakhand can take rapid strides in children's education and development, why cannot Bihar? In the context of child development, the government must ensure qualitative and time-bound implementation of the three main programmes of the Central Government in addition to other central and state-level schemes. The first key programme is the *Sarva Shiksha Abhiyan* ("Education for All" in Hindi) and related to this, is the mid day meal scheme. The second programme is the employment guarantee scheme, under which all adults are entitled to at least 100 days of employment. And the third is the National Health Mission. Unfortunately, we have countless evidence that show that in several districts of this state, corruption and fraud are rampant in these schemes.

Bihar has witnessed a mushrooming of voluntary organisations. Some of them are working very dedicatedly and effectively but, unfortunately, there is a huge gap in terms of coordination among them. In the absence of a highly aware, motivated and active society, a government or administrative system would work only to the extent it does in Bihar and in other similar states. It does not behove social organisations to blame the government, and wash their hands off the issues. All of us must come together to transform the image of Bihar from a backward, corrupt or poor state into one with self-confidence and dignity.

□

(—May 2009)

Why is Child Labour Not Justifiable?

There is a lot of uproar in the media on the government's announcement prohibiting domestic child labour. It is as if the government has achieved a revolutionary feat as a result of which millions of children will be taken off work and pushed onto the roads on the morning of 11th October. The government ban on child labour in households, road construction, restaurants, hotels, etc. takes effect from the 10th of October.

First of all, it must be made clear that this gazette is not a new law but one of the amendments being done to a 20-year-old piece of legislation from time to time. The law to prohibit child labour in some industries, and to regulate it under certain conditions in other industries was passed in 1986. Under the Child Labour (Prohibition and Regulation) Act (CLPRA), 1986, 13 industries were placed in the prohibited category because, as per the recommendations of the health department, these occupations were considered dangerous. These included the carpet, *beedi*-making, leather products, fireworks, mining industries, etc. However, there was no child labour prohibition for agriculture (in which most child labourers work), the construction industry, domestic work and restaurants, among others.

The constant pressure exerted by social organisations working against child labour, changes in the standards of international labour reforms and intervention of courts, has together resulted in the inclusion of a few industries and processes in the prohibited category through government gazettes. Now, since it is domestic child labour that affects the middle class, there is much hue and cry. It is worth noting that the prohibition on domestic child labour is also not entirely new. Through a gazette issued on 14th October, 1999, the Central Government amended the service rules for government employees, under which a government official could neither make a child work as a child labourer, nor keep them as a servant.

Since then, questions have been raised on the continuation of domestic child labour in other sectors. If child labour is a detrimental practice, why should there be policy pertaining only to government officials and not to others? That is why the gazette issued on 2nd August was a governmental decision that had been put off for a long time. For this reason, voluntary organisations are citing it as a moral victory against child labour. However, in this context, I must not forget to mention an innocent child, Ashraf: omitting his name will not only be denying a historical event. It will also be immoral.

On 12th September, 1996, *Bachpan Bachao Andolan* (BBA) learnt that a 6-year-old domestic child labourer, Ashraf, was beaten up severely by his master, Hamid Hussain. The activists rescued him after conducting a raid on Hussain's house, a Delhi-based senior IAS officer and the then Under Secretary of the Ministry of Agriculture. The child was not in a condition to speak. The torture he went through was heart-rending and an eye-opener about the hidden reality of domestic child labour for the whole country. A hungry Ashraf, who took a few spoonful of left over milk from the glass of his master's son (who must have been his age), was branded with hot iron tongs by Hussain and his wife. The child kept crying in pain and fainted. The neighbourhood watchman somehow communicated this to Ashraf's mother. Given that Hussain was an influential person, it was impossible to file a police case against him.

When all our attempts in this direction failed, we went to the house of Justice Ranganath Mishra, who was then the President of the National Human Rights Commission, and made an appeal. Despite it being a Sunday that day, Justice Mishra held a special court at his home to hear the case and instructed the Delhi Police to take immediate action.

BBA did not limit this case to demanding justice for Ashraf alone. The Commission was requested to recommend to the Government of India that keeping children as domestic servants should be made punishable for all government officials. The Commission, taking it seriously, issued instructions to the government in that direction. On three occasions between 1997 and 1999, the government refused to accept these instructions.

Meanwhile, voluntary organisations brought up several cases of murder of domestic servants and the rape of young girls working as domestic labourers before the Commission, as well as the government. BBA, in order to pressurise the government to act, organised a week-long march across the nooks and corners of Delhi and made the common people aware of the dire condition of domestic child labourers. Finally, in 1999, the Central Government was forced to accept the recommendation.

It is essential to hold an honest debate on the questions being raised about the new gazette. First of all, it is being said that millions of kids would suddenly become unemployed and destitute, and be forced into a life of crime or prostitution. This is ridiculous: how can a middle-class society, which does not tire of criticising the government's inability to comply with laws, suddenly believe that with one stroke of the pen, the entire government system will become able, active and honest in a day? *It is another matter that this is how it should happen.*

The second question is concerned with the sudden surge of emotion in favour of poor children. Feudal and convenient middle-class mentality gives birth to arguments that try to give immoral acts a garb of morality—all for their own selfish reasons. Nobody is ready to accept the fact that innocent girls are kept as domestic servants because they are the cheapest labourers: they would not raise their voices against any atrocity, or, unlike adults, would not need to return home in the evening. On the other hand, she readily accepts the squalid living conditions and interminably long working hours. In the middle-class society, there is often stress and tension arising from strained relations between ladies and their mothers-in-law, besides the work pressure and the race to show off one's wealth—which often translates into abuse and beatings for the child servant. But the argument proffered is this: we are being kind to these children, they are just like our own kids, etc.

The third issue is related to justifying the continuation of child labour because of poverty. To keep children trapped in labour on the pretext of helplessness because they or their parents are poor and illiterate cannot be the hallmark of any civil society.

If the supporters of child labour are so sensitive to society, why do not give full-time employment to an adult in their homes or shops? Recently, the International Labour Organization (ILO), revealed in a report that if a country spends one rupee on ending child labour, it would later reap a benefit equivalent to seven rupees. This is because by educating and fully developing these children, the economic prosperity of the country will grow as well.

At a conference in Paris organised by UNESCO on 'Education for All', the various United Nations institutions agreed that the educational objective cannot be achieved without ending child labour. Here, it goes without saying that in the current age of capitalism, communication and globalisation, no country can rid itself of poverty without providing quality education to all its citizens. This has been endorsed in all the reports of the World Bank and UNESCO.

One must not forget that in our country, elementary school education has been made a fundamental right of all children. It is completely against the Constitution to make children work in homes, hotels, restaurants, etc. It is the responsibility of the government to provide for the strict enforcement of the law against child labour.

In conclusion, we must believe that the ban on domestic child labour is not only a legal government initiative but is also essential for a country like India, which is taking rapid strides on the road towards economic development. The education of the girl child can be an effective step in the direction of judicious control on the population growth, to curb the spread of HIV/AIDS, and to end gender discrimination, etc.

The global community has set the goal of providing free and quality education to all children by the year 2015. In that direction, it was also pledged that by 2005, the world's schools will have an equal number of boys and girls. India is among the 83 nations who have failed to achieve that aim. It is worth noting that our neighbour, Bangladesh, has already achieved this objective. United Nations Girls' Education Initiative, a UN group formed under the aegis of UNICEF, has made it amply clear that domestic child labour is the biggest hindrance to achieving the goal of girls' education. □

(—October 2009)

Making India Child Labour Free

The issue of child labour is deeply connected to social justice. Since now the International Labour Organization (ILO) has also accepted it, this assumes significance in several respects. One, child labour is concerned not only with development and welfare, it is a violation of human rights. Two, the economic exploitation of children cannot be continued on the pretext of poverty alleviation of the family or of the country. Three, child labour deprives children of their due involvement in economic, social and political activities. Four, it snatches away their basic rights to education, freedom and equality. And five, child labour is universally a crime.

Over 60 million children in India are victims of one form of child labour or the other. They are condemned to lose their childhood and future in agricultural fields, stone quarries, brick kilns, factories and sweatshops, roadside restaurants and hotels, and common households. This is not just a humanitarian issue but also a constitutional and legal crime, a violation of human rights, a cause as well as effect of poverty, the biggest source of adult unemployment and the toughest obstacle to social and economic justice.

The ILO's move is a good beginning, because usually, the three goals of education, ending child labour and catalysing development are viewed through separate lenses. At an international level, the UNDP is working on the Millennium Development Goals, including poverty eradication, which are to be taken up by all countries by

2010. The responsibility for achieving the six objectives under 'Education for All' by 2015 lies with UNESCO, while the ILO is responsible for ending the dangerous forms of child labour by 2016. In most countries, there are separate ministries related to child labour, education, development and poverty alleviation. Forget collaboration, these ministries have little policy coordination. Against this backdrop, combining child labour eradication and education to form a joint ideology and taking a practical step is a welcome one.

More than 215 million children across the globe are working in different kinds of child labour today. 70 million have never been to school. According to a study, most of the education-deprived children are engaged in child labour, with 94 percent of them belonging to poor countries. Out of these, South Asia accounts for 35 percent and West Africa 40 percent. It is not a mere coincidence that child labour dominates these two regions.

In our country, child labour is considered a humanitarian issue or helplessness of the poor, besides a crime or violation of human rights. But a lot of people would find it odd or shocking that this social evil is deeply connected to the systemic corruption. Corruption and child labour have a cause-and-effect relationship—just like it is a chicken-and-egg situation in connection with child labour, poverty and illiteracy.

There are 60 million children in the country engaged in child labour, whereas 65 million adults are unemployed. According to various studies, an employer spends a maximum of ₹ 20 per child labourer for their food, clothes, daily wage or salary, etc., whereas in the case of an adult labourer, this amounts to ₹ 120. Even that is below the minimum wage rate as set by the government. Children are made to work at least 12 hours, while adults work only 9 or 10. What this means is that if 60 million adults were to be employed in place of children, then the employers would need to spend nearly ₹ 100 more per labourer from their profits. This in turn implies that by giving work to children instead of adults, the employers save roughly ₹ 600 crore every day—which is nothing but black money.

One must know that labour costs entail a large portion of the cost of production. For handicraft and small consumer goods, in particular, this amounts to almost 30 to 40 percent. In all documentation and accounting ledgers, the expenses on labour, however, cannot be shown to be lower than the minimum wage set by the government; so, out of the total amount that is shown to have been spent in records, a major proportion is saved as black money by resorting to employing child labour.

It is evident from basic facts that because of child labour, at least ₹ 18,000 crore per month or ₹ 2.16 lakh crore annually is generated as black money in the country. Where does this huge amount of black money go? For sure, a portion of it goes towards the election of local leaders and political parties. It is also spent on bribing government officials.

Strict laws are necessary to end child labour. Even today, there is no complete prohibition against child labour in agriculture and similar industries. And where it is prohibited, the law is not properly enforced. There is no child welfare law in the country, or a law prohibiting child labour, which can ensure the accountability of the so-called upholders of law for their incompetence, failure, apathy and complicity with violators. There should also be an initiative to implement the law on Right to Education together with the law on the prohibition of child labour in a holistic manner. There should also be effective measures to educate and rehabilitate the children rescued from child labour.

However, it is not appropriate to leave everything to the government and sit idle. Society will also have to take the initiative. If the stain of child labour is to be removed from the country, then us common citizens must protest against it.

You should pledge not to have tea at the restaurants or even have water at houses where children work as labourers.

We are proud of our great customs, culture and history because, prior to the colonisers, every boy and girl in the country used to get the best education. This was the reason India used to be called *Jagadguru* (world teacher). Even today, it is not the politicians who are restoring our lost glory across the globe but young men and women who are proving Indian talent in computers, software engineering, biotechnology, medicine and management internationally. If each and every child of the country can be freed of child labour and exploitation and given quality education instead, then we can become the biggest power in the world in just a few years.

□

(—November 2009)

Bringing Accountability into the Movement

I remember the time when I, along with some of my like-minded young friends, started our social life: how passionate our generation used to be! We observed the injustice and oppression and wanted to bring about a fundamental change in the whole system. We dreamed of creating a society in India that reflected what Gandhi, Lohia, Jayaprakash, Chandrashekhar, Bhagat Singh and Subhash Chandra Bose had in their minds. At that time, one could not even begin thinking of social work if one's mind was not brimming with idealism.

To create an alternative public policy against the Indian politics of that time – characterised by 'the appeal of power and attachment to wealth'—became a crucial part of our lives. We had not heard the vocabulary of career, money, resources, projects, non-government organisations (NGOs), funding agencies, etc. It was not that I, and other students like me lagged behind in studies. It was on the strength of good marks that many of my friends and I got admitted into engineering colleges, but our concern for the society ran much wider and deeper. I am astonished to see the huge change that has come about in the personality and character of our society within a single generation. The ability and standing of the prime ministerial candidates of today pales in comparison to those political leaders who had to struggle, despite their stature, for the chief ministership of provinces. Today, finding leaders with the qualities and leadership exemplified by the likes of Govind Ballabh Pant, Chandra Bhanu Gupta, MGR, Pandit Dwarka Prasad Mishra and Karpoori Thakur is next to impossible even at the national level. The same situation prevails more or less when it comes to the stature of personalities in journalism and social activism.

I am not a Gandhian, but there is enough energy and moral strength in Gandhi's personality and expressive style to inspire social revolutionaries for a long, long time. The unique style of the public agitation of Gandhi that has impressed me the most is how he could transform spiritual and religious ideals and values into the weapons for a movement. Such is the power of *Ahimsa* ("non-violence" in Sanskrit) and *Satyagraha* ("insistence on truth" in Sanskrit). Sensitivity to children is similarly an eternal value, but never before has there been an attempt to make it a people's movement. A few friends joined me in taking the first step in that direction, and even succeeded in establishing a movement for the rights of the most exploited, even enslaved, children and taking their cause across the globe.

In our culture, teaching has traditionally been held in very high esteem, but never before have we seen the struggle for the birthright to education reach the streets of the country. The belief that every consumer today is also a father, brother, son or human being has led to a different dimension with regard to outcomes: millions of people, who are guilty of buying things for which children were exploited, have shaken the foundation of corporations with billions of dollars in profit, thus giving rise to a new culture of Corporate Social Responsibility (CSR).

The foundation of our worldwide movement against child labour and in support of education was not built with funding from rich countries or governments, nor is its edifice made up by the brick work of so-called professionalism. When we started our war against bonded child labour in 1980, our office was set on fire in the stone quarries of Faridabad. One of our colleagues, Dhoom Das, was martyred (1984). Back then, the word NGO had not been heard of in India and the people who got associated with us took inspiration from the ideals of Ashfaq and Bismil. They boldly faced Haryana's stone quarry mafia and criminal gangs of builders-owners that ran influential construction companies and brick kilns in Delhi and many other places. None of them was familiar with the definition of a project, or funding, or more. To this date, our colleagues try and do everything possible to keep the basic character of the movement alive while organising resources internally as well as externally.

Terms like child slavery or bonded labour were not in vogue at that time. No UN institution or any other charitable organisation of the Western world paid attention in this direction. There was no judicial intervention in favour of enslaved children in any court. Barring rare exceptions, the intellectual section did not have this issue in sight, nor was any book in any language published on this subject.

The start of the 1980s was a time of idealistic despair resulting from the disillusionment with the non-Congress, Janata rule. All the same, it was also the time when many talented young men and women were trying to find an alternative way of changing society, through individual or collective efforts. It was during these days that the historical movements for farmers, landless labourers, unorganised workers, fishermen, women and the downtrodden began. However, if we deeply analyse the past two-and-a-half decades, we will find that there has been rapid commercialisation of revolutionary idealism and revolutionary agitations inspired by the scientific assessment of society.

When we began our movement in 1980, child slavery was a 'non-issue' and there was a general lack of awareness and consciousness about it. Poor children labouring in agricultural fields, factories and homes was a part of everyday life—akin to how women have been discriminated against for ages. Educated people, journalists and even the legal fraternity were oblivious to the fact that making children work as child labourers destroyed their childhood, opportunities for education, and their human dignity and future. Common people were aware neither of the atrocities and sexual exploitation that children were subjected to, nor of the damage to their delicate limbs. *Bachpan Bachao Andolan* took the media into confidence, knocked at the doors of the courts, pricked the conscience of political leaders connected with social work, and made the very children who were victims of exploitation, the arbiters of their own freedom. The reaction to all this happened in the second phase. On the one hand, a few sensitive people worked with us on this issue and, on the other, in organised fashion, governments and other watchdogs emphatically denied the existence of this evil.

Then a third phase arrived, in which the voices against child labour became stronger and more vocal. All the same, the vested interests became violent and vindictive. This aroused the curiosity of the national as well as international media and of human rights organisations. Our strategy of direct intervention for rescuing children from bonded labour, dangerous though it was, provided a new plank for TV channels and newspapers all over the world. International welfare organisations based in Europe and America spotted a new opportunity to raise funds. They understood quite well that on questions such as these, common people, the church and their governments would loosen their purse strings – and that was what happened. And then, in almost no time, hordes of NGOs working on the issue of child labour appeared overnight in several third-world countries, including India. There was a flood of people who could create and run a 'project' in immaculate language and at a professional level.

The ardent beginning intended to rescue childhood by eliminating exploitation, injustice and inequality widespread in society suddenly began to shift into institutionalism. In the 1990s, on the pretext of child labour, people started running these 'agencies' dealing in foreign aid and government grants on every street, corner and village of India. These were the kind of people who employed children in their own houses to do cleaning, washing, etc. and whose lifestyle and character were miles away from the winds of social change. This does not mean that all voluntary organisations or NGOs are like that. In India, many social workers are still toiling away – expending their youth and life in such inaccessible, dangerous and amenity-less places where even the government has not taken any initiative. Their efforts have borne positive results.

It has become difficult, if not impossible, to verify the truth today. Societal ethics and human values are not lived but used cleverly as stepping stones to success. To now think that the wheel of time will turn back and our hearts and minds will reverse their march away from the razzle-dazzle of the market or the rat race of life, would be nothing short of hollow idealism. What remedies exist, then, to at least keep some fundamental values alive among the people and organisations engaged in social work currently? In my opinion, the first requisite is mutual accountability. To keep a governmental or legal pincer-grip on organisations working in the fields of child rights, development, environment, human rights or social justice is nothing but unconstitutional or coercive. This only works to the benefit of government departments already neck-deep in the quagmire of corruption. Indeed, the organisations should be made accountable to the people for whom they work or from whom they have raised funds.

The first condition with regard to this accountability is economic and managerial transparency and the second is participation of the affected people in the decision-making process. The third is to ensure the strengthening of these people, whilst the fourth condition is decentralisation followed by the transfer of rights. If these benchmarks are ensured at the basic level or, better still, voluntary organisations can embrace it as part of their work culture, then I think we can prevent the rapid erosion of ethical values. The society, media, and other stakeholders will also have to become aware and responsible in this direction – but often the reverse is still visible.

It now seems that there is an avoidance of, or denial of accountability at every level of society. After all, who is accountable to whom? What is the accountability of those who make legislations or of those government servants who, while living off the hard-earned money of the public, are supposed to enforce the law? Likewise, newspapers, voluntary organisations, even the courts of justice – to what extent are they accountable and to whom? The corporates and markets anyway do not seem to be accountable to anyone but to themselves. It appears that the time is ripe for a new *Satyagraha* agitation: an accountability movement, wherein the public will take stock of everyone's accountability and make decisions. Laws and regulations seem to exist merely as formalities: the governments or the NGOs would not mend their ways unless and until the common people hold those in positions of responsibility accountable.

Here, I would like to give an example. *Bachpan Bachao Andolan* has always maintained it as an ideal that the children who are victims of slavery and exploitation should become their own rescuers and leaders. A national secretary and a treasurer in our organisation are two young men whom we rescued from bonded labour around 10 to 12 years ago and whom we then rehabilitated and trained. Likewise, we have a child in Rajasthan, Om Prakash, freed from bonded labour. In the *Bal Ashram*, a rehabilitation home for former child labourers run by BBA, he got the chance to nurture and grow his talent. While studying at the Ashram he got birth registrations done, in his spare time, for more than 500 children from his village. He also fought against the unlawful extortion of money going on in schools despite the fact that primary education was free. The result: this 15-year-old child received the world's biggest prize.

A Netherlands-based institution, Kids Rights, honoured him with the International Children's Peace Prize. As per a statement issued by the institution, the child will be given a memento, and a sum equivalent to ₹ 45 lakh will be given to a world organisation working on child rights, which was to be decided later. However, some over-zealous journalists from a well-known newspaper in Rajasthan, without trying to understand the seriousness or prestige of one of the world's most successful experiments, started to turn it into a 'story'. One of these young men went to the child's village and tried to incite his father and other village folk. He asked them, "How much did you get out of the 45 lakh rupees? Did the NGO keep it all?" The rustic, simple-minded father could not see through the ploy and simply said that he had not received anything. And lo and behold, the story was ready: 'Where did the child's prize money disappear to?' The sad part, which crosses the bounds of ethics, is that before the story was published, Kids Rights had clearly communicated that the prize money had not been given to Om Prakash, *Bal Ashram* or *Bachpan Bachao Andolan*—nor would it be given to them. The decision to award the prize money would be taken in 2007. But this newspaper, in an act of one-upmanship with other newspapers, threw journalistic principles out of the window and came out with exaggerated 'stories' written in misleading language. It is time to look back to where India rose from and embrace those ideals again.

□

(—July 2012)

CHILDHOOD ON SALE

"There is no greater violence than to deny the dreams of our children."

1. **A serious crime like child-trafficking was defined and provision for punishment provided for the first time in the Criminal Law (Amendment) Act, 2013.**
2. **Children who fall victim to child trafficking are used in illegal activities, such as forced child labour, sexual exploitation, pornography, domestic child labour, etc.**
3. **According to statistics from the Ministry of Labour and Employment of the Government of India, between 2008 and 2012, 452,679 children were victims of child-trafficking all over India.**
4. **Between the years 2008 and 2012, 25,006 cases of child-trafficking were registered; only 3,394 cases resulted in convictions.**
5. **As per the National Crime Records Bureau report, 38,555 children fell victim to child-trafficking in the year 2014, out of which only 30 percent of the children could be traced.**

Child Trafficking and Sociology

Human trafficking is one of the largest illegal trades in the world today. It can be compared to the black money-generating businesses of drugs and weapons. Statistics suggest that every year around 12.5 million people are bought and sold like inanimate objects and those who indulge in it make black money worth some ₹ 2 lakh crore. Obviously, such a huge business cannot be run without the complicity of politicians and corrupt officials, nor can the large sum be distributed without their proper knowledge. There are multiple ways in which human trade, especially child trafficking, is carried on in our country. Going by its international definition, hundreds of thousands of children are bought and sold within states or among districts. There are many who are bought and brought to India from neighbouring countries, like Bangladesh and Nepal. Besides child prostitution, these children are used in forced or bonded labour, domestic work, child marriage, forced beggary, entertainment and other businesses, and even as child jihadists.

Around two years ago, *Bachpan Bachao Andolan*, along with its associated NGOs in India, Bangladesh and Nepal, organised the 'South Asian March Against Child Trafficking'. Starting from Kolkata, the march travelled along India's border with Bangladesh and Nepal, winding its way through a lot of villages, towns and districts, and reaching Delhi after covering as many as 5,000 kilometres. Hundreds of thousands of people took part in the march.

I had the opportunity to organise the leadership for the march. There were many astounding experiences in this journey, which was aimed at creating public awareness and putting pressure on governments. The March revealed that human and child-trafficking is rampant in all the border areas, and that the middlemen were raking in money. The efforts of NGOs, however, were barely noticed and their voices went largely ignored. There was little awareness among the poor folks in the village about the abominable trafficking. The parents whose children had been lured, or snatched from them in return for paltry sums of money, were meek or helpless. They did not have the courage to report it to the police and feared getting entangled in a legal mess. In the rare case if one of them dared to do it, it would only amount to a lot of trouble for themselves.

Children from Bangladesh, Nepal and India walked with us in the march for almost a month. Spending their days in different programmes, they would sometimes talk to one another and exchange their tales of misery and pain. One of these evenings, three kids from the three nations were talking to one another. A girl from Jharkhand said to the others, "I was bought as a domestic servant for ₹ 2,000, and later sold a couple of times by different agents. Has something like that happened to you too?" Pat came the response from the Nepalese kid, "Sister, you proved to be quite expensive—the middleman bought me for a mere ₹ 500!" Next, the Bangladeshi girl said, "Then I'm expensive, too, for I was sold for 2,500 takas." And then the kids related how the buffalo is much better than any of them—a buffalo fetches ₹ 25,000 in the market. This small talk by the children is a huge slap on any society that calls itself civil. All those deliberations on development, progress, human rights, constitution, law, religion and culture, is just meaningless and empty when you hear from the mouth of a young child, that a buffalo is twenty times more expensive than she is.

The annual Trafficking in Persons (TIP) report issued by the US Department of State last year, stated that the world's largest democratic country, India, was the one most affected by human-trafficking. It further noted that despite bonded labour being a grave concern here, no stern measures were taken to punish those exploiting bonded labourers. The most important thing about this report is that for the first time, attention was focussed on child trafficking done in the name of child slavery at the international level. The law in India related to preventing human-trafficking and child trafficking does not have the provision to stop human trafficking done in the name of child slavery. It is not even included in the definition of human trafficking. The reality is that the main purpose of inter-state child trafficking in India is for forced or bonded labour. In this age of prosperity and development, the third biggest 'business' in the world is the sale and purchase of human beings as if they were animals or dead objects. Every year, around 700,000 to 800,000 children, women and men are traded across countries. The human trafficking numbers within countries would be much larger.

It is indeed sad that there is no law in our country to stop the smuggling of human beings or trafficking of children like this, or to punish the perpetrators. There is also a lack of social consciousness about the ills within the society. The situation is compounded by the imprudence of the children's parents, neighbours and the village folk. The police and other departments regard the child victims as if they are criminals, not the complainants. What is more, nothing much is done to attend to their emotional, social and/or economic needs, or to send them home and rehabilitate them. In this context, some immediate steps need to be taken: for instance, enacting a strict law to stop child trade for the purpose of forced labour, so that the middlemen, employers and others involved in this crime can be punished severely. The accountability of government officials should also be ascertained in areas where child trafficking is prevalent.

There are five main reasons why this horrible trade is prospering in India: First, the lack of political will. Two, deficiency in social consciousness and concern. Three, an expensive, complex and bureaucratic legal system. Four, collusion amongst criminals, political leaders and the police. Five, lack of honesty and ethics in the common people. Issues like child trade and forced or bonded labour have not yet been made political issues. There is seldom any open debate on them. In election rallies, rarely does a candidate touch upon these issues. The election candidates do not understand these issues, nor do they find any purpose in them. The laws in India are insufficient; those laws that do exist are openly flouted. No initiative is taken by our governments or opposition leaders towards punishing the criminals or those who are complicit in the crimes. Special programmes on adult education, awareness and economic development ought to run in areas from where children are taken away for trafficking, but the governments do nothing in that direction.

The lack of social awareness and concern is clearly visible. Most people still do not see girls at par with boys. Girls are usually the unwanted children, so no attention is paid to their upbringing, health and education. As if they are born for domestic work only, they are often pushed into child labour or prostitution. Generally speaking, there is negligible knowledge of children's rights in our society. Child marriage is a common practice in several regions of the country. In some places, for example, in the regions of Andhra Pradesh and Karnataka, there is misconception among the cotton growers that if unwed girls plough the field, it will result in a good crop. Thus, thousands of girls from the neighbouring districts are taken there for cotton farming. The *devadasi* tradition, in which adolescent girls and widows are handed over to the temples as gods' servants, has still not ended: in practice, they are made to work in the sex trade. Among the girls who are employed as housemaids, most fall victim to child trafficking. There is a rapidly growing demand for child maids among the burgeoning and prosperous middle class of India.

Often the middle-class people do not hesitate before indulging in any dishonesty or corruption for the future of their children. They would readily spend inordinate amounts of money to get their children admitted to the most expensive English-medium schools, but feel no shame in employing the son or daughter of a poor man as a domestic servant. The demand for cheap and 'trouble-free' child labourers has bred a new criminal business in all metropolitan and many major towns. In Delhi alone, there are more than 2,200 so-called placement agencies. These agencies are thriving on nothing but human trafficking. Children, girls and women are enticed with good jobs and brought to Delhi. Later on, depending on the demand, they are made to work as housemaids or prostitutes. All types of abominable deeds are done to them. All this happens around us. Given the shamelessness and lack of sensitivity of the society, this business is thriving unabated.

As mentioned above, there is no clear law in India for forced child trade, and whatever laws exist, are not effectively implemented. No employer engaged in child trade or bonded labour has been sentenced and sent to jail under the provisions of any law whatsoever. It is just not possible for the families of these children to travel thousands of miles to where these lawsuits are registered and run from pillar to post between the court appointments, often after selling their land or houses, and facing constant danger.

In the web of human trafficking, between India and other countries, including Bangladesh and Nepal, everyone is involved—leaders, criminals and the police. Several shocking incidents came to light in the country in the last few days. Members of Parliament (MPs), leaders and celebrities from various fields were arrested in *kabootarbazi* (a practice in which people are sent abroad by fraudulent means). When we conducted raids on several placement agencies in Delhi and rescued children, girls and women, we were astonished to see that the criminals running these agencies had hung framed photos—showing them with MPs, ministers and even chief ministers and police officers—on their walls. The remarkable thing is that these placement agencies are human trafficking shops plying illegally without registration.

We live in a society where children are said to be God's embodiment on earth. Women are worshipped in the form of Saraswati, Lakshmi and Durga—the goddesses of knowledge, wealth and power respectively. Children are also called *bal-gopala* (Gopala being one of the names of Lord Krishna). During Navratri, young girls are worshipped, and giving them food is considered an act of redemption—and yet, not a single day passes when the papers do not carry news of the rape of innocent girls. This hypocritical mindset of ours is most responsible for child-trafficking. We witness incidents of atrocities on innocent, trafficked children around us—in our homes, shops and factories—yet we feign ignorance. Millions travel on trains and buses everyday but ignoring the fact that someone sitting next to them could be a middleman committing an act of child trafficking there and then.

A strong initiative is necessary to remove this public stain on society. The main components of such an initiative should be: making new laws and taking responsibility to implement them; voicing concerns against child-trafficking; punishing the guilty by completing the judicial process in timely fashion; making special efforts towards the education and rehabilitation of children rescued from child trafficking; providing useful and high-quality education to children free of cost; and providing opportunities for economic development in districts that are perceived to be the hubs of human-trafficking, among others.

□

(—August 2009)

The Plight of the Missing Child

The incidents of children going missing are continuously on the rise in India. Today, the situation is such that a child goes missing every six minutes in the country. According to government statistics, 68,227 children in 2009, 77,133 in 2010 and 90,654 kids in 2011 went missing. Around 40 percent of these children could not be located. The irony is that no law has been made in the country to prevent this heinous crime, nor has the Parliament ever expressed concern on this matter and raised the issue for debate. If a Member of Parliament (MP) does submit written questions once in a long while, the secretaries of the government departments prepare stock answers, which are repeated in the House just as perfunctorily.

You may perhaps remember the Nithari incident of missing children in India a few years ago, one which shook humanity with shame and disgust. One fine day, the government sweepers found bits of children's bodies from a gutter in Nithari, a village adjoining Delhi and a part of the Noida suburban area. The whole village was stunned. Prior to that, whenever the parents of missing children went wailing to the nearby police station to file their complaints, they had to go back insulted and disappointed. It later came to light that cannibalistic savages in the form of men used to drink the blood of these children, cut them into pieces and gorge on their flesh. What can be more shameful than the fact that even such an atrocious and heart-rending incident failed to prick the conscience of our government? Nor could it sustain the then outraged scruples of our society for long.

Nothing can be more punishing and unbearable for parents and families of children than to have no clue about them when they go missing. It is a crime that no civilised society should tolerate. Most of the missing children are from poor or weak sections of society: they live in slums, or belong to displaced families that have come to the city and settled here from far-flung villages and towns in search of work. Since such folk are not well-connected with important people and have little by way of identity and voice, they are ignored by the police and media, even by their neighbours. The parents of such children are usually uneducated and timid by nature. Owing to the lack of knowledge, they keep looking for their children themselves for hours, even days, instead of reporting it to the police. If the society and police are alert enough, they can help prevent the kidnapping of children and many such crimes can be curbed.

But all of us know very well how the monitoring agencies of the government make a mockery of the country's laws and how court decisions are disregarded. It would be a fallacy to think that the same policemen who are wallowing in black money hoarded by child traders and kidnapping gangs would, of their own accord, comply with the court's decisions. Court directives can only be useful if someone is willing to step forward and get them followed through. While you need social awareness to prevent incidents of children going missing, the role of an alert and active civil society in holding the government system accountable is just as important. If we want to break the vicious cycle of people going missing, child trafficking, bonded labour, forced begging, etc., we will have to launch a collective drive against all these crimes.

The correct identification of every child is necessary to take preventive measures for crimes against children. The birth registration of every child should be mandatory for all *Panchayats*, municipal bodies and other institutions. Just like adults are issued *Aadhaar* (a form of identity cards) cards, every child should be issued a certified identity card. Criminal proceedings under a separate law should be initiated against factories, workshops, industries, homes, schools, child homes, etc. that employ children without these identity cards. Wherever children are found without identity cards—on the streets, footpaths or other public places—action should be taken against the officials and policemen responsible for those areas. Unless we properly know the whereabouts of the children, who they are, what their background is, etc., how can their safety and security be ensured? It is on the basis of information such as this that we can ascertain which children have been kidnapped, whether they are victims of child labour, malnourished or deprived of education, what diseases afflict them and how their problems could be solved. This will also help us ascertain the governmental budgetary allocation required for the benefit of children.

It is possible that the hungry and naked child you give alms to at a red light at a crossroad is the same one for whom a mother somewhere in this country has been waiting for years on end. The delicious food you are enjoying at the home of a friend and relative has possibly been cooked by a young or adolescent girl servant, whose aggrieved parents are looking for their daughter everywhere in Odisha, Jharkhand or Assam. It is necessary that all of us fulfil our social responsibility by boycotting all things made by child labourers or in which child labour plays a role. This will go a long way in preventing the kidnapping of children for trading them like commodities and forcing them into cheap labour.

□

(—June 2013)

The Role of Law in Breaking the Nexus of Trafficking and Exploitation of Children

A barbaric incident of sexual torture of an innocent six-year-old girl in Delhi put the whole country to shame and disgrace. The initiative and activity of media and non-governmental organisations (NGOs) kept the issue of child rape burning for a few weeks. Not that the incidents of rape and sexual exploitation of girls suddenly escalated and stopped during that month alone. In reality, the TV channels and others became occupied with other sensational happenings soon after—and the screams of innocent children somehow got lost in the ever-changing din.

The rising incidents of child rape are heinous enough, but other sexual crimes committed alongside are no less shameful. A few years ago, a shocking study on child abuse was published by the Central Government and UNICEF. According to the study, 53 percent of children in India fall victim to some form of sexual exploitation. Most children are abused by persons known to them or by the very people responsible for their care and safety: relatives, neighbours and teachers.

The beastly incident with a little girl had brought to the fore the insensitivity of the society, police and government, the criminal incompetence, abominable corruption and lousy politics of the day. Forget quick action and investigation regarding the complaint of the parents, not even a First

Information Report (FIR) was registered for the first six hours. The child was found by luck rather than through the efforts of the police. The limit of cruelty was breached when the police officials offered a bribe to the child's father to keep his mouth shut. On top of that, all manner of old and new political party leaders reached the hospital, where the child was admitted to enquire after her—but not without their big banners, flags, caps and what not.

This is not just about that little girl from Delhi: in the case of thousands of innocent children, often multiple crimes such as sexual abuse, rape, bonded labour, forced begging, trade in body organs, and more, begin with children going missing. Children are first kidnapped, and then, they are tortured in several ways. Every hour, 11 children go missing in the country, which is a heinous and torturous crime against the children and their parents and relatives—one that is indeed shameful for any civil society.

Bachpan Bachao Andolan, under the Right to Information Act, gathered information from all districts of the country, which revealed the fact that nearly 120,000 children go missing every year. Most of the missing children are from poor or weak sections of society, who live in slums or belong to displaced families from remote villages. They cannot approach people in high, powerful positions and find little voice in the media. Lacking knowledge, they look for their children themselves for a long time, rather than report the incident promptly to the police.

A recent significant judgement of the Supreme Court has brought a new ray of hope in the lives of missing children and their parents. The historical judgement, given in response to a petition filed by *Bachpan Bachao Andolan*, has directed all state governments and the Centre to consider each case of a person going missing as a potential crime and, therefore, lodge a First Information Report (FIR) for the same. It is well-known that there is no law in our country to tackle the cases of missing children. The law that does exist is only in the case of kidnapping, and even under this, the complainant is bound to name someone on the suspicion of kidnapping their children. Only then is an FIR registered. And since the parents of those children who have been kidnapped by strangers cannot pin their suspicion on anyone, no FIR is lodged by the police. For this reason alone, according to government statistics, out of the 117,000 cases of missing children from 2008 to 2010, FIR could be lodged merely for 16,000. The court ordered the police to lodge an FIR and start investigation within one month for all the cases of children missing since 2009. In the government records, for the years from 2009 to 2011, as many as 75,808 FIRs will have to be registered. Now the police will have to view the cases of missing children from the perspective of child trafficking and kidnapping.

Activists like me have constantly been repeating that the matter of missing children should be seen at par with organised crime. Children are not inanimate objects, like an umbrella, purse, shoes or mobile phone, which are left forgotten in different places. Every child that goes missing needs a place to sleep, something to eat, water, etc. on the very first night so that they can raise an alarm by shouting. If a child has been missing for days, months and even years, then somewhere there has to be an arrangement for food and water to keep her alive. In fact, all children that go missing are victims of child trafficking. Cunning criminal gangs mark certain colonies from where they steal kids and then sell them off to other criminals. Else, they send them hundreds of miles away to some of their partners in crime. The children are controlled through beatings, drugs, narcotic injections, etc. and then sold for different jobs. They are employed for child prostitution, bonded labour, slavery, or forced into begging after being turned into cripples. They are even forced into child marriages and, sometimes, different organs of their body are sold for organ trade.

Eleven-year-old Santosh (name changed), who was rescued a few days ago as a result of efforts by BBA, told us that he was sold several times. For many years, he was made to work in fields as a bonded labourer. Another rescued child was kept as a bonded worker by a circus in Punjab. Some years ago, two girl students who were returning from their school in South Delhi went missing. They were rescued many years later from a village in the Alwar District of Rajasthan. They were forced into prostitution there. In another instance, kids stolen from a few villages in Jodhpur by a gang were being forced to beg in Delhi.

Against this background, the judgement of the sovereign court of our country can prove to be a milestone. Each police station must now appoint at least one trained police officer who, as a juvenile welfare officer, will investigate crimes related to children. In addition, one paralegal volunteer will be deputed to every police station with the help of the National Legal Services Authority. The volunteer will keep a watch on every action being taken on criminal and other complaints related to children, including the missing children's cases. Also, a Standard Operating Procedure (SOP) will be effected at the national level to ensure the proper implementation of laws related to the incidents of missing children, child labour, trafficking, kidnapping and exploitation, besides helping in the search for missing children and dealing with those who do return. Besides this, a computerised network will be set up between various important departments and institutions related to children, such as the Child Welfare Committees, special police forces, all police stations, Juvenile Justice Boards, district and state level Child Protection Units, etc. A central database will also be built.

The Supreme Court judgement should be seen together with two other important legal weapons. One is the Criminal Law (Amendment) Act, 2013 and the other is the Protection of Children from Sexual Offences (POCSO) Act, 2012. The passing of these laws is indeed a remarkable achievement for social welfare organisations. In the law that came into effect in April this year in India, it is for the first time that human trafficking has been defined. In Section 370 of the Indian Penal Code, it is outlined while interpreting different aspects of human trafficking, that inducing a child or adult and taking them away or kidnapping them or deceiving them or transferring them from one place to another is a crime. Furthermore, under Section 370(A), provisions for separate punishments have been made. This means if the police investigates or takes action in a case of the missing children on the instruction of the Supreme Court, then it will be possible to punish each person guilty of child trafficking. The POSCO Act, passed in November 2012, gives detailed interpretation of the sexual crimes against children up to 18 years of age. The provisions for punishment have been kept in accordance with the given definitions of different types of sexual exploitation. The crimes committed by officers or workers associated with child welfare are regarded as heinous one. Legal and judicial procedures have been made safe, dignified and friendly for children.

Besides legal safeguards, several other strong measures are necessary to stop crimes against children and curb instances of children going missing. First, creating awareness among parents and children and generating a sense of social purpose among neighbours, so that a watch can be maintained on strangers in the area. There is a special need to create awareness among people, who work at schools, religious places, hospitals, bus depots, etc. An attempt should be made by parents, teachers and the responsible people in society to inculcate good habits right from childhood for a dignified and spontaneous relationship with children, especially girls.

Second, it is necessary to create at the national level a central database of children who go missing – children who live on the roadside, children working in agricultural fields, factories, mines, etc., and children in juvenile homes, reformatories, orphanages, child rehabilitation centres or asylums, government or non-governmental child homes, etc. This database should also be linked to all the states. Nobody knows which child from which state is languishing in another part of the country or whether she is living as a bonded labourer, beggar, slave or a victim of prostitution. So, it is essential to centrally collate information on all the children of the country in one place.

Third, the police and other investigative agencies should be sensitised, trained and provided with resources. In addition, they should be made accountable. The most important thing to do is to ensure the accountability of the police officers. Action should be taken against the officers of those police stations from whose jurisdiction children are stolen, time and again. For all this, it is essential to create sensitivity and concern among the common public as well as inculcate political will in the governments.

□

(—July 2014)

Fighting Child Trafficking in Assam

India is the largest democracy in the world with considerable economic growth. It is a land of great civilisations, cultures and religions, but at the very same time, it reels under the stigma of being home to the largest number of trafficked and enslaved children in the world. Children belonging to poor, marginalised and socially oppressed sections of society are already victims of adverse circumstances: they are further victimised and violated by being engaged as cheap labour.

Over the years, the north east, in particular, the state of Assam has emerged as one of the biggest source areas, transit routes and destinations for trafficking of children for forced labour. A painful combination of frequent natural calamities, surmounting insurgency by extremists, abject poverty, illiteracy and ignorance, weak law enforcement and adverse geographical structure of Assam make it a breeding ground for child traffickers to thrive. Moreover, trafficking of children is a global phenomenon and is the third most lucrative illicit trade in the world after small arms and drugs.

I have come across dozens of incidents where Assamese girls have been victims of modern-day slavery in the national capital. Very often, these girls are forced to work as domestic child labourers under inhumane conditions in urban centres of India and countries with which we share borders with.

Nefarious elements from West Bengal, Assam and Meghalaya have set up placement agencies for supplying domestic help in major metropolitan cities. There exists an organised nexus between such people and local procurers based out of the North-East. Taking Delhi as a case in point, 36 placement agencies have been identified to be trafficking Assamese children-mainly girls – to the states of Haryana and Punjab and several other cities. The agents are paid ₹ 4000 to ₹ 5,000 per girl by the placement agencies, which in turn take ₹ 25,000 to ₹ 30,000 from the families where these girls are employed. Although the girls and their parents are promised a monthly remuneration of ₹ 3,000 to ₹ 6,000, yet in most cases, very little or no wages are paid at all. Additionally, these girls are frequently abused and sexually exploited behind closed doors.

Girls trafficked from this region are also forced into child prostitution across the country. A pimp supplying a girl for prostitution earns anywhere between ₹ 50,000 to ₹ 200,000 depending upon the girl's age and virginity. At the other end of the spectrum, a large number of children are trafficked to Assam from other parts of the country to work in bondage at tea plantations, brick kilns and the mining sector.

We have been receiving reports of several heart-wrenching incidents of trafficking of children for forced labour, slavery, sexual assault and even gang rape from the survivors themselves and their parents, ever since BBA's campaign against child labour and trafficking kicked off in Assam in December 2012.

We have further observed that more and more aggrieved people are mustering the courage to step out of the shadows to share their stories of exploitation and repulsion.

Sunita (name changed) was one such girl, who was lured and trafficked by a middleman with six other girls from her village Tunnijaan in Lakhimpur district of Assam. They were taken to Delhi under the false promise of a good future, but to their horror, all of them were sold to a placement agency. Sunita was employed as a domestic help at Paschim Vihar in West Delhi. One day, she was raped by the owner of the placement agency when she refused to go to work.

The owner threatened to sell her off if she dared to open her mouth about the incident. Somehow, she managed to escape and reached home. She was not paid a single penny for the two years of services rendered. Adding to her woes, she was recently discovered to be pregnant. Her life had become a living hell.

In a similar story, Poonam (name changed) was duped by a middleman from her village Lookampur in Lakhimpur district of Assam. He brought her to Delhi. She was promised back wages of two years of service that she had delivered. Additionally, she was ensured a new job with good salary.

Instead, in Delhi, she was gang-raped by three youth in Shakurpur area. Despite the police registering her case at Khayala Police Station, nothing has been done so far. Poonam is still awaiting justice.

A few months ago, I was personally involved in the rescue and repatriation of 16 adolescent Assamese girls who were trapped in bondage at various places in Delhi. They were trafficked through local agents, Mangal Marandi and Ranjit linked to placement agencies called Pooja Domestic Servant Services and Bansi Domestic Services based out of Shakurpur in Delhi.

On the basis of complaints from desperate parents who had travelled all the way to Delhi from remote villages in Kokrajhar, BBA managed to rescue the girls through multiple raid and rescue operations in cooperation with the authorities and police. All this was not easy. Upon rescue, these girls were sent to our transit rehabilitation centre, Mukti Ashram, for a couple of weeks while their repatriation formalities were underway. None of them had been paid any wages for at least 16 to 17 hours of back-breaking work per day, seven days a week. Almost all of them had common tales of woe, entailing verbal abuse and physical torture but Geeta's (name changed) story is even worse. On being rescued, she was hesitant in returning to her home. When the women activists accompanying me probed a little, Geeta opened up and it was absolutely shocking. She had been raped frequently and was pregnant. She was depressed to the extent of harbouring thoughts of ending her life.

Besides being trafficked to work as domestic helps, thousands of minor girls and boys from the north east are held in bondage in *zari* (embroidery) and the garment manufacturing industry of Tamil Nadu and Karnataka. Additionally, a large number of adolescent girls are duped under the garb of decent employment, only to land up in prostitution or sold as child brides in states like Haryana, Punjab and Himachal Pradesh.

The trafficking of children for forced labour continues to remain a serious issue. An estimated 70,000 child labourers from Nepal and Bangladesh work under slave-like conditions in the coal mines of Jaintia Hills district of Meghalaya, and Ledo, Makum, Margherita and Mikir Hills of Assam. Such children are eventually forced into bonded labour. Many children working in brick kilns and tea gardens spread across the entire north eastern region are trafficked from Jharkhand, Bihar, and even Bangladesh. Trucks loaded with coal cross the border of Bangladesh and on the way back, return with children who have been lured by false promises, purchased by middlemen or abducted from their homes. It is also important to note that children from Bangladesh and Nepal are taken to different parts of our country via Assam.

Human trafficking and slavery, particularly when children are the victims, not only violate fundamental human rights but also account for an utter failure of our religions, cultures and civilisations – casting a blot on the Constitution and legislation, thereby perpetrating a developmental disaster.

It is a manifestation of systemic injustice, disparities, discrimination, a proof of corrupt governance and an apathetic society. Therefore, it has to be dealt with in the composite context of crime, development, human rights and social evil. No singular approach can eradicate this problem in toto. Education for all, decent employment for adults in healthy and safe environments and total elimination of child labour are three interrelated issues to ascertain our upliftment, sustained economic growth and the development of our country.

In my opinion, the trafficking nexus in Assam and other north eastern states must be properly investigated and systematically dismantled by taking stringent and punitive actions against all those who are involved in this heinous crime. Establishing fast track courts and initiating summary trials for such matters could prove to be very effective. The media, civil society, the government and village institutions particularly *panchayat*s and village defence parties (VDPs) should work hand in hand in source areas of child trafficking to educate and empower the local community.

In addition to this, child labourers must be thoroughly identified, rescued and rehabilitated thoroughly. The government must proactively ensure free, quality and meaningful education while working towards the enrolment of out-of-school children and their sustained retention in the school thereafter. The government should run centrally-sponsored schemes for the rehabilitation of trafficking victims.

Special Task Forces should be established to combat trafficking at major railway junctions en-route to the north-eastern states. There is a serious need of slate level inter-departmental coordination in Assam. The Central Bureau of Investigation (CBI) and other government agencies should take up the cases of trafficking in Assam as a priority, and track down the missing children with a sense of urgency.

Although the recent incident of gang rape in a moving bus in Delhi has invoked an unprecedented outburst of emotions and anger across the length and breadth of our nation, the cases of crimes perpetuated on helpless Assamese girls remain unnoticed and unheard in Delhi. Moreover, no police action has been taken against the perpetrators despite several such heinous incidents being reported. We are preparing to file Public Interest Litigations in the Assam High Court soon.

I request the Assam Government to establish Fast Track Courts on an urgent basis to ensure the fair and speedy trial of all child trafficking-related cases originating from the state. I strongly appeal that fast-track courts be set up in all the states as well as at the Centre to cater to cases related to child trafficking and all kinds of sexual abuse, especially those of girl children.

□

(—February 2013)

Saving Children from Trafficking in the Time of Calamity

The National Commission for Protection of Child Rights, alluding to the state government, has made a startling revelation: 1,227 children went missing because of the Uttarakhand tragedy. The statistic is on the local children of the state, and many of them might unfortunately have died. But, in all probability, several of these children could also have been made victims of child trafficking through kidnapping, enticement or coercion. The statistics, however, have become quite controversial because different ministries of the district, citing sources and the basis for the figures, are passing the buck to one another. In a government statement, it was announced that if no information about the children was found, they would be declared dead. In our view, doing that would sadly be very ironic.

The Uttarakhand tragedy has many aspects—both in terms of what caused it and its effects. The loss of life and the damage to property are effects that are visible immediately. But the far-reaching consequences are no less dire. In the circumstances ensuing from the natural disaster, thousands of children have been affected in one way or the other, besides those that lost their lives. Merely completing the formality of gathering information about them or expressing sympathy for them will not do. The educational infrastructure for thousands of children in 4,000 villages have been devastated. The livelihoods and homes of their parents have been destroyed. Many children have been separated from their families. These circumstances are totally conducive for the children to go missing, via child trafficking, child prostitution or bonded child labour. Obviously, for the illegal child trafficking, such disaster-hit areas become a potent source of children being availed at cheap rates.

On the second day of the tragedy, I myself contacted the State Commission for Protection of Child Rights, requesting them to caution the administration, police and all relief agencies against the potential danger of human trafficking. And they did so. Besides, I had written to the Chief Minister of the state in this regard, requesting for a strict vigil on relief camps and flood-affected areas. But when many of our colleagues and the pressmen spoke to the senior officers of the police and the administration, it seemed that this issue is beyond their understanding or priority. Unfortunately, it is not just the case with the state governments. Even the Centre has no understanding of tackling disaster management, relief and rehabilitation in a way that is child-centric or child-friendly. To do all of that in the backdrop of child rights is even more far-fetched for them. This work should be done not only from the point of view of compassion and disaster management, but also from the perspective of child rights.

It is to be noted here that the tragedy-stricken children are worthy not just of pity. According to the Juvenile Justice Act, every such child up to the age of 18 years has the legal right to care and security. It is not necessary that the child be without parents or an orphan. Through the Child Welfare Committees set up in each district, the needy children should be immediately sent to Child Protection Units, where the government is responsible for their care, security and education. In spite of huge strides in technology and communication, the thought and strategy on tackling disasters still appears to be a century old.

Child trafficking flourished in the tsunami-affected areas of Indonesia, Sri Lanka and India. Likewise, incidents of kidnapping of children were witnessed in the 2008 Kosi River flood in the state of Bihar, in which thousands of families were affected. I had conducted raids in the Kosi region and rescued children from the clutches of child traffickers. Learning our lessons from the tsunami, BBA ran an intensive awareness campaign against child trafficking in the relief camps and villages affected by the flood. BBA also took the initiative to create awareness among Indian as well as foreign relief agencies, government departments, the police and the volunteer organisations working in the area. We also conducted three separate raids at bus depots and railway stations and rescued 12, 9 and 3 children respectively from the grip of child traffickers. Despite all the efforts to prevent trafficking, nearly 3,000 children were smuggled out in the three to four months following the flood. Till today, the flood-affected areas of Kosi—Saharsa, Darbhanga, Madhepura, Madhubani, Sitamarhi, etc. – are among the largest hubs of child trafficking.

The state of Uttarakhand has long been a source of young boys and girls for child traffickers. Adolescent girls from the villages of Pithoragarh are sold through middlemen for child marriages and prostitution. Many children from several regions of the state, including Uttarkashi, are taken to Dehradun, Rishikesh, Hardwar, Haldwani and other places in Uttar Pradesh as well as to the homes and restaurants in Delhi for the purpose of child labour. A sad thing about Uttarakhand is that there are only three children's homes in the entire state. There is not even a single Child Protection Unit. What is surprising is that the state government has opened eight juvenile justice homes, which means that the government believes that in Uttarakhand, a lot more children are occupied in crime than those who need care and protection. Fortunately, the State Commission for Protection of Child Rights in Uttarakhand is more sensitive and active than any other such Commission in the country. In the past one year, the Commission has been instrumental in the intensive training of government machinery, police officers and District Child Welfare Committees on the social and legal aspects of child rights—but these Committees are crippled in the absence of resources. Most of them do not even have a place to sit and work.

The callousness and inertia of the state government has no bounds: the Integrated Child Protection Scheme (ICPS) of the Central Government has not been implemented in Uttarakhand till date. In the past four years, ₹ 600 crore have been distributed under the scheme among various states, but the Government of Uttarakhand has never asked the Centre for money—nor has the Centre come forward to contribute on its own. The reason why this has not happened is utterly shoddy. A few months back, I learnt from various sources that there was a cold war between the state's Social Welfare Ministry and the Ministry of Women & Child Development over seizing control of the huge funding that one could receive under the ICPS. Had this scheme been running properly in every district of the state, then in the tragic time of the floods, the Commission, Child Welfare Committees and the concerned departments could have immediately taken the affected children into their care and protection.

The Uttarakhand tragedy is being termed a national disaster, but tackling it is limited to rescuing the pilgrims that came here from across the country, keeping them in relief camps and taking pictures of the afflicted people waving green flags at trucks laden with relief material. For some others, rebuilding the Kedarnath Temple premises at an international level may be akin to national duty. But the need of the hour is for the Prime Minister's Office to establish coordination between different ministries and the Government of Uttarakhand, so that the child-traffickers are unable to take the affected children out of the state and into the confines of other states. For this, at the order of the Home Ministry, police in all the bordering states should be alerted. The needy children should be identified and sent to Child Protection Units that are equipped to provide them care and protection. The Central Ministry of Women & Child Development and the Ministry of Social Welfare should make honest and accelerated efforts in this direction. The country's Ministry of Education along with the State Government should ensure that the Central law of Right to Education, when it comes to implementing it in Uttarakhand, does not get washed away in the flood waters of Bhagirathi. The concerned Central ministers should work together for the livelihood of the poor families whose children are susceptible to being pushed into child labour. Likewise, the Central Health Ministry should come forward to help thousands of afflicted children get over the trauma and psychological ill-effects of the floods. Only then can we really tackle this national calamity.

□

(—July 2013)

PROTECTING CHILDHOOD

"Childhood protected and nurtured will bring value to our world while wasted childhoods will erode all prospects of a promising tomorrow."

1. To protect children from sexual exploitation, the Government of India has enacted the Protection of Children from Sexual Offences Act, 2012.
2. According to the National Crime Records Bureau, 8,904 cases of sexual crimes against children were registered in the year 2014.
3. According to the National Crime Records Bureau, in the year 2014, 8,990 children fell victim to sexual abuse.
4. In the year 2014, the guilty were punished in only 1 percent of the cases of sexual exploitation.
5. According to the National Crime Records Bureau, in the year 2014, 14,535 girls were victims of rape.

Wanted: Laws to Protect Childhood

Today a government report revealed something that has again put us all to shame. Unfortunately, it was not splashed in the media, but the fresh report of the Ministry of Child and Family Welfare about the sexual abuse of children is enough to expose the boastful claims of our economic development, culture and civilisation. In an India that never tires of calling upon its great traditions of protecting women, an under-aged girl is raped every 155 minutes. The government report also says that India is home to the largest number of sexually exploited children than anywhere in the world.

On 1st May, while the government was discussing this report in the Lok Sabha, a yoga instructor was sexually exploiting a 9-year-old class IV student barely a few miles away from Parliament House. And just one day before that, on 30th April, the Delhi Police registered three similar cases. In the Swaroop Nagar area of the capital, a child was abused by his neighbour when he was playing in the municipal park outside his home. In the same area, a 14-year-old girl was raped by her 24-year-old neighbour. The third incident is even more despicable. A 40-year-old policeman, whose job was to protect the life, property and dignity of citizens, raped a girl in broad daylight on Tughlak Road – only a few metres away from the homes of the Prime Minister, Central ministers and court judges. There is no dearth of such abhorrent incidents that occur, day in and day out. And when this is the situation that prevails in Delhi, one might well imagine how insecure would be the lives of children in far-flung areas of the country.

Nobody knows how many children face abuses and insults as they make their way back home from schools, hospitals, entertainment centres, temples, police or other government departments every single day. Worse still, there are many who are not lucky enough to come back alive. They are condemned to torment in brick kilns, factories and quarries, crying silently or breathing their last there and then. Many more die of malnutrition, hunger and disease. And then there are those children who are crushed to death on the roads by buses, trucks and cars – quite often the courtesy of rickety buses, or drunk or novice drivers.

In our society, there is a clear and acute lack of awareness, preparedness and honest attempts when it comes to safeguarding children. The biggest reasons why such incidents keep happening time and again: an apathetic social mindset towards children, an irresponsible attitude and the all-pervading insensitivity. Therefore, it is necessary that the dangers to the lives of children and any acts of violence against them are understood from a wider perspective; also, an all-round solution should be sought out.

There is a general lack of sensitivity and responsibility towards the security and rights of children in all areas. It appears that more than half the children suffer sexual exploitation and violence at the hands of their own acquaintances, relatives or teachers. Among the children who go through such situations, 70 percent do not tell anyone anything about what happened. Our society, in general, is not a friend of the children. Friendship itself is a safety shield and the best way to groom a child. Just taking pity on children or caressing them does not make us their friend. That is why, maternal or paternal uncles or other close relatives often do not miss a chance to sexually abuse children. They are able to sexually harass or exploit children because they know that the kids are not likely to tell anyone, and even if they do complain, denial would be very easy. Millions of children are taught right from their childhood that they should "respect the elders", "not say anything against seniors" or "not argue against what they say"—precepts that have now turned into instruments for silently bearing the agony. Despite suffering sexual abuse, the children cannot even point a finger at these elders.

Consider the so-called elite: highly educated families. Burdened under the beneficence of expensive education provided by their parents, children in these families are pushed hard to get over 90 percent marks, or to become the little dancing stars a la Boogie Woogie, or to win medals in sports competitions everytime, but the pressure to perform makes them lose their self-confidence. Such behaviour of parents does not bring them closer to their children; on the contrary, it creates such a huge gulf between them that they are unable to summon up the courage to complain to their mother or father about the sexual exploitation occurring within their home.

No training regarding sensitivity to the children is given to the labour inspectors and officials appointed to curb child labour in India. Neither the rights of children nor their dignity are kept in mind when they are interrogated by officials. The police usually behave with children in a crude, insulting and unfriendly manner. Unfortunately, the same is the case in our courts.

Among the efforts needed in this direction: creating public awareness about the laws related to child safety, creating the political and administrative will to get them implemented, providing enough resources, providing complete damages instead of a token relief amount in case of accidental injuries and deaths, and punishing the guilty through fast track courts.

The most important thing, however, is to create

sensitivity towards children and awareness about their rights among all those people who come in contact with children – be it the school bus driver, staff in educational institutions, teachers, or workers in hospitals and health centres. This is even more important for workers and officials of juvenile justice homes, the police, courts, etc.

Our government must hold all those who are entrusted with the implementation of laws and schemes related to children as well as instructions of the courts accountable. For how long can we give excuses about the delay in justice or relief and allow our children to be crippled, raped, burned, murdered or made victims of violence?

□

(—May 2007)

Child Rights and Law: Going Beyond the Books

Last year, an important law was passed in the country that was little discussed: the Protection of Children from Sexual Offences Act (POCSO). This is the first special law for protecting children from crimes which are sexual in nature. We will talk about the main provisions of this law later on. First, I want to relate an incident pertaining to the hurdles coming in the way of its implementation. Last week, a young man from the Kokrajhar District of Assam met me in Delhi; two of his relatives from Ghaziabad were also with him. They had reached us with the help of a local journalist. The youth Shafiqullah (name changed) was running from pillar to post in search of his 17-year-old sister Shakila. He burst out crying several times as he told us about it. A few months back, a local middleman and two persons from the Pingod Village in Haryana's Palwal District abducted her after enticing her on the pretext of marriage. The village *maulvi* even made a nuptial agreement. The handicapped father and the brother of the girl kept looking for her for several months. They even sold their land for a ₹ 30,000-bribe to get it reported in the Kokrajhar police station, but nothing came of it. Last month, somehow, Shakila was able to call up her brother. According to Shafiqullah, his sister is trapped in a place where many people are raping her in the name of marriage. When he reached Pingod and discreetly met his sister, he saw scratches and wounds on Shakila's face, neck, hands and legs. All his appeals for the return of his sister to the family were to no avail.

When our colleagues, along with Shafiq and his relatives, reached the Palwal police station, nobody was ready to listen to us. Forget the low-ranking officials, even the inspector had never taken any action against crimes like child trafficking, sexual abuse, bonded labour, etc. When we referred to Sections 370 and 370A of the Indian Penal Code (IPC), which have new provisions related to human trafficking, along with the Juvenile Justice Act, then they reacted, "Are you talking about the law in America?" The inspector believed that such marriages happen in each and every village of the area, so there was nothing new or illegal. It took several hours of locking horns with them and showing them the directives of the Supreme Court along with copies of IPC, POCSO and other laws – even translating these in Hindi and explaining their main points – that they finally agreed that the laws did belong to India. Even then, the police refused to go to Pingod to set the girl free.

The inspector was annoyed with the constant pressure being exerted by our workers. He said, "Go and first get the registration certificate of *Bachpan Bachao Andolan* (BBA) and the authorised ID cards of all people, only then will any further action be taken." They also had no fear or shame in shooing away Shafiq. The senior members of BBA then spoke to the district's Superintendent of Police and the D.I.G. of the area. Somehow, a police contingent was sent with us to rescue the girl. Hundreds of villagers, along with the *maulvi*, gathered there in protest. The police looked afraid. With the help of a couple of conscientious policemen, however, our colleagues succeeded in getting Shakila out of the house from the back door and driving off with her.

But it was back to square once we reached the police station. While her brother had brought Shakila's government school certificate as a solid age proof, the police insisted on getting a bone test done. And if the doctors did not find her to be below 18 years of age, she would be duly handed back to her husband and family. If she wished, she could later file a separate lawsuit. In the police station, Shakila was made to sit along with her rapists. And even though the policewomen were there, the initial interrogation was done in everyone's presence. There is no government shelter for girls or women in Palwal, nor is the Child Welfare Committee present in any form. So, after getting the medical check-ups done, she was presented the next day at the court of a local magistrate – who sent her 200 kilometres away to a women's home in Karnal instead of entrusting her to her brother and relatives.

The officials at the women's home in Karnal told our colleagues that since the case is under the jurisdiction of the magistrate of Palwal, they will not hand over Shakila to Shafiq without the magistrate's permission. Our worry grew as a new piece of information came in. It was found that in the past few days, two girls had committed suicide at this women's home – which was the only one in the entire state. Surely, the situation at this government institution was grave. It was obvious that in this entire process, mockery was made not just of the POCSO Act but of every single law related to crimes against children.

In another incident, only last fortnight, we rescued 16-year-old girl Maria (name changed) from Sonepat in Haryana. She had been trafficked from the Lakhimpur district of Assam. An illegal placement agency of Delhi had sold her off as a domestic maidservant to a rich businessman for ₹ 22,000 three years ago. Maria's mother came to Delhi, where she too was sold off as a bonded labourer a year ago. The SHO of Sonepat had chided and driven away the associates of BBA. The girl could be freed only after two days of gruelling work. The most unfortunate part of this incident was that the girl, who had continuously fallen victim to rape, was two-and-a-half months pregnant.

POCSO was used for the first time in the Sonepat case. The two culprits are now in jail.

In the Palwal case, only one person, that is Shakila's alleged husband, was arrested. Cases were filed against him under Sections 3 & 4 of POCSO, Section 370 of IPC which is related to trafficking of person and was added after amending criminal law in 2013, and Section 366A, which corresponds to forced sexual relations on the pretext of marriage. It is evident how an organisation like the BBA, which on several occasions got the Supreme Court and high courts to pronounce historical judgments, had to move heaven and earth for the use of POCSO in this case. It would be hard to imagine how this law could be implemented for common victims in police stations in far-flung areas. Possibly, only a handful of women's organisations, lawyers, experts and a few sensitive officers would be familiar with POCSO, or who might be ready for the struggle to obtain justice for the aggrieved. The POCSO Act gives detailed interpretation of the sexual crimes against children up to 18 years of age and also provides for punishment in accordance with the given definitions of different types of sexual abuse. It is the only law that takes a child-friendly approach into consideration and takes cognisance of the dignity of children. Hearing of the cases under POCSO is to be done in special courts, which will help the victimised children in getting compensation for their medical and rehabilitation needs, none of which happens in reality.

For a proper understanding of sexual abuse, it is necessary to understand a few other aspects related to it, especially when sex crimes are committed at a large scale in an organised and systematic way. Children going missing, child trafficking and sexual exploitation of children should not be viewed separately. Barring exceptions, all these crimes are deeply interconnected. Many crimes, such as child abuse, rape, bonded labour, forced labour, organ trade, etc. often begin with children going missing. Most children once lost are never traced back later. A majority of them belong to families residing in far-flung places, displaced families and belonging to the weaker sections of society. Such people hardly have any voice. If the society and police can help prevent the kidnapping of children through alertness and caution, a large number of crimes against children can be stopped.

Some important amendments have been made to the criminal justice law after considering the broader context of rape and sexual crimes. In the new law that has been enacted, human trafficking has been defined for the first time. In Section 370 of the Indian Penal Code, several activities have been identified as crimes, which includes luring a child or adult with something to abduct or deceive them, taking them from one place to another, etc. There are also provisions for separate punishment for different crimes in Section 370A of IPC. This will make it easy to bring the perpetrators to book if the Supreme Court gives directives in this regard, or if the police investigates a case and takes action.

The biggest challenge, of course, is to get these sections implemented, along with the provisions of the POCSO Act, which was enacted on 14th November 2012. It is obvious that governments that thrive on the economic, physical and emotional exploitation of children and an apathetic society will not allow it to be implemented so easily. Therefore, it is essential to challenge the unholy nexus between the criminals and businessmen, who trade children like cattle and exploit them for labour and prostitution, and the politicians who fill up their coffers with the black money thus generated. Conscientious people and revolutionary groups must come forward against child exploitation and use the justice systems as weapons to fight this battle in an organised way.

□

(—July 2013)

THE CHAINS OF SLAVERY WILL BREAK

"I refuse to accept that the combined capacity, compassion & courage of nations is unable to wipe out the scourge of child slavery."

There are six laws in India for ensuring the protection, education and safety of children:

1. **The Child Labour (Prohibition and Regulation) Act, 1986**
2. **The Prohibition of Child Marriage Act**
3. **The Right of Children to Free and Compulsory Education Act, 2009**
4. **Protection of Children from Sexual Offences Act, 2012**
5. **The Criminal Law (Amendment) Act, 2013**
6. **The Juvenile Justice (Care and Protection of Children) Act, 2015**

Our Strength Lies in Our Laws

In the new laws proposed in the Indian Parliament in the past few years, one law also relates to child labour. However, no discussion has taken place on this because it is not a priority of any political party, including the ruling party. It is clear that the country's politics is based on mass votes. In the mathematics of elections, children do not count as vote banks. They are considered as mere footnotes lying outside the margins of politics. It is another matter that all candidates fill up the election form with an oath to protect the Constitution. Perhaps no one pays any heed that the same Constitution not only ensures the fundamental rights given to all citizens and to every child up to the age of 18 years, but it also guarantees their safety, development and dignity. Besides, there are several other important laws as well. Chief among them are the Juvenile Justice Act, 2000, the Right of Children to Free and Compulsory Education (RTE) Act, 2009, and the Protection of Children from Sexual Offences Act (POCSO) (2012).

The law pending in the Parliament we are referring to here is a statute related to the prevention of child labour. Essentially, it is related to a few amendments in the Child Labour (Prohibition and Regulation) Act of 1986. Its objective is to ensure consistency between the current law on child labour and several other laws and constitutional provisions. The Central Cabinet had given its green signal to the draft of this Act sometime back. From this standpoint, technically speaking, the Parliament should have no problem in passing the amendments.

According to non-governmental statistics, there are around 50 to 60 million child labourers in India, whereas the government puts this number at nearly 12.5 million. But whatever is the figure, no one can deny the fact that millions of children, who should be going to school in India, are labouring in agricultural fields, stone quarries, brick kilns, factories, restaurants, homes, entertainment centres, etc. Various national and international studies have established the link between child labour and other social ills, such as poverty, adult unemployment, illiteracy, etc. – besides becoming a big hurdle to personal development and economic growth. How then can its perpetration be justified?

A few significant recommendations have been made in the proposed draft. Chief among them are a complete ban on child labour for children up to 14 years of age, and a ban on employment for children of 14 to 18 years of age in hazardous industries and related processes. Second, there is a suggestion to make child labour a cognisable offence. Third, for employers who harbour child labourers, it is suggested that a higher punishment be awarded. Even though these proposed amendments can address the inconsistencies in Juvenile Justice Act and the law related to right to education to some extent, they cannot completely eradicate child labour, nor would they protect the constitutional rights of children and international agreements. In the 1986 Act, child labour for up to 14 years of age has not been completely prohibited. The ban exists only for hazardous industries and related activities. Furthermore, under the existing law, 18 industries and 65 related processes that come under the hazardous category no longer apply to the age group of 14-18 years.

Now, only the mining industry, industries making explosives, and some other dangerous industries, which are listed under the Factory Act of 1948, are included in the total prohibition of child labour for children up to 18 years of age. This implies it will not be legally prohibited to employ child labourers in homes, agricultural fields, restaurants and roadside hotels, entertainment centres, etc. It is worth noting that nearly 80 percent of children in India who are employed in child labour work in these very industries. This situation will be against several provisions of the Juvenile Justice Act, which guarantees security of children up to 18 years of age against all kinds of exploitative and harmful circumstances.

Another shortcoming of the proposed amendment is that the changing perspective on crimes against children has been completely ignored. Today, around 10 children go missing in India every hour. Half of them fall prey to child trafficking. Every year, hundreds of thousands of children are lured and pushed into child labour or by persuading their parents. Most of these children are victims of child labour, bonded labour, forced begging, domestic forced labour, etc. This issue of missing children is certainly connected to child labour directly. But this grave concern has been completely ignored in the proposed law. The third shortcoming is related to the process of rescuing child labourers, and the lack of provision for their rehabilitation. Neither the existing law nor the draft of the amendment mention these matters. If a child is a victim of bonded labour, then under the Bonded Labour System (Abolition) Act, 1976, the judicial magistrate has been entrusted with the responsibility to rescue the bonded labourer. But there is no clarity on who will free the child and how. The law is completely silent on where the rescued children would go, and how they would be rehabilitated economically, and socially, and also in terms of their education. Without economic rehabilitation, it is very difficult for any such law to be successful.

If the intentions of the government were honest, it could have included various directives given by the Supreme Court from time to time in the draft of the amendment. For instance, the important 1996 judgement of the honourable Supreme Court, in which the employers of child labourers were required to pay penalties, and the money was to be spent on the rehabilitation of children. Or giving employment to the parent or an adult member of the family of the child that has been rescued. Besides this, one judgement of the Delhi High Court directed the employer to pay full compensation to the child for the duration of his employment as a labourer. The government should ensure that there are legal provisions for mainstreaming the education of children rescued from child labour. The same law should also provide for the vocational training of children above 14 years of age, so that this law becomes their legal right and no rescued child ever has to fall into the trap of child labour again. The fourth shortcoming concerns the same old insincere attitude of the government when it comes to punishing the employers of child labourers. From this point of view, the existing law has proven to be completely blunt and ineffective. Under the law, thus far out of 1,360,117 cases, only 49,092 resulted in prosecution, and merely 4,774 cases in convictions.

As a mere formality, the penalty has been raised from ₹ 20,000 to ₹ 50,000 under the proposed draft amendment, but viewed from the angle of inflation, then the ₹ 20,000 in 1986 translate into ₹ 10 lakh today. This small amount will not instil any fear in employers.

In cases of child labour, a minimum punishment of three years' imprisonment should be meted out. The sentence for the crime of forced labour should be at least a seven-year term. For those knowingly employing children who have been victims of trafficking, a minimum five years' punishment should be given. If someone is caught having engaged in child labour for the first time, then the license of the factory or establishment concerned should be suspended for a week and, if the offence is repeated, the license should be revoked. Simply making child labour a cognisable offence will not be enough. In addition, it should be made non-bailable. We should not forget that frequent amendments to welfare laws are not done easily.

Take the law related to child labour, for instance. After the constitutional provisions of 1950, it took 36 years to give it legal shape. Only in 1986 did the new law come about, and that in half-hearted fashion. Child labour up to 14 years of age should have been banned at that very moment. Now, 27 years later, there is some discussion on amending this law. This is still an opportunity: one that must be taken with complete honesty and foresight.

□

(—August 2013)

Government Accountability and Sensitisation

For media, the burning issues of today are confined to the coal scam, corruption, black money and *Jan Lokpal*. Besides these, other important issues and happenings are dealt with in a paragraph or two in the newspapers. Nobody can deny that the issues on which the media is focussing are important questions before the nation, but providing freedom, justice and equal opportunities to children who are victims of physical, mental and economic exploitation is no small issue. It is another matter that the media seldom pays any attention to this. In the history of the Indian Parliament, our honourable Members of Parliament (MPs) have not been able to spare even a single day for a complete debate on child labour, and to try and discharge their constitutional responsibility by finding a solution. But those fighting against child labour finally achieved a significant victory. A few days ago, the Central Cabinet gave its nod to the amendment of the 1986 law on child labour. Now, it remains to be passed in the Parliament.

Under the new law, child labour up to 14 years of age will be completely banned. Furthermore, adolescents in the age group of 14 to 18 years will not be allowed employment in any hazardous industry. Child labour will become a cognisable offence, punishable with up to three years' imprisonment and up to ₹ 50,000 in fine. This is a welcome step, but there are several challenges and hurdles in getting it implemented.

The first difficulty is the lack of political will, owing to which there is no compliance with the fundamental rights or the principles of equality and justice enshrined in the Constitution, nor has it been possible to implement the laws and schemes that favour the poor, exploited, aggrieved, women, children or other weak sections of society.

Since 1950, there has been a provision in the Constitution for the ban of work that is hazardous for children. Despite that, until 1986, no law could be made in the country to prevent child labour. In these 36 years, at least two generations grew up in child labour. In the early 1980s, a few people like us used to stage demonstrations at the Parliament House and struggle to inspire some conscientious MPs to enact laws against child labour. This resulted in the law to prevent child labour in 1986, but it basically turned out to be a law that was against childhood. Keeping just 10 to 15 percent of the businesses in the prohibited category, it gave legal sanction to child labour in the remaining 90 percent. I remember burning copies of this toothless law together with hundreds of parents of child labourers who used to work in the stone quarries of Faridabad and the brick kilns of Delhi and Ghaziabad. Now, after 26 years of strenuous efforts, it has been proposed for this law to be up for an amendment.

The second challenge in implementing the new law relates to the accountability of the government machinery. It is an open secret that in some areas and industries of the country, there is rampant child labour, bonded labour and child trafficking. Besides stone quarries, brick kilns and roadside restaurants, domestic child labourers and children that are forced to become beggars can be found in every corner of the country. In the carpet industry of Mirzapur, coal and mica mines of Jharkhand, the glass industry of Ferozabad, the lock factories of Aligarh, the brass workshops of Muradabad, the fireworks industry of Sivakasi and Virudnagar, and the embroidery industry of Tirupur, Jalandhar and the National Capital Region, millions of child labourers are generating wealth for the rich—at the cost of their own health, childhood, education and freedom. In all these places, the labour inspectors and commissioners are not only revelling in the salaries paid to them through taxes imposed on the hard-earned income of the public, they are also the beneficiaries of industrialists who break the law. Child Welfare Committees have been set up in most districts. Above them in several states as well as at the Centre, there are Commissions for Protection of Child Rights. Millions of rupees are spent on these institutions set up for monitoring, but in more than three decades of struggle against child labour, I have not come across a single example in which an official of a department or commission has been dismissed for failing to save children. Clearly, the irresponsible officials, flanked by red-tape on one side and their patrons' beneficence on the other, are free from all accountability, simply ignoring the grave situation.

The third challenge is the lack of capability in the government system responsible for the implementation of the law. The main reasons for this incapability includes insensitivity towards child rights, the lack of understanding of laws related to child labour, the shortage of human resources and other means, and the lack of regular training. Under the amended law, the ambit of implementation has been widened from the labour department to the police. Now every police post or station will be legally bound to act upon complaints or information on child labour. However, the anti-people and corrupt character of the police are often in plain sight. One can imagine how they will behave with child labourers or their utterly poor parents. This is why it is necessary that efforts are made to train and sensitise police officials and workers with a new approach.

It is not that the erstwhile law had no provisions for punishment. Imprisonment of up to two years and a penalty of up to ₹ 20,000 were included in the 1986 law, but not even a single employer who kept not one or two but hundreds of children as labourers and slaves ever had to serve the full jail term under the aforementioned law. As a so-called fine, only ₹ 15 to 20 were collected in some cases. What better bargain in the world can there be for an employer who snatches away the childhood of a child? The Central Government conceded last month that since the law against child labour was enacted, only 1,360,117 inspections were done, whereas 12,500,000 child labourers were counted in the 1991 census. In these 26 years, only 49,019 cases were filed, out of which only 4,774 employers were convicted, which amounted to the paltry fine of a few rupees.

The fourth challenge is the lack of intent to obtain correct information on the number of child labourers. According to the government, only 5 million children today are engaged in labour in the country. Ten years ago, this number was cited to be some nearly 12.5 million. This means that at least 7 to 7.5 million children have been rescued from child labour. But if less than 5000 employers were found guilty during this time, then the question arises: What legal process was used to free up so many children? Thankfully, the pseudo-Godmen, who deal in miracles, black art or sham, are not claiming that it is they who have transformed the hearts of the common people of the country. Nevertheless, the government says that the rising enrolment in schools has brought down child labour. This is only partially true. Wherever children are regularly getting mid-day meals along with free and good education, children have started going to school instead of working, but in several districts of the country, the number of children enrolled in schools is only shown to be 25 to 30 percent of the total school age-going children.

In the past year, *Bachpan Bachao Andolan* (BBA), with the help of the government, has rescued nearly 1,100 child labourers in Delhi alone. These children were trafficked from states like Bihar, Jharkhand and Uttar Pradesh. Out of these children, the names of around 750 of them were registered in the ancestral schools of their villages. Quite possibly, the mid-day meals meant for them went into the bellies of the local government officials.

The fifth, and perhaps the biggest, challenge pertains to the rehabilitation of children rescued as a result of the implementation of the new law. So far, only one government scheme has been running: the National Child Labour Project Scheme. It is said to be operational in 266 districts, but its supposed beneficiaries are only 600,000 children. In the government's own monitoring reports, various scams have been discovered in which it was found that in several cases, there were no beneficiary child labourers at all. In the name of scholarships etc, the benefits were being given to children from well-off and influential families. Taking non-governmental organisations' estimates, 40 to 60 million children are victims of child labour, but even if the government figures are considered, then as many as 5 million children up to the age of 14 years will have to be rehabilitated. Besides, 1.5 to 2 million children in the age group 14 to 18 years will become free under the new law. Obviously, they will not start studying in the first or second grade. For them, vocational and employment-oriented education and training under a special syllabus will be needed. The government must get ready for this from now on. Certainly, such an undertaking will require a budget several times higher than what is currently being allocated.

The sixth challenge is to establish good coordination among the various ministries and departments after the law is passed. There is already a rabbit's nest of laws and schemes for the protection of child rights. After the new law comes into effect, this challenge will only grow. Preventing child labour is the job of the Ministry of Labour, but now the police department will also be involved. For children's rights, there are Child Welfare Committees, which come under the purview of the Department of Women and Child

Welfare. Under the Juvenile Justice Act, these committees have enough powers. Above them are the Commissions for Protection of Child Rights at the state and central levels. Those, in turn, come under the Union Ministry of Women and Child Development. They are the custodians of the Right to Education Act, whereas ensuring education is the responsibility of the Ministry of Education. If a child is the victim of child labour or trafficking, then it comes under the jurisdiction of the deputy magistrate. Very clear directives and regular training will be required for the coordination among all of them. One good thing about the new law is that the District Magistrate (DM) of every district has been given the responsibility to implement it, however it is necessary to train and sensitise the DMs in this direction.

Finally, one cannot sit idle and leave it solely to the government to take the responsibility of properly tackling all these challenges. Unless the hands that wield the law like a weapon are strong and active, the law is nothing but a bunch of papers. An aware and conscientious public can become those hands. We will have to accelerate the ground movement in order to put pressure on the government on one hand, and make Indian as well as foreign industrialists accountable on the other. The end of child labour is also the end of inequality, exploitation, poverty and injustice – and it is only possible through a mass movement.

□

(—June 2013)

Towards an Effective Juvenile Justice Act

The Juvenile Justice Act is once again in the news. The suggestions of the Minister of Women and Child Development are being opposed not only by most opposition parties but by organisations concerned with child rights as well. It looks like this matter will only create more ruckus, especially when the government does not have a majority in the *Rajya Sabha*. After the Nirbhaya tragedy, the debate around reducing the age for being considered a 'juvenile' has not died down. Incidents of rape and murder every now and then by adolescents below 18 years have added fuel to the fire. Even the politician Subramanian Swamy has filed a petition in the Supreme Court demanding the reduction in the age limit, but he has not succeeded in this.

The unfortunate thing in the whole episode is that ignoring the reach of the Act and other important aspects, the entire debate has remained confined to punishing the juveniles involved on a par with adults, or just taking corrective measures. The reality of the existing law is that, despite its shortcomings, there are important arrangements to ensure the safety and care of children and adolescents. It is to be noted that the foundation of this law is built on the United Nations Convention on the Rights of the Child (CRC). Almost all governments of the world, including the Indian Government, signed this treaty in 1990. Several campaigns are behind this important document, which is considered the Bible of child rights. I also had a role to play.

Enacted in the year 2000 and amended in 2005, there are two aspects to the Juvenile Justice Act. One, the state is to give full security and care to every child up to the age of 18 years who needs it. Two, if under any circumstances, a child goes against the law of the land, then instead of treating him as a common criminal and making him go through the judicial process, or stuffing him into a prison cell, he can be sent to a juvenile justice home for a period, ranging from three months or up to three years. This decision can only be taken by Child Welfare Committees or Juvenile Justice Boards.

It is unfortunate that the governments of this country have proven to be incapable and unsuccessful in honestly following these two aspects. Millions of children, despite being legally entitled to security and care, are begging on the streets, living on pedestrian paths a life that is worse than an animal's, being bought and sold like objects, are deprived of quality education, trapped in marriages like toys, condemned to engage in child labour or bonded labour, or just living a malnourished life amid severe deprivations. Countless children can be found not only in juvenile homes but even in prisons, in the absence of any legal help.

Despite being defined under the Juvenile Justice Act, why do these children remain invisible to the government and politicians? Many of these children and adolescents fall easily into the grip of criminal gangs. They are used in crimes as varied as pickpocketing, to selling and smuggling drugs. Terrorist organisations active in Kashmir and Maoist groups use brain-washing techniques, enticement or sheer force to hand over these children bombs or guns. Criminal gangs deploy adolescents in thefts, robberies or even murders. The fundamental question is that if the government and society had honestly striven to take care of their childhood and constitutional rights, then would it not have been possible, in most cases, to prevent them from entering the world of crime? Besides, crimes committed by children can also be stopped to a great extent by taking strict and quick action against the adults responsible for the situation.

The Minister of Women and Child Development is stating that the rapist adolescents should get the same punishment as adult criminals. However, organisations working for child rights are adamant that no amendment should be made to the existing law. In my opinion, both kinds of thinking are extreme in nature. As far as redefining the 'juvenile' age is concerned, it is totally inappropriate, because in addition to other things, it is contrary to those international treaties and declarations that India has accepted. At the same time, one cannot ignore the fact that heinous crimes are also committed by children in the age group of 16 to 18 years and, quite often, by children just 3 to 4 months shy of 18 years. They cannot be treated in the same way that a child of 12 or 14 years is treated. So, instead of being obstinate about one thing in this matter, it is necessary to find a practical and appropriate way out.

I think for involvement in serious crimes with punishment starting from a sentence of 10 years up to life imprisonment, juveniles should be kept in a separate category. The Juvenile Justice Board should be empowered to send cases in this category to the regular court. If the court finds any such juvenile guilty, then for punishment, he should not be sent to the common jail. Because, if he were to live with other hardened and professional criminals, then, instead of being reformed, he is more likely to become a hardened criminal himself. In such cases, special juvenile reformatory and protection centres should be created where the children can be kept. In these centres, there should also be programmes for psychological counselling and societal transformation. When the child attains the age of 21 years, then his behavioural changes should be analysed in court.

If the judge is satisfied with the rehabilitative process, then the young man can be released, or else, he would have to be sent again to the centre for another three years. This review cycle can be done every three years.

There is ample scope for improvement in the provisions for the care of small children and adolescents. Take, for instance, the matter of poor children who are deprived of health services completely. The sorry state of government hospitals is there for everyone to witness. The sheer lack of facilities, rampant corruption, gross negligence and the inhumane attitude of workers at these hospitals can barely provide health and life to the children. What remains are the 'private enterprises' running in the name of healthcare – whose very business is to burn a hole in people's pockets. It is hard to think that the children of the poor can benefit from these places. It is our suggestion that under the Juvenile Justice Act, every non-governmental hospital should be made legally responsible for providing treatment to all the needy and ailing children. Medicines and treatment of up to ₹ 2 lakh should be completely free. Legal action should be taken against hospitals that do not treat sick children under the new law.

It is a similar situation with poor children not having access to private education. Under the Right to Education law, it is mandatory for schools to ensure that of the total students enrolled, at least one-fourth are from the poor sections of society. Nowadays, there is a whole gamut of institutions providing private tuition for preparation of all kinds of competitive exams. The fees are so high that it is impossible for poor families to afford it. Under the amended law, it should be made compulsory for such institutions to provide free tuition to at least one-fourth of the adolescents.

Whatever law is made, if there is a lack of knowledge and awareness about it in society, it will be difficult to implement. Even more important is the political and governmental sensitivity, the will to implement laws, the sufficiency of resources and capacity-building of enforcement agencies.

□

(—July 2014)

Note: *The amended Juvenile Justice Act was passed in the Rajya Sabha on 23rd December, 2015.*

Disregard for the Laws Protecting Child Labourers

One of the significant initiatives of the Central Government is the prohibition on domestic child labour. In an era of open markets, domestic child labour is rapidly growing in the developing countries of the world along with the growth of middle-class society. Most of these labourers are young children, especially girls. Among the rich countries too, there is a growing trend of having young boys and girls from China, Sri Lanka, Thailand, etc., as domestic servants. Recently, there was huge hue and cry when an incident concerning UN officials keeping child labourers came to light.

In every town and city of our country, you will find children working as labourers in all kinds of homes doing all kinds of work – from washing, cooking and cleaning, to looking after the children of their employers. Shameful incidents of torture on these children often leak out, which include beatings, branding them with hot iron or tongs, rape or even murder.

We must go beyond looking at the prohibition on domestic child labour as a mere routine legal process. Most of the labour laws have remained confined to factories, mines, brick kilns or small-scale industries, whereas now their purview has spread to hundreds and thousands of homes, villages, and small tea shops in towns. Therefore, the most important thing is that if this law is not strictly implemented, then there will be widespread lack of credibility and faith not only in the laws related to child labour, but also in all laws concerning the welfare of society. If mockery of the law is practised in each and every home, then its worst psychological impact will be rising arrogance towards our legal system.

Against this backdrop, it is necessary to have an honest review of the important legislative procedures related to child labour. The lacunae that allow the existing law to be mocked at should be removed.

Let us first take a look at the compliance of this law. In 1986, 13 industries and over a dozen processes were considered hazardous and child labour in these industries and processes was completely banned. These included carpet making, leather research, fireworks and quarrying, among others. But everyone knows that in the explosive cracker workshops of Sivakasi in the state of Tamil Nadu, and several other places, children are blatantly employed as labourers.

These factories are prone to explosions that often occur even at the slightest negligence – and children constitute a majority of those who are injured or killed. The number of children working in other hazardous industries appears to be rising rather than declining. This includes children melting hot glass to make bangles in Ferozabad, children harming their lungs in the making of carpets using coloured woollen threads, and those working in brick kilns or stone quarries, among others. There are provisions of a jail term of up to two years for the crime of employing children as labourers under this law, but there is not a single instance in the country in which anyone was sent to jail. In most such cases, a fine of ₹ 20 to a few hundred rupees is issued as a mere formality. In this way, this Indian law has just become a sham.

Along similar lines is an important incident: the historical Supreme Court judgment of 10th December, 1996. In the judgement of the case M.C. Mehta vs. The Government of India, a division bench of Justice Kuldeep Singh had termed child labour a heinous crime against humanity and directed the Indian Government to hand over to the court – within six months – state-wise lists of children working in hazardous as well as non-hazardous industries. A country-wide survey was to be conducted for this. At first, the government expressed its inability to conduct the survey in six months. Later on, it made inexcusable mockery of the court's decision. The dates of the surveys to be conducted for identifying child labourers were advertised on radio and in newspapers. Government staff was then deployed in these surveys and, as was expected, no child labourers were found. It was like announcing that all thieves should be ready at work, and the police would come on the specified dates and mark them out. The report that the state and central governments presented to the Supreme Court six months later were even more disappointing and ridiculous. After all this hard work, only a few thousand children were identified.

In this judgment, the most important clause was a few suggestions to tackle the grave problem, the first one being the order to immediately slap a fine of ₹ 20,000 per child on the owners of hazardous industries and processes where child labourers were employed. The government was asked to add another ₹ 5,000 to this amount, with the resulting figure of ₹ 25,000 to be spent on the education and rehabilitation of the former child labourer under a fund created for the purpose. But all this remained only on paper. No child anywhere in the country benefited from this. Barring a few cases in Uttar Pradesh's Bhadohi and Gyanpur, no fine was collected from employers. Another important order in the judgment was that in the event of an owner being unable to pay the fine, he would provide employment to an adult member of the child's family – again, it was not done even in a single instance.

Here, it would be pertinent to cite a third legal initiative. In a notification issued on 14th October, 1999, the Central Government had amended certain rules for government employees under which they could not employ children as domestic labourers or servants. This was the result of a National Human Rights Commission directive in connection with a six-year-old child, Ashraf. An IAS officer in Delhi had branded the child with hot iron for the 'crime' of drinking the leftover milk in his son's glass. BBA had rescued the child and raised the issue with the Commission.

The gazette was issued by almost all states in the country. This implies that no government official in the country is allowed to keep a domestic child servant, but it has met with the same fate as other legal prohibitions. In the past seven years, no government employee has been dismissed from his or her job for the crime of child labour. It would be meaningless to talk about the government taking its own initiative. Even in places where the voluntary organisations and NGOs put their lives at stake to rescue children and have brought such cases to light, no action was taken against the government officials.

In this context, the most important question concerns the rehabilitation and education of children who have been removed from labour. Today, education is not just a welfare scheme of the government but for every child up to the age of 14 years, it is a constitutional right. Anything or anyone who is an impediment to it will be considered to be violating the constitution. To protect the Constitution is the government's supreme priority and responsibility. So, it is necessary that every child be provided free, compulsory and useful education. This also includes mid-day meals and the provision of special facilities and discounts to children and their parents who have been victims of certain circumstances. The gazette on the prohibition for government officials to keep domestic child labour should be seen and implemented with this perspective.

There are around 100 districts in India where there is an unfortunate mixture of child labour and poverty, unemployment, illiteracy, population growth, lack of health facilities, etc. Therefore, it is most important that the central schemes are focused on these districts. There should be uniformity and harmony in the implementation of programmes on poverty eradication, village development, free and quality education for all, and ending child labour. Sadly, not only in India but in most poor countries of the world, there are separate departments and ministries for poverty, child labour and education – with little coordination in their policies and schemes. The United Nations organisations have proven that people are illiterate not only because of poverty, but that they are poor because they are illiterate. A similar relationship exists between poverty and child labour.

Now that the gazette on the amended law has been issued, it is everyone's moral responsibility that honest efforts be made to implement it. The government should recruit well-trained labour inspectors in sufficient numbers and give them time-bound responsibilities. Also, our suggestion is that the legal accountability of employees from the labour, industry and police departments be ascertained. That is, if children are found working as labourers in areas under the jurisdiction of these officers, who have been appointed with the hard-earned tax money of the common people, then punitive action should be taken against them. The responsibility should also be given to *Panchayati* systems, NGOs, etc. Voluntary citizen groups can also be formed for conducting raids at places suspected of employing child labourers.

In conclusion, we should consider the prohibition on domestic child labour not only as a legal initiative by the government, but as a necessity for a country like India, which is making rapid strides on the highway to economic growth. □

(—October 2012)

Adopting a Friendly Attitude Towards Victimised Children

Over the past few days, there was news of 42 children dying in a bus accident at Bodeli in Gujarat, which was covered at length by the media the day it happened. According to some newspapers, the accident occurred when the driver lost control after an axel broke; others wrote that the bus fell into a drain while trying to overtake a truck at high speed. Several called it negligence on the part of the driver. This incident found space in media for another couple of days, after which it became one of those matters which drag on for years in government investigation and court proceedings.

The same day, three other incidents were reported. In the pilgrimage city of Gaya in the state of Bihar, a 14-year-old girl was carrying her younger brother who was seriously injured in a road accident when some vermins abducted her. They took her to a field nearby and gangraped her. Later, they murdered her by throttling her, burying the body of the innocent girl right there. The second incident is from the city of Bhuj in Gujarat. A few days ago, a teacher forced himself on his student and threatened her with dire consequences if she were to speak about it. In another incident in Delhi, the capital of India, a 13-year-old girl committed suicide owing to her constant failure in the English subject.

There is a fundamental similarity in all of these seemingly separate incidents – our society is lacking in awareness about the protection of children, our readiness to protect them and honest attempts to do so. Such incidents are repeated because of a lackadaisical societal mindset towards childhood, the irresponsible attitude and the widespread insensitivity. The need of the hour is to understand, from a broader perspective, any act of violence against children and the threats and insecurities in their life. A holistic solution must be sought.

After all, how long can we think of these incidents as merely sad and unfortunate? There is only temporary sympathy with the grieving families of the children, as they cry their hearts out looking at pictures of the dead. We are disturbed for a while with such incidents, but reports of large-scale violence against children do not even make a dent in society. Statistics from UNICEF have revealed a very sorry picture of India, which is home to a disproportionately large number of malnourished and exploited children in the world. And behind every such statistic, there are real children with real names and identities such as the ones in the incidents in Bodeli, Gaya, Bhuj and Delhi.

The Gujarat bus accident is not something unique: school children are routinely crippled or killed by vehicles on the road. It is only these big incidents which cause a furore for a few days, and then it is back to square one. Similar instances were the deaths of 19 children last year in a boat tragedy in Kerala or 100 children burning to death in the kitchen fire of a school in Kumbakonam in Tamil Nadu or, a few years ago, 29 kids losing their lives when a tractor trawley carrying them turned turtle in Madhya Pradesh.

Around 10 years ago when 29 school children died in an accident at Wazirabad in Delhi, the Supreme Court issued some benchmarks in the context of school buses: that every bus will have a helper; parents can travel in the school bus along with the children for their own satisfaction; the provision of a box for school bags under each seat so that children do not have to sit uncomfortably laden with their bags; and a 'School Bus' board in the front and rear of the vehicle. In addition, there was to be a special registration process for school vehicles. Such vehicles had to have first-aid material and be equipped with a fire extinguisher. Old, dilapidated buses were to be banned. These instructions were issued for the whole country. But forget small towns, these are being openly flouted even in the national capital.

The number of private vehicles ferrying children to school has grown along with the rapid commercialisation of education and the mushrooming of private, expensive schools. The fleet includes everything from old, ramshackle cars and vans, to small and medium vehicles and buses. Every morning on the streets of Delhi, you can see overloaded Maruti vans – stuffed with 15-20 children each – on their way to schools. Significantly, each van is licensed to carry only five passengers, which is what its defined capacity is. In addition, private buses are also hired for ferrying school children. Some of these buses are not even registered. One such unregistered vehicle crushed a 4-year-old girl student of a school in Ashok Vihar on 28th February. The girl was saved, but her parents say that she may not be able to walk for the rest of her life.

The lack of safety of children and sensitivity and responsibility towards their rights has become far too common everywhere. The squalid conditions of juvenile justice homes (considered as a jail by almost all children residing there) are enough to support this.

A key deficiency in the Indian system is that there is no training given to labour inspectors and officials as far as the rights of children and sensitivity to those rights are concerned. The situation with the police is even worse. The way the policemen treat children when they question them in cases concerning victimised children is not only rude, but insulting and anti-childhood as well. No government training is given to constables and inspectors for adopting a friendly attitude towards children.

In addition to creating awareness about the laws related to the safety of children and implementing them with the political will and sufficient resources, compensation must be given to the families of children injured or dead in accidents – besides bringing the culprits to justice through fast track courts. The government officials and workers in schools, hospitals or other places, the common public should also be made aware of measures for child safety. □

(—April 2008)

Madiba: A Source of Inspiration for Child Rights Movements

(This chapter was written after the death of Nelson Mandela.—Editor)

Nelson Mandela, the towering moral force in the world of modern politics and a great advocate of human rights, is no longer with us. In the intellectual and political realm, much has been written about the various aspects of his life, especially after his death. But one facet of his life's philosophy is almost hidden. It is his sensitivity, concern and successful initiatives with regard to child rights. In my lifetime, I have had the opportunity to come face-to-face with him on four occasions. On two of these instances, I was fortunate enough to have a conversation with him as a child rights activist. When he first came to visit India in 1994, I was proud to stand next to him and shake hands with him, even if for a fleeting moment. But I was fortunate in 1997 when, as part of the preparations for the Global March Against Child Labour, I arrived in Johannesburg to receive his support and blessings. We were to start one phase of the march, which was to begin in 1998, from South Africa, while two more phases were to commence from Manila (Philippines) and Sao Paulo (Brazil).

We wanted to begin the Africa phase from outside the Robben Island prison in Cape Town, where Nelson Mandela had spent 23 years in captivity. It was with regard to this plan that I met him one morning at his residence. He was sitting in an easy chair outside. I briefly outlined to him our global campaign against child labour. In a very encouraging tone, he said, "This is a very ambitious and brave step." Just sitting near him and talking to him filled me with immense excitement and courage.

During the chat, Madiba told me about an incident signifying the involvement of youth and children in protecting child rights. Mandela is affectionately called Madiba, which refers to his ancestral clan. Once he was passing through a street in Cape Town. Noticing a group of children playing football on the roadside, he stopped his car and started chatting with them. The children cried in excitement, 'Madiba, we love you!' At this, he asked them, 'Why do you love me?' One of the children quickly responded, 'Because you spend a lot of money on us.' Madiba told me that he really liked the children's candid clarity and, inspired from this incident, he established the Nelson Mandela Children's Fund in 1995. Later, the Fund went on to become a large centre for promoting democratic values in African children and youth, fighting diseases such as HIV/AIDS amongst children and ensuring a dignified life for them. The centre also spread out beyond Africa, to America and Britain.

Even though Madiba could not attend our programme due to ill health, he sent us a written note, given to me by his wife and world-renowned human rights leader Graca Machel. In his message, he wrote, "I extend my hearty congratulations on this occasion. I am really worried about the large number of children becoming victims of child labour in South Africa and the world. A journey and campaign like this will create huge public awareness about preventing the snatching away of childhood from children and the violation of their rights. It is due to an effort like this that children can be freed of child labour and a whole new generation can be prevented from falling victim to it." Eventually, this march of ours, having passed through 103 countries, not only concluded successfully at the Geneva office of the United Nations, but it also resulted in our demand being met for the enactment of an important international convention to prevent child labour under hazardous and worst conditions. Later on, Graça Machel told us that Mr. Mandela was very happy and excited about the success of this Global March.

On another occasion, I got an opportunity to meet Madiba and obtain his support and blessings for a new movement. In 1999, we had started the Global Campaign for Education. Through this campaign, a mass movement was established among the international community as well as the common people to free every sixth person in the world from the bane of illiteracy. In this connection, in the early days of 2002, I met Madiba. The meeting this time took place at the Nelson Mandela Foundation, which was formed to give shape to his thoughts and ideals. He was already aware of our efforts towards the right to education, as we had been in constant touch with Ms. Machel in this matter. Both of them gave me ample support and encouragement. This was a matter of great inspiration for me in my role as the international head of this campaign. Through a letter, Madiba and Graça told us, "Millions of parents, teachers and children across the globe are partaking in the mass movement to get free and quality education for children from their respective governments. They are involved in this Global Campaign for Education and the two of us are also joining hands with them to lend our support to this movement." I exchanged correspondence with them several times during the campaign. In one of the letters, they wrote, "Education is the most effective weapon to change the world." Every year, we organise the Global Action Week for Education in more than a hundred countries. Under this programme, child representatives associated with our movement met Madiba in 2006 (I myself could not go to meet him that time). Madiba had a lot of fun with the children and inspired them a lot – something that became valuable to the children for their whole life.

Madiba's health continued to deteriorate in the later days, but even during that time we kept in touch with his family. His wife, Ms. Machel, not only regularly participated in our programmes on child rights, she was also involved in a high-level panel on education initiated by us. She, Gordon Brown (the former Prime Minister of the United Kingdom) and I are co-presidents on this panel, whose members include the former UN Secretary-General Kofi Annan, former Australian Prime Minister Kevin Rudd and a former Prime Minister of Norway, among others. Ms. Machel not only participated actively in the panel meetings, she also suggested several significant steps. My humble requests to her are to urge African governments and heads of state to end child labour and do something about education on the basis of many of her important initiatives. During the last World Cup in 2010, we campaigned extensively for the right to education in South Africa. That was the last time we had a glimpse of Mr. Mandela: he was in a wheelchair and could not speak, but I will always remember that raised hand and smiling face of his.

Just as people will remember this great personality, Mr. Nelson Mandela, a great proponent of human values, dignified life and freedom, as a warrior against racism, the builder of a new South Africa and an embodiment of peace and generosity, likewise, there are many like me, who will remember him as an upholder of child rights and a constant source of inspiration. I offer my humble tribute to this great individual on behalf of our movement and all the children of the world.

□

(—December 2013)

EDUCATION IS THE KEY TO FREEDOM

"It is education and education alone, which can turn the tide in favour of the oppressed."

According to the Annual Status of Education Report (ASER) 2014 by Pratham, a Non-Government Organisation:

1. **In India, around 233.6 million children are in the age group of 6 to 14 years. Under the Right to Education (RTE) Act, all of them must be given free and compulsory education.**
2. **In India, 6,064,229 children are deprived of education—children who should have been in schools as per the RTE Act.**
3. **The percentage of children unable to even identify letters in the alphabet was 13.4 percent in the year 2010, which increased to 32.5 percent in 2014.**
4. **There is no arrangement of drinking water for 25 percent of school children in the country.**
5. **Toilets in 33 percent of government schools in the country are unfit to use. In the worst conditions are the toilets for girls. In 50 percent of schools, the toilets are unfit for use by the girls.**
6. **Mid-day meals are not distributed in 15 percent of the country's schools.**

The Role of Education

Education is a fundamental human right enshrined in the Universal Declaration of Human Right as well as in the constitutions of many countries. The purpose and objective of education for all, as has been defined by scholars, has caught the world's attention, time and again, and recent research and studies have generated empirical evidence that education is not the only the determinant, but is also a key factor in economic growth and sustainable development.

In the 19th century, large landholdings that introduced new technologies of irrigation and cultivation in agricultural fields were among the prime movers of growth and development. Investment in human capital was not a priority for most countries. The 20th century witnessed a pivotal change: human resources development, innovations and technological advancement, as well as investments therein, were considered catalysts for economic growth. During this century, primary and secondary education, skills formation, on-the-job training, research, acquiring knowledge and new technologies became crucial determinants of 'human capital', 'human capacities', productivity and economic growth. The 21st century is the century primarily driven by market forces. Economic growth is directly connected with market trends, and hence, the fast movement of information and knowledge plays the most important role. In other words, the journey between the 19th, 20th and the 21st century is a shift from "the age of material capital to human capital, and now the knowledge capital." Therefore, education does not remain just a virtue or a value or a human right, but has transformed itself as the backbone of the world's economy.

Thus, investments in education is a high return and low risk initiative in enhancing productivity, boosting participation and share in development, social justice and gender equity, the creation of participatory and transparent democracies, attaining better health and nutrition, reducing child, infant and maternal mortality, and increasing life expectancies, better population control, preventing HIV / AIDS, reducing hunger, and contributing to a growing understanding of environmental responsibilities. These are not only the key development indicators but are also the driving forces for economic growth.

The countries of the Asian region cannot be generalised in terms of establishing any common indicators of economic growth. Situations vary from South East Asia to South Asia, and also between the countries in these sub-regions. There are several variables like governance, the political environment, government policies and programmes, trade policies and investors' interests, geographic and environmental factors, and aid and debt issues. Educational variables include access, equity, inclusion, quality, and compulsory years of schooling. The relationship between education and economic growth can be seen in the following areas:

1. **Building Human Capital:** Education helps to build, maintain and hone human capital. It is essential to creating, applying, and spreading new ideas and technologies which in turn are critical for sustained growth. It augments cognitive and other skills, which in turn increase labour productivity. Its empowering nature aids in equipping the citizens as socially, economically and politically self-reliant, leading to greater understanding of the competition and challenges, mutual tolerance and co-existence.

All of these are translated into economic gains, especially for the women labour force.

One important factor stated by the World Bank in an early 1990s report on the Asian economic success story is getting the basic rights including the accumulation of human capital by providing universal primary education and secondary education. For example, faster productivity growth in Hong Kong is associated with its higher education standards whilst Singapore also priotises education in fostering innovation which impacts economic growth.

2. **Education and Income:** Education equips people with the knowledge and skills they need to gain employment and increase their incomes, with better bargaining power in competitive market situations. This is a pre-requisite in overall poverty reduction and growth at the national level. One study suggests that people's earnings increased by 10 percent for each year of schooling that they receive. This translates to a one percent annual increase in GDP if good quality education is offered to the entire population.

   Another study suggests that enhanced education leads to better income equity which is more likely to favour higher growth rate. Yet another study suggests that a one percent increase in the labour force with secondary education would help to increase the income of the bottom 40 to 60 percentile by between 6 and 15 percent.

3. **Education and Productivity:** Besides creating the basic foundations of literacy and numeracy through primary education, secondary and tertiary education play an important role in the acquisition of skills towards technical and industrial know-how. It has been established that the social returns

of primary education far exceeds those of secondary and tertiary education, whilst secondary and tertiary education have direct bearing on productivity and economic gains at the national level.

Agricultural productivity has increased manifold due to access to education. Educated farmers are far ahead in acquiring and utilising modern technologies for farming in comparison to their illiterate compatriots. In Thailand, farmers with four or more years of schooling were three times more likely to adopt fertilisers and other modern input than the less-educated farmers. Another study in Nepal reveals that at least seven years of schooling contributes to increases in wheat productivity by 25 percent and rice productivity by 13 percent. Education has proven to be a key contributor to a rise in industrial productivity in China, India, Korea, Taiwan and Sri Lanka, among others.

4. **Education and Trade:** The impact of education has been a remarkable contribution to greater trade openness and investment practices. This has in turn has affected the aggregate growth rate, which is another way in which human development influences the macro perspective. A World Bank study on the economic growth rate in sixty developing countries from 1965 to 1985 proves that the growth rate was higher in those countries that had a combination of higher education, macro-economic policies and openness to trade. Higher education brings greater adoption of foreign skills, knowledge, and technologies as input to their domestic industry and market, which facilitates higher exports and global market accessibility. This has been particularly true for many Asian countries, beginning with Japan and Korea, and now also China and India.

While there has been remarkable economic growth in a number of countries in Asia, others are still stuck with domestic problems including political instability, growing terrorism, dependency on foreign aid and mounting debts, mass illiteracy, chronic hunger, and natural calamities. These have grossly hindered their prospects for social justice and economic prosperity. Despite the heterogeneous situation in Asia, some important lessons can still be drawn:

1. No country can achieve sustainable development and steady economic growth without providing good-quality education to its people. Education is indispensable for the creation and maintenance of a just and equitable society and economy.
2. The completion of secondary education is the core component in social mobility, increased productivity and higher income, with higher bargaining capacity.
3. The distribution of economic gains, and control and power of the economy directly corresponds with the acquisition of higher and good quality education in the society. This is clearly reflected in the growing influence of the middle class in the market economy and the politics of a country.
4. As education plays an important role in market development, investments in education, especially higher education, are influenced by market dynamics. This has been noticed in China, India, and other countries. In the 2009 annual budget presented in India, the emphasis was on higher education with an eye on its high and immediate returns, at the cost of basic and primary education. If this trend continues, we would face a situation where the quality of education sees a downward fall, especially for primary education. Instead of meritocracy in education we would be heading towards mediocrity, thus stifling innovation.

5. The liberation of human potential on one hand and creating a balanced, aware and mutually responsible society on the other, is the core value of education. However, it has been seen in East and South Asian countries that education is viewed with the end goals of jobs and economic gain. While education helps in economic mobility and reducing hunger, the impending deterioration of the human value and quality of education would not return a high yield in building and maintaining human capital.
6. The inclusion of hard-to-reach people, especially children from the socially deprived sections of the society, child labourers, victims of HIV/AIDS, children with disabilities, girls, minorities, indigenous children, and children of migrant and immigrant communities, must be provided with good-quality education so that they can benefit from the overall economic gains in a country. Deprivation from education leads to the denial of their human rights, social justice and participation, which can eventually create irreparable social tension, civil unrest and violence.

The burning issue here is to translate the achievements in growth and productivity for economic growth and sustainable development in a way that promotes social justice and equity. The education issue has to be seen in totality, which has been defined well in the Dakar Framework of Action on Education for All, which the international community has promised to achieve by 2015. The economic growth in Asia and worldwide, must also be determined in the context of attainment of the Millennium Development Goals, another political obligation to be fulfilled by the international community.

In times of economic crisis and fiscal prudence, investments in education must be encouraged for a healthy and decent labour force, thus maintaining productivity and keeping the gears of the economic cycles rolling. It is not just necessary, but absolutely urgent, especially now, that we provide every girl and boy, man and woman with a right to education. Education has to be the long-term policy tool to help us achieve not just economic growth, but sustainable growth at all levels – from a remote village to the metropolises of the world.

□

(—July 2009)

Right to Education: In Pursuit of a Dream

For someone like me who always dreamt of a world where all children are in school, enjoying education and growing as responsible citizens, piecemeal development would never be enough. However, today is a very important day in my life. Today is the day when millions of children in my country won their legal right to receive free education.

Education has always been considered a charity or one of the many state welfare measures. Starting today, it would no longer be the same. It is now a legal and constitutional right in India.

I recall the face of that six-year-old cobbler boy who unknowingly changed the course of my life forever. I could not do much for that particular boy but what I have been doing perhaps is attributed to that incident.

In 1980, when I started my journey against child labour along with a handful of friends, I strongly advocated that the elimination of child labour and education for all children are two sides of the same coin. One can never be accomplished without other. It was not an academic conclusion or judgement but a heartfelt opinion of an ordinary activist. Now I am pleased to see that the World Bank, the International Labour Organization (ILO) and other United Nations agencies infer and opine on the inter-linkages between the two. My heartfelt thanks to those academicians and researchers involved.

Today, I would like to congratulate and express my immense gratitude and respect for all the volunteers, activists and members of *Bachpan Bachao Andolan* (BBA), particularly the children who dared to share the dream that education shall become a universal fundamental right one day. I would also like to applaud individuals, NGOs, politicians, celebrities and teachers' organisations who campaigned to make it happen.

As I write this, I recall those days of *Shiksha Yatra* ("Education March" in Hindi) in 2001, when we were marching across the length and breadth of the country to demand that education be made a fundamental right. We met thousands of children and their parents who did not even know which country they belonged to! One such mother along with her daughter, who worked in a matchbox factory, was listening to me very intently in a public street meeting. When the meeting was over, she rushed to me and asked "Do you mean to say that my daughter will be able to go to school and will become a *ma'am* (teacher)? If so, when will that be?" Had I known the whereabouts of this mother somewhere in the state of Tamil Nadu in the south of India, I would have told her that it is possible now.

I am reminded of another incident which happened in a village called Pilkhua in the state of Uttar Pradesh. After a street play by the marchers, a young boy, who must have been between 10 to 12 years old, came to me and gave me all of his earnings of two days and said,"This money is all I have and I give it to you for liberating children like me so that we can be in schools." I can narrate innumerable heartrending incidents from those days of the *Shiksha Yatra*.

We braved the rains, the mud, the sun, the cold and floods in different parts of the country during this 15,000 kilometre, six-month-long physical march. We were sheltered in schools, temples, mosques and paddy fields. We spent nights at a stretch at road junctions and roadside hamlets. With every step we took and every mile we covered, our confidence multiplied by witnessing people being convinced that education was their right, no matter how poor, oppressed or discriminated they had been against for generations.

In the 1990s, we started the Parliamentary Forum on Education with concerned Members of Parliament of both the Upper and Lower Houses. Interestingly, 166 Parliamentarians across party lines joined hands with us under the leadership of Shri Ravi Prakash Verma. Several of them held the flag high by raising questions in Parliamentary sessions. This further strengthened our movement.

The BBA could be credited for major accomplishments in bringing about a paradigm shift in education as a human right. For almost two decades now, BBA has been the pioneer in initiating, building and spearheading a movement on the right to education. We have also been able to successfully establish the theory of a triangular link between child labour, illiteracy and poverty through real life experiences and practices. Now the cause-and-consequence relationship between the three is largely accepted. We strongly believe that education can act as the key to open all doors for all human rights.

We still recall that eventful morning in 2000 when hundreds of children knocked on the doors of Parliamentarians and woke them up from their slumber in their North and South Avenue residences in the capital, at the break of dawn. The high-profile Parliamentarians were shocked to meet children who handed over symbolically empty slates challenging them,"Why are our slates clear even after 53 years of independence?" Some sensitive and engaged Members raised the matter in the Parliament that very day and demanded a debate on the status of education in the country. This happened for the first time in the history of the Indian Parliament.

I remember several meetings these children had with former Prime Ministers like V.P. Singh, I.K. Gujral, and Atal Bihari Vajpayee, the current one Manmohan Singh and former President like K.R. Narayanan and current President A.P.J. Abdul Kalam. They were reminded to fulfil the dreams of the forefathers of the nation by providing education for all.

Almost a decade ago, there was not even a single national or regional political party that considered education to be an important issue. There are umpteen instances when our fellow activists and I would wait for hours for the manifesto writers to emerge from their offices for us to convince them how important it was to include the issue of education in their election campaigns.

I can recall some interesting anecdotes from our campaigns during national and state elections. The BBA launched an intensive and unique election campaign to approach all key contestants from various political parties requesting them to sign pledges for the eradication of child labour and ensuring free and quality education for all children. Many of the candidates initially threw away those letters but when it struck them that education could influence votes, they realised the popularity of the campaign. The same contestants would then call us to sign their letters. Of course, those who totally declined were declared as 'anti-children candidates'. The BBA and our partners had huge success in garnering support on this issue in more than half of the constituencies in the country.

Due to the unprecedented popular demand for education generated through *Shiksha Yatra* in 2001 and the intense Parliamentary lobbying, India's Constitution was amended and education became a fundamental right. But this was not enough. We did not settle for it without making it a law. It took us eight long years to translate it into reality. As I mentioned above, the present law is not sufficient. Therefore, the struggle for free, quality, compulsory and equitable education will continue. We are winning the battles but the war is yet to be won.

The good news is that numerous civil society organisations and their networks have emerged during the last decade in our country. We must appreciate their commendable work in the field of education. It is about time that such forces join hands on a common minimum agenda for action. Besides the NGO community, some of the most important partners who have ensured that this law becomes a reality are the National Coalition for Education (NCE), the All India Primary Teachers' Federation (AIPTF), the All India Secondary Teachers' Federation (AISTF) and the All India Federation of Teachers' Organisations (AIFTO). BBA has worked with these organisations over the years and I believe we will continue working together in the future to make this vision come true.

First of all, we have to challenge the discrepancies in the data and figures of out-of-school children. The government should be honest and admit the actual number of such children. 7.7 million is a grave underestimation when the National Sample Survey of 2005 to 2006 had estimated 46 million to be out-of-school. An independent study by AC Nielsen ORG-Marg in 2001 indicated that 85 million children are out of school. Secondly, the common people need to be aroused and mobilised against an inherent tendency towards commercialisation and discrimination under the present education system. The proposed voucher system in the 11th Five-year Plan of the Union Government is highly misleading. It is a diversion from the state responsibility of universal primary education and an attempt to encourage privatisation. Complaint redressal and legal activism has to be enhanced. It is a pity that the responsibility and authority of ascertaining a constitutional right which was naturally supposed to be with the regular judicial system has been given to a unit under the Ministry of Woman and Child Development, i.e. the National Commission for the

Protection of Child Rights and state commissions, which are not constituted in most states.

Government agencies and local governance institutions like the *Panchayati Raj* Institutions, etc. have to be held accountable for enforcing the law. The special efforts for the inclusion of hard-to-reach children like trafficked and bonded child labourers, disabled children, children especially girls belonging to indigenous communities, Dalits and minorities, have to be made. Their retention in schools and the quality of their education should be ascertained. We also have to address the biggest challenge of adequate resources being made available in the Central and State budgets and spent in genuine fashion. The civil society has to work as equal partners in planning, implementing and monitoring all education plans. We have to work with committed officials and institutions to make this a reality. This clearly means that your continued cooperation and support is not only invaluable, but inevitable.

Despite these important caveats, there is definitely a reason to celebrate today, as it is the day millions of dreams come true. Cheers!

□

(—April 2010)

Education for an Equal and Equitable World

Today every seventh person in the world is an illiterate. Out of these, 60 million children have never been to school and around 120 million left school after just a couple of years. Among those who continue to study in schools, 250 million cannot properly read a text in their own language, nor can they do basic calculations.

A good education is not only a human right but also the most effective weapon to attain freedom from mental, social and economic slavery. And while civil society understands the power of education, it is accorded much more importance by violent, religious fanatics and terrorist organisations. That is the reason they are scared of the educated schoolchildren and are attacking them everywhere. In Nigeria, Boko Haram had abducted and kept in captivity over 200 girl students over a year ago – out of which there is no information on more than half of the girls. Only last month, terrorists entered a college in Kenya and butchered almost 150 students. A few months ago at a school in Peshawar in Pakistan, 145 people, including 132 innocent kids, were riddled with bullets. In certain parts of Syria and Iraq, 3000 to 4000 young and adolescent school girls are being abducted and pushed into abominable sexual exploitation and prostitution.

Against this backdrop, an education conference of the United Nations was held in South Korea from 19th to 22nd May. Education ministers and official representatives at the highest level from almost all countries attended the conference, which was held under the auspices of UNESCO. In addition to the UN Secretary-General Ban Ki-moon, leaders and officials from the World Bank, UNESCO, UNICEF, etc. participated in it. I had been invited to address the inaugural session of the conference. This was considered the most important international occasion so far on the future of the world's uneducated children and illiterate adults. Before this, global conferences on the issue of education were organised in 1990 and 2000, but this conference is significant from the viewpoint of ensuring the role and importance of education in setting the developmental goals for the world. It is to be noted that in the UN General Assembly conference to be held next September, new developmental goals will be assigned.

In 2000, the United Nations General Assembly had set eight Millennium Development Goals. These goals, which are joint pledges for the world community, are considered to be solid programmes to rid humanity of poverty, disease, illiteracy, unemployment, environmental destruction, etc. over the next 15 years. It is ironical that in the past 15 years, the face and character of global politics has changed quite a lot. The fear of terrorism and the continuing violent struggles and wars have certainly pushed back development priorities. Meanwhile, the world has also had to face a dire economic downturn. As a result, there have been drastic cuts in the development grants of rich countries and in the budgets of developing countries for social expenditures.

Education is likely to be given an important place in the draft agreement on global development at the next UN General Assembly. I seriously believe that no development goal can be achieved without providing free, qualitative, inclusive and equal education to all. The continued development of society rests on four basic pillars, and without strengthening them, the continuity of development cannot be ensured. The four pillars are:

people, environment, prosperity and peace. Education is the common link connecting them all. The welfare of the people depends on security, justice, participatory democracy and good governance. Blind faith and terrorism have stoked racial sentiments in both rich and poor countries. The locals are increasingly filled with suspicion and hatred for the communities immigrating and settling in from other countries. Non-liberal parties, as a result, are gaining quick popularity. These developments are dangerous for the people and for democracy.

The solution to these rising dangers lies only in education. Education helps the growth in liberalism, harmony, participation, responsibility, accountability and transparency. Another point to note is that infant mortality rate have reduced by half in the case of educated mothers, compared to uneducated ones. With education alone, almost 700,000 people can be saved from fatal diseases such as HIV/AIDS over the next decade.

The second pillar is the environment. The earthquake in Nepal and the floods in the state of Uttarakhand are fresh examples of nature seeking revenge. Climate change and global warming cannot be tackled without the finest scientific and technical measures. It is our moral responsibility to ensure education on saving the earth be given right in primary school. The production of alternative, harmless energy, besides the conservation of water and energy, has only been possible through high quality education.

The third pillar is prosperity and economic development. In today's world, we are living in the age of economics of communication and knowledge. The market and trading systems are connected and controlled by the wireless system of communication technology. It was revealed in a recent study in 50 countries that the annual education given to the entire population of a country can increase the gross domestic product of that country by 0.37 percent. And if the education is of high quality, then the growth is at the rate of 1 percent per annum. Other studies by the World Bank, UNESCO, etc. have proven that every year of study of a child in primary school results in an increase in his income, upon attaining adulthood, by 10 to 15 percent. In the case of higher secondary education, this increase in income has been observed to be in the range from 15 to 25 percent. Girls benefit even more than that.

The fourth important pillar is peace. Peace is not merely the sermon given by religious leaders and sacred books at religious places; nor is it merely a subject for academics or seminars. It is also not just the negotiations occurring at diplomatic events. Everybody wishes for peace in their personal and public life, as peace is not only an individual's basic character but also a right as well. Continuous development is not possible without it. Education engenders logical, tolerance and the will to understand each other. But it is unfortunate that, in the name of religion and morality, education is turned into a weapon to spread narrow-mindedness, hatred and violence. One challenge before us is to provide an education that begets human values, ethics and global citizenship.

For the education of all children in the world, only a sum of US$22 billion is required per year. This is equivalent to four days from the annual global defence expenditure. Not only that, it is one-fifth of the money spent by European consumers on cosmetics and one-fourth of that spent by Americans on cigarettes and tobacco. The Incheon city of Korea is going to add a new chapter in history. It is now incumbent upon global governments and the world community to give top priority to education for social development. It is not difficult to do. Political will, moral accountability and sufficient funds can help achieve the goal of education for all.

□

(—May 2015)

The Marginalised Tibetan Children

In several cities of India one can easily spot Tibetan refugees selling woollens – short-statured, button-nosed, and wearing brown overalls or those adorned with colourful stripes. Primarily, the Tibetans in India are settled in Dharamsala in Himachal Pradesh, under the leadership of their spiritual guru, Buddhist monk and Head of State the Dalai Lama, but they have also settled in groups in many other cities. Majnu-ka-Tilla is one such colony in the capital Delhi, where hundreds of students and young men from the nearby Delhi University can be seen thronging each evening – as much for the special alcoholic beverage, called '*chhung*', as for the fair-skinned, beautiful girls who sell and serve the drink from the *dhabas*. Several cities of North and South India have Tibetan markets selling woollens, stone necklaces, leather jackets, etc. Such markets also abound in many cities in Nepal.

But this is not the real life of these Tibetans living in their own little world. The roots of their identity and heart and soul lie in the ancient, mountainous and beautiful land of Tibet and its remote villages, a land under occupation by China. The Tibetan lifestyle is deeply rooted in their religious beliefs and rituals. For that reason, they could not easily embrace China's society, nor could they commingle with the local communities of India and Nepal where they live in refugee colonies.

The struggle for Tibet's autonomy has been going on relentlessly for the past four to five decades. The most distinguishing feature of this struggle is its continued non-violent and peaceful nature. The six million or so Tibetan people are mainly Buddhist. The Dalai Lama is counted among the foremost religious gurus and upholders of world peace. That is why millions of his followers and Tibetan movement supporters are found all across the globe, including Europe and the United States. At a practical level, the Dalai Lama has agreed to consider Tibet as a part of China and favours the restoration of peace along with the religious freedom of Tibetans and the protection of their human rights, provided greater autonomy and a special status is given to Tibet. However, several small sects of young Tibetans – who lack patience and tolerance – have taken shape. All the same, there is a long tale of suppression of Tibet by a domineering China. The situation was worse in the days of hard-core communism. Not only that, China has always considered the Dalai Lama as its enemy. The Panchen Lama, Tibet's second highest religious leader after the Dalai Lama, has been imprisoned in a Chinese jail since childhood.

The Olympics are going to be held in China this year. What better chance could there be to highlight the Tibetan issue on the world stage? Thus, the protestors accelerated their movement. In the peaceful demonstrations by Tibetans in China, there has been violence and turmoil for the past couple of months. The Chinese army has attacked Buddhist monasteries, villages and towns. The Chinese Government has accused the Dalai Lama of inciting violence and stated that the Buddhist monks are causing armed mayhem, whereas the Tibetans allege that it is the agents of the Chinese army who, disguised as monks, are spreading violence and thus suppressing the movement at a large scale. Worldwide, including in India, demonstrations are being held to stop the Olympic torch, especially in Europe. In Paris, the capital of France, the Olympic torch was extinguished. Forty people were arrested.

One thing that is getting marginalised amidst all these political allegations, counter-allegations and demonstrations is the matter of the rights of Tibetan children and adolescents. Whether they belong to Kashmir, Kosovo, Afghanistan, Iran or Sudan, children do not cause wars or create violence, nor do they attack people or stir up turmoil. On the contrary, in the violent history of the world, they are the biggest victims. Regardless of whether the parents of children are fighting in an army or on the side of the terrorists, whether they are the innocent citizens who fall victim to bullets and bombs or refugees uprooted from their motherland – all these children have to suffer deep mental trauma, anguish, irreparable psychological disorders, crippling violence and even collective deaths. These horror-struck children are cut off from mainstream of society. In several places, their schools are turned into war cantonments or refugee camps; in others, they become afflicted with fatal diseases such as HIV/AIDS. Children are smuggled into other countries and pushed into the darkness of slavery or prostitution in large numbers. Elsewhere, terrorist groups snatch away their toys and books and hand them guns instead.

Tibet is not impervious to all this. On 16th March, the shattered body of a 16-year-old girl, Lundup-so, was handed over to her family. She was clasping her school bag to her bosom. On her way to school in the capital city of Lhasa, she was hit by a bullet in military firing. According to her relatives and school teachers, she was the most promising and studious girl in the entire village. Six days prior to that, a Buddhist monastery was sealed from the outside in Lhasa – forcing people to starve to death, including small children. When 15-year-old Lopseng raised his voice against it, he was arrested and taken to an unknown place. The education of children all across Tibet are being hindered. The nearly two million children living there are already deprived of their rights to education, health and development; they are also living a life with a deep uncertainty about their future.

On one hand, China, in addition to becoming the fastest-growing economy, is the biggest threat to the market system of America and Europe; on the other, the province of Tibet under this country has seen a worsening of its economic situation. According to the human rights reports of the United Nations, 54.8 percent of Tibetans are uneducated. One-third of Tibetan children have never been to school. The health situation is also very poor. There is great gender imbalance in education, that is, the number of girl students is even much smaller.

In China, only nine out of 100 Tibetan children get admission to high school. In the past 20 years, in the old and famous district of Tinghi in Tibet, a mere 15 children were able to finish high school. No scope of good employment and career is visible for them. Nevertheless, as per a white paper issued by the Chinese Government in 2001, there are a total of 956 schools of all kinds in Tibet. It is worth mentioning here that in the name of education in schools, there has been major interference with the children's religious freedom, cultural heritage, history and language. The curricula imposed on Tibetan children are causing the students to get confused and deluded. A direct consequence of these circumstances is that the Tibetan people, especially youngsters, are compelled to flee their homeland in large numbers. Every year, they turn up with their families in Nepal or India as refugees. The most worrisome situation is that one third of those escaping alone or through middlemen are under the age of 18. It is difficult to say anything about their mental state and future prospects – or when, where and how their anger, suppressed since childhood, will erupt. But one thing is for sure: at least India and Nepal cannot remain untouched by that.

In these circumstances, it is necessary for the Chinese Government to pay heed to child rights protection in Tibet and ensure that their education and health are given top priority. Clear budgetary allocations should be done in this direction. Curricula should be ascertained along with Tibetan representatives, and the expenditure on and quality of education should be monitored. The places where children can be found – schools, monasteries, hospitals, colonies, etc. – must be protected from all kinds of violence. Human rights, especially child rights, should be restored in Tibet. What is more, we should also keep our natural expectations from the Dalai Lama, and all other groups and international cooperative organisations associated with the Tibetan movement, that they will keep the issue of protection of child rights on their list of priorities.

□

(—April 2008)

CHILDREN AND RELIGION

"I challenge the passivity and pessimism surrounding our children. I challenge this culture of silence, this culture of neutrality."

1. The people of India primarily follow these religions: Hinduism, Islam, Sikhism, Christianity, Buddhism and Jainism. As per the Census of India, 2011, the proportion of Hindus in the country is nearly 80 percent, of Muslims around 14 percents, and Christians and Sikhs are each around 2 each; whereas, those who follow Buddhism are 0.7 percent and the followers of Jainism are around 0.4 precent. People who follow religions other than these number around 0.7 percent.
2. Human compassion is the foundation of all religions. That is why, in our scriptures, there is ample discussion about affection towards children, and their dignity and security.
3. In the Vedas and Manusmriti, instructions have been given for the dignified education and the impressionistic and holistic development of all children. But the reality is exactly opposite to that. The followers of Hinduism spend huge amounts of money on rituals and worship in temples, on the installation of idols and the construction of grand buildings, whereas poor, starving children are seen begging for alms outside those very temples.
4. It has been said in the Holy Quran that no child should be murdered because of poverty. As per Islam, the light of God shines on the spotless face of an innocent child playing in her mother's lap. But today, under the garb of religion, terrorists are abducting thousands of innocent daughters, selling them and sexually exploiting them. They are kidnapping adolescents and children and turning them into fidayeen (suicide squads), handing over to them AK-47 guns and making them kill innocent people.
5. There are sermons in Christianity on love and compassion towards children. Jesus Christ has even said that let children approach him first. Children should not be deprived of the divine kingdom, because it is meant for them. But, even in Christian countries, evils, such as sexual exploitation of children and child-trafficking exist. Despite that, Churches and the clergy do not raise their voices against it.

Let's Not Give Children a Communal Identity

The relationship between religion and children is quite peculiar. At birth, the child enters the earth a simple being. Thereafter, it is the adult society that gives her/him a communal identity – through baptism, rituals of *Kalma* (the first pillar of Islam) or *Khatna* (Circumcision), tonsure and *Janeu* (sacred thread) or *Kada*, *Kesh*, *Kripan*, etc. (the five Ks under Sikhism). The day they are branded Hindu, Muslim, Sikh, Christian, Buddhist, Jain, or any other religion is the day, in my view, when humanity is once again divided and another crime against God is committed.

All over the world, more than one billion children are victims of abject poverty. More than 210 million children use their delicate bodies to do laborious work for others. Every minute, 10 malnourished children die in the world. 70 million children have never been to school and another 150 million quit school before finishing the fifth standard. Millions of children are victims of trafficking and there are open markets where they are sold. There are many who are kidnapped and their kidneys, skins and other delicate organs are extracted and sold. Brought thousands of kilometres away from their parents, the trafficked children are enslaved in agricultural fields, factories, brick kilns and brothels. Over 5,00,000 children have been forcibly kept as child soldiers in terrorist, private and illegal armies. Children who should be holding toys and books instead wield dangerous weapons, such as AK-47s and AK-56s.

In spite of the influence, prosperity and abundance of churches, mosques, temples, *gurudwaras* and other religious places, children across the globe are in miserable condition. Once in a while, these religious institutions do something that is significant and commendable, but it is as little as a drop in the ocean.

There is a commandment to raise children in a proper manner in the Quran-e-Majeed and Hadiths. Prophet Mohammed had only one progeny, a daughter. He called daughters the biggest blessing of God and considered families without a daughter unfortunate.

A few years ago, we rescued a child from a glass-bangle-making factory in Ferozabad. This 7- or 8-year-old used to melt glass in furnaces. His whole body had turned black from this work. Far away from his parents, the factory owner had kept him as a bonded labourer. Whenever the child missed his mother, the owner used to beat him up. Suddenly, my eye caught the palm of the child: it had a big hole. Upon enquiring, it came to light that by mistake hot, molten glass had fallen on his hand, piercing the palm like a bullet. The owner, instead of getting the child treated medically, mercilessly beat him for this mistake. My head bowed in shame when I learnt that this innocent child was named Mohammed, after the Prophet, and moreover the factory owner was a renowned local leader of the Babri Masjid Committee.

I would like to quote a similar incident from Mirzapur in the state of Uttar Pradesh. When we raided a carpet factory to rescue some girls, who had been abducted from the Rewa district in Madhya Pradesh, 11 girls emerged happily, but I saw a 14- to 15-year-old girl sobbing, with her face next to the wall of that hovel-like room. I brought a local lady magistrate with me and again entered that room, and told the girl that she was now free; we would take her to her parents. At this, she began crying even louder than before. She told us she did not want to go back. Later on, we learnt that she was a frequent victim of rape, and that the innocent girl was carrying a child in her womb. All of us, including the magistrate, felt ashamed when we came to know that the girl was called Sita. How would you have felt if you also saw the large flag fixed to the door of the owner's house, which read, "Master Lord Ram we will come, and build a temple on that very site."

It is certain that there is no connection between crimes like these and religion. But how can one ignore the public and private character of people who continue to run their shops or remain leaders through religious and communal frenzy? If one were to investigate the mutts, *madrasah*s (Islamic seminaries), missionary schools or religious education centres being run in the name of service and charity, it would become clear that the delicate minds of children are being poisoned under the garb of building character and virtue. Most of the people who run such institutions are more skilled in enforcing mental slavery in the name of discipline, than respecting children's rights and the freedom of children. Incidences of homosexuality, eve-teasing and the rape of girls are not uncommon in these places. Under the disguise of religion, child marriages, discrimination against girls, and untouchability in schools are common. In many countries, perversions such as genital mutilation of little boys and girls or, in the name of celibacy and *Brahmacharya*, forced unnatural sex are rampant.

Religion, beliefs and traditions are different entities, but how many religious teachers oppose customs that have a stamp of religion on them? Through 24×7 television channels, these *guru*s create propaganda for their religious doctrines, loud-mouthed publicity and self-praise, besides promoting medicines and talismans, collecting donations, spreading malpractices and hypocrisy, and stoking fears of the future, planetary conditions, horoscopes – thereby causing the rise of superstitions, confusions and false miracles. How many among them embrace the essence of religion and spirituality or live a life of human compassion and sensitivity and, with moral courage, raise their voices against injustice and inequality?

There is fundamental similarity between the religious doctrines and the revolutions in support of justice and equality all over the world. The roots of all religions and revolutions sprout from a deep human consciousness. It is from this consciousness that a deep connect with human values and actions is established, through people and groups against oppression and evil. This can also be called the path of spirituality. Another path is the one of struggle for changing the social, economic and systemic reasons that engender and sustain oppression and evil. This is the path of all the big and small revolutions in the world.

From these two paths, emerge a few other paths as well. The metamorphosis of the main path of spirituality, which is organised religion, can breed rituals, hypocrisy, communalism and even terrorism, over a period of time. On the other hand, in its basic form, religion is involved in helping others, establishing peace, equality and brotherhood, and restoring the dignity of the oppressed and underprivileged sections of society. Likewise, while one path of social, economic and political revolutions keeps alive the continual struggle for human pride, justice and equality, another one leads to political sham, verbosity, hypocrisy and power-bred corruption. All in all, there has been the grave downfall of both religions and revolutions. Perhaps, for these reasons, childhood is being destroyed so rampantly in the world.

There are about 6,00,000 villages in India. According to an estimate, there are around 650,000 alleged *sadhus*, hermits, *maulvis, fakirs*, *bhikkhus*, missionaries, *babas*, *mahants*, etc. It will be a bigger number if you add up all the priests of the temples, mosques, *gurudwaras*, churches, etc. Now imagine the social awareness that would be created if all of them, who earn their bread and respect in the name of God, were to strengthen their voice against the oppressions – child labour, slavery, child trafficking, torture, foeticide, etc. – faced by the most beautiful progeny of God, that is, children. With that, all the religious *guru*s and their followers will once again explore the very reasons of their emergence. Only then they will realise that in the absence of sensitivity, concern and activism towards children, they are not following their religion but doing something entirely aberrant.

□

(—August 2012)

Can You not See Little Lord Ram Begging on the Streets of Ayodhya?

At the invitation of the Shri Ramkinkar Trust, I had the first opportunity in my life to visit Ayodhya. During my two-day visit, I experienced four primary but serious contradictions. First and foremost, something any one passing through the alleys and streets of this ancient town can witness are the poor conditions of its ancient buildings that are built in Avadhi architecture and which recount their own sad tales. Second, its simple people, who have cherished the inherited pride of being the citizens of this capital of Ram for ages and yet, do not usually harbour any hate or anger for non-Hindus. On the contrary, there is an amazing brotherhood amongst the Muslims who grow flowers, the gardeners and priests and abbots – which continue to grow unrestrained for reasons of necessity, custom and employment. The same brotherhood was on display in the very delicate circumstances following the breaking of the Babri Masjid structure. When the whole country was engulfed in an atmosphere of mutual hatred and distrust and violent riots broke out in several places, at that time, not only did the Hindus and Muslims of Ayodhya and Faizabad stand by each other's side to maintain calm in their area, they were also spreading the message of peace by taking out harmony processions in different places. Still, leaders from both the communities were able to breach the local groups and organisations and succeeded in getting a little toehold in Ayodhya.

Third, the poor have been greatly attracted to education, as a result of which literacy has increased to 70 percent in Ayodhya-Faizabad. But one anomaly here is that compared to the male literacy rate of 80 percent, the literacy rate among women is only 60 percent. I think the roots of this go back to Ram Rajya. Had it been a Sita Ram-Rajya, then perhaps it would have been a different picture in Ayodhya-Faizabad. Possibly, the history of our country would have been different.

Fourth but the most significant experience is related to *Ram-janmabhoomi* and Ram Lalla. Out of curiosity, I went to visit with my wife and a few friends the controversial spot that is the biggest cause of emotional aggravation and communal disharmony between Hindus and Muslims. Owing to my work in the fields of human rights, child labour and education, I have had opportunities to visit the most dangerous places in more than a hundred countries. This includes countries engaged in border disputes and civil wars which have been under the control and supervision of United Nations peace-keeping forces. But we had to struggle much more to reach the makeshift structure created in the name of a temple on the alleged birthplace of Ram Lalla. We had to pass through at least five or six security posts. In every nook and corner, thousands of security personnel were deployed, armed with weapons. Our mobile phones, wallets, identity cards, pencils, etc. were kept at the police station. On top of that, we had to go through thorough body checks at five places. Not only that, it was not possible to veer off the cage-like path that was made up of thick iron rods. The large number of security personnel, weapons and strict arrangements on that path that is almost a kilometre long would perhaps not be matched even during the rule of Dashrath or Ram.

After leaving, we were afflicted with scorching heat, sweat and thirst, but we could not get water or a cup of tea for ourselves at the multiple sweet shops and small restaurants surrounding Hanuman Garhi – because almost everywhere, we could see child labourers working in soiled clothes and pitiable conditions. Me and my colleagues boycott places, people and products in which child labour is involved. Fortunately, we found a shop selling food, which was run solely by an aged gentleman. We stopped there and had some chilled water, but, in a short while, our car was surrounded by child beggars, which included not only Hindus but a few Muslims as well. All of them were barefooted, in torn clothes and had thin, slender limbs.

This was such a contradictory scene that I would never forget it in my life. On the one hand, you had the stone idol of Ram Lalla, who had turned away from his kingdom to assemble and organise oppressed tribal groups and end the life of Ravana, a symbol of tyranny, who had the power of rule, wealth and knowledge, the Ram Lalla who, of his own accord, had spent fourteen years in poverty and mendicancy while establishing a relationship of dignity and equality with the people of lower castes. On the other hand, you had these little children of Ram, who were condemned to beg or be engaged in labour. If the children of Ayodhya are not Ram *lallas*, then who are they? (*Lalla means baby in Hindi.*)

This scene is no different from what you see at Deoband town in the state of Uttar Pradesh, where *fatwa*s (Religious edicts in Islam) are issued on irrelevant matters, or the alleys and streets around Delhi's Jama Masjid or the *dargah* (mausoleum) of the Khwaja of Ajmer. The owners of furnaces, factories and shops, under the garb of brotherhood, are sucking the blood of innocent children. During a raid to rescue bonded children, my colleagues and I had to face violent attacks, when religious kingpins spread the rumour that a few *kafirs* (non-believers) are snatching the children away from the *madrasa*s. Generally, in almost all the religious places of Hindus, Muslims, Buddhists, Sikhs and Christians, the exploitation of children continues unabated. It is unfortunate that priests and devotees never catch sight of these children of God.

As has been written above, it is not the common public of Ayodhya who is responsible for the temple/mosque controversy, but the religious leaders and politicians sitting in Delhi, Lucknow, Banaras, Aligarh, Mumbai, etc. It is the religious gurus who, for their own selfish gain, reached Ayodhya to play with the emotions of millions of people in the name of temples and mosques, thereby creating disharmony. They can see neither these Ram *lallas* nor the area where Ram would have been brought up.

If those who parrot the couplet by Tulsidas, *'Siyaram may sab jag jani'* (from the Hindi: "The whole world is full of Siyaram"), were to embody even a slight bit of it in real life, then the 60 million children of the country today would not have been deprived of education and would not have fallen victim to child labour and exploitation. The sex ratio would not have come down to 918 as a result of female foeticide. Around 70 percent of the country's Ram *lallas* would not have become victims of physical abuse and 53 percent of 'daughters of *Janak*' would not have been sexually exploited.

If the religious teachers of all doctrines were to use their voices and the power of reverence of the devotees to stop the atrocities against children, then to a great extent, the blemishes of child slavery, child-trafficking, foeticide and illiteracy could have been removed from the country. There should be no hesitation in accepting the fact that even today, the kind of impact that the messages and sermons of religious gurus can have on their followers, cannot be matched by any government advertisements or the public awareness efforts of social activists.

□

(—July 2011)

Ram Lalla in an Identity Crisis

There have been several reactions to my article 'Can't You See Little Lord Ram Begging on the Streets of Ayodhya?'. As Goswami Tulsidas had rightly written in *Ramcharitmanas, 'Jaki rahi bhavna jaisi, prabhu moorat dekhi tinh taisi'*, that is, one sees that form of God which reflects one's own emotion. Most people are used to seeing the form of God in temples, mosques, *gurudwaras,* churches, idols, graves, stones, trees, pundits and priests, *maulvis,* scriptures, etc., but there are a few who see God in the form of God's children. In my opinion, children are the most guileless, spotless, transparent, bias-free and beautiful forms of life, who truly epitomise godly qualities. Such children, whether they are slaves or beggars, whether they are condemned to prostitution or forced to commit crimes with guns handed to them by terrorists, in all these circumstances, these children are Ram *lallas* for me.

Now, let us talk about the social character of religion, which begets spirituality. The basic elements of religion, *'Vasudhaiv kutumbakam'* (the whole world is a family) or *'Sarve bhavantu sukhinah'* (Hindi: "Let everyone be happy") or *'Sagachhadweim'* (Hindi: "All walk together") or *'Sam wo manaansi gyanataam'* (Hindi: "Let us all jointly create knowledge") or *'Sah nau bhunaktu'* (Hindi: "All consume together"), even if they are treated as impossibly idealist sentences, but our religious books, sermons of gurus and our prevalent traditions are full of infinite respect, dignity and compassion towards children.

Hindu religion considers children to be God's embodiment. The child plays of Ram and Krishna are an indisputable part of Hindu culture. All over the country, during Navratri and other family and religious ceremonies, there is a tradition of worshipping and providing food to adolescent and young girls. The basis of the Varna system has been to allow children to have compulsory, equal and quality education and to let adolescents choose their profession as per their interest and activities. Under the *gurukul* tradition, Prince Krishna and poor Sudama used to live and study together. The education of girls was common and compulsory, just like it was for boys. In the Bible, Jesus Christ had given a clear message by saying, 'Let the children come to me first'. As such, in principle and practice, the first priority should be given to children and their concerns. Christianity is full of messages of inculcating compassion towards children. There are plenty of examples in Islam in which affectionate and empathetic messages have been given for children; even the religion that consider God to be formless, talks of feeling the light of God on the smiling face of an innocent child playing in the lap of her mother. A child has been spoken of as the most beautiful gift of Allah.

Now, let us look at the reality. The group that worships girls during Navratri does not feel ashamed in raping innocent girls that are just one or two years old. Fifty-three percent of children in the country are victims of one or the other form of sexual exploitation. It is the same religious leaders and so-called patriotic people who talk of shedding blood for their country, who do not hesitate to kill Sita, Savitri, Lakshmi and Parvati right in the wombs of their mothers. People who snatch away the most beautiful gifts of God from the laps of their mothers and buy or sell them at prices lower than cattle's, are the same ones who continue to maintain their existence in the name of religion. Jesus Christ never said he would embrace Christian children first; he loves all children equally, but the places that convert people and children to Christianity under the garb of mission and service are doing a roaring business in tribal and backward areas. Those who snatch away books, notebooks and even the Holy Quran from children and adolescents in Pakistan, Afghanistan and Sudan, and hand them guns and bombs instead, never tire of calling themselves the protectors of Islam.

In India, the practice of human sacrifice of children is prevalent even today. I would like to cite an incident related to that. Around 10 years ago, a child was brought to our children's rehabilitation home for former child labourers, *Bal Ashram,* located near Jaipur run by *Bachpan Bachao Andolan* (BBA). The child had been rescued from a tea stall in Ajmer. Deepak (name changed) must have been around 6 to 7 years of age at that time. The head of the child was badly wounded and bandaged. He was under such trauma that he would not utter a word to anybody on his own, but whenever someone went near him, he would start trembling to his bones. It took us years to properly treat him physically and mentally. After much investigation, we found out that right from after his birth, Deepak's mother used to remain seriously sick. Coincidentally, that village of Rajasthan also suffered a drought for about two to three years around the same time. A tantric laid all the blame on Deepak, calling him a ghoulish spirit. As a result, the child was completely abused. Later on, the same tantric suggested sacrificing the child in the temple of the Goddess Durga and said it would cleanse the sins of the family. During Navratri, one midnight, the sleeping child was taken to the temple on the hill some distance away for sacrifice. After all the rituals and mantras were over, when that butcher tried to cut of the throat of the child, the child suddenly woke up and the sword missed its mark, hitting the child on the forehead. Thinking that the child was dead, all the people ran away from the spot, but the next day some villagers took the injured boy to the district hospital in Ajmer. He was released from the hospital in a few weeks. Considering him to be helpless, the neighbouring teashop owner kept him as a servant. *Bal Ashram* was able to locate Deepak's family a few months ago. Deepak has taken his Class XI exam, having lived in *Bal Ashram* for about 10 years, but still, despite countless attempts, his neighbours and family folk did not take the child back because their blind faith in the tantric remained intact.

Under the garb of religion and community, children are exploited excessively. With the help of the court and the police, BBA rescued 1,092 children last year, out of which around 60 percent were Muslim kids brought from in Bihar, West Bengal, etc. Most of their agents as well as employers were also Muslim. Poor parents easily believe those who make false promises of education and progress in the name of community, but, later on, they are forced to run from pillar to post in search of their children. At times, the heartless employers kill the children like butchers.

A similar incident happened with the child Moin. Ten-year-old Moin, who had been trafficked from a village in the Madhubani district of Bihar, was murdered a couple of months ago. An agent named Kalimullah had brought him to Delhi, where he kept him as a bonded labourer in his own bangle factory. Whenever the children committed any mistake, he would hang them from a ceiling fan or beat them with a stone tied in a cloth. Once, not satisfied with beating him mercilessly, Kalimullah threw young Moin at a wall, and the child dropped dead on the spot. A young man working as a sweeper at Azadpur cemetery, who brought up the matter of a blood-drenched body of a boy being buried in a rush. After much struggle, we were able to get a case of murder registered against Kalimullah. The most shameful incident happened when, after three days, I went with my wife and two other colleagues, together with the mother and grandmother of Moin who had been brought to Delhi from Madhubani, to again bury the dead body of the boy. Suddenly, around half a dozen local Muslim leaders, clad in gaudy, expensive muslin pyjamas, shirts and caps, descended on the cemetery. At first, they made an ugly display of mourning. Later on, with sheer shamelessness and cunning, they implored Moin's mother and granny to go along with them. They wanted to persuade and lure that poor mother, who was constantly falling into a half-fainted state, in the name of mosque, community and religion, so that it would be easy for them to cover up their heinous crime of murdering the child.

I know very well that the heart of poor and aggrieved people is crystal-clear like a mirror. Our eyes became moist when Moin's mother, wearing a torn sari and walking in broken slippers, a small cloth-bundle on her head, came towards us herself. She then joined her palms together and said to those religious leaders, "You have already snatched away my son. What more do you want from us?" That put an end to their hidden agenda.

May I ask, 'How can we call ourselves religious when we have moved away from the human sensitivity that is the foundation of all religions?' Those who torture an innocent person are the worst sinners according to the Ramayana, which says, '*Par peeda sam nahi adhamai*'. But those who see religion and human sensitivity as separate, and continue to ignore the atrocities against innocent children are in no less measure criminals. The need of the hour is to kindle the '*Siyaram may sab jag jani*' sight within ourselves that can help us recognise the millions of Ram *lallas* struggling with an identity crisis.

□

(—July 2011)

God's Religion and Social Change

Thanks to advertisements and TV channels thriving on viewership ratings, the market for God, religion and yoga has scaled new heights. New *baba*s, miraculous yogis and tantrics arriving at the scene every other day have been able to milk money off the god-fearing masses, constantly struggling with serious and petty ailments and on the lookout for shortcuts to success. Likewise, the so-called civil society experts, specialists, panellists and debaters are in great demand. Media and 'social revolutionaries' are necessary for each other in equal measure. In this context, a serious and healthy debate on the reality and relevance of God and religions as well as on the fundamental values and character inherent in attempts at societal change is only natural.

Religion is nothing but the continual struggle in society for everyone's betterment and justice. Spirituality is the eternal value on whose foundation such struggles are carried on, while true God is the inspiring and resolute force of inner consciousness that gives continuity, integrity and universality to these values. On no other subject do we have so many studies, brainstorming, writings, debates and discussions as on the topics of God, religion, spirituality, etc. In every corner of the world in all eras, everyone in one way or the other, is connected to these subjects; but as the thoughts, analyses and deliberations flourished, so did the differences, fears and confusions – perhaps the latter more than the former.

On one hand, religious gurus and religions have played a historical role in making society disciplined, temperate, cultured, mutually cooperative, organised and welfare-oriented, on the other, doctrines and religions have been built on the foundation of sacrifices, human compassion, pure resolve and benevolence of great saints that have proven to be the exact opposite.

Over time, in most cases, the hypotheses, explanations and definitions of God have become mere instruments of fear, redemption, greed, selfishness, violence, hedonism, robbery, cleverness, mediation, and collective hysteria.

Organised religions became a cause for division in human society and, perhaps, among the biggest and easiest centres of power and money. Against peace, equality, justice, human dignity and rights, they are thriving as systems giving a principled base to alleged religion, beggary, *guru*dom, superstition, hypocrisy, casteism, racism and social and sexual inequality. At the physical, political and psychological level, this system is so deep and widespread that the basic element of religion, that is, true spirituality and God, has become lost in its midst.

The foundation of religion is spiritual essence and the soul of spirituality is the true form of God. But over thousands of years, everything has become so muddled that, at the practical level, it has become extremely difficult to view them separately, or to analyse their inter-connectedness. Despite all this, one cannot ignore its presence and impact on different aspects of an individual's life or for the society at large. So, it is necessary to first understand their true reality and assimilate this understanding. An honest attempt must be made to adopt it in one's life and, following that, it should be given the shape of a social mission. This is a long journey or, better still, a journey of struggle that will be undertaken not by full stops but with question marks.

The real relationship with God is one of consciousness and experience. It cannot perhaps be described in words. Another relationship is with our minds and hearts (emotions). There are limits to the logical as well as to the emotional mind of a human being. While there are several philosophical and elemental aspects of the acceptance of God's existence on one hand, on the other, there is emotional devotion, *bhakti* and surrender before God. Mind and heart cannot alone experience the joy of God. Yes, we can certainly learn from His qualities, benefit from them and attempt to create a new society based on equality, justice, tolerance and peace.

For instance, if God is omnipresent, then why do we have differences pertaining to temples, mosques, Hindus, Muslims, Christians, Brahmins, Dalits, Americans, Africans, rich-poor, male-female, employer-labourer, etc? And if He is not omnipresent, then what would be the difference between a dictator and God?

If God is the creator of the universe and the upholder of justice, then the acts of robbing nature, violence, destruction, space war, power-grabbing, struggle for stature and money, and wide differences in the distribution of resources for consumption and production…all these will be considered anti-God. And if God takes sides, then it is better for Him to not exist at all. In this manner, there is a need to analyse the various qualities of God with an open mind and explore their universal and contemporary context.

Let us think of a different aspect: the small and large efforts towards societal change. Since time immemorial, the human race has been inventing new ways for its physical comfort and convenience on the one hand, and, on the other, there have been individual and organised attempts towards justice, equality and peace. The thing to note is that these two streams are so co-mingled now that it is difficult to see them distinctly. The internal reasons for this admixture are characteristic weaknesses and the erosion of personal and societal values and the external reasons include consumerism, capitalism, political ambitions and corruption, among others. Still, movements to bring about societal change are continuing in some form in our country as well as in the rest of the world.

Everyone knows that today, politics is based on the lure of power, attraction to wealth and criminalisation. The necessary conditions for politics have become corrupt behaviour, cunning, falsehood, verbosity, communalism and sycophancy, but even after knowing all this, social movements are not untouched by the attraction of power and its resources. The easy argument is that how can lasting change be brought about without ample resources or without power (or governing power)? It is the kind of convenient argument that builds a circle of comfort around most groups of activists involved in social movements or revolutions.

In this context, it is necessary to throw light on the challenges for non-governmental interventions and their fast-changing character and priorities. In the 1980s, the word 'non-governmental organisation' (NGO) had not been invented or imported into our country. The efforts of NGOs were usually based on Gandhian thought, and were universal and voluntary. Cultural, social and religious institutions used to run numerous programmes for human welfare, women's liberation, the emancipation of Dalits, etc., which has been our country's tradition for ages. For instance, in our country, one can see inns and lodges all over, where people could stay for free. Society has given more water wells, fruit-laden shady trees, free clinics, *piaos*, charity kitchens, etc., than any single king or regime. Such deeds have been considered pious and religious. Public welfare has been an integral part of our society for eons, a major influence of which has been seen in Gandhian attempts.

In the 1970s, the anger of youth against the tyranny of the erstwhile government took democratic and creative shape. With the aim of re-establishing democracy, millions of youth entered this movement, which resulted in regime change. While a few joined the government in 1977, there were thousands of young men and women who, armed with the resolve of bringing about a new social consciousness, did not return to their universities and careers. Some of them formed groups and took residence in villages, where they set out to create public awareness for equality and justice, while some other idealistic youths, disillusioned with the political system, turned to Naxalism and marched towards mountains and jungles. The debates on women's rights, environment, proper rural development, people-centric economic policies, the rights of Dalits, unorganised bonded labourers, farmers, landless labourers, fishermen, children, etc. became aggressive, as a result of which many remarkable organisations and movements were established in the country. But then, gradually, on these same issues, new kinds of institutions assumed shape.

There was a major change in the character of this domain in the 1990s. It had to do with the influx of foreign money, thoughts and methods. In the West, a lot of noteworthy work was done on human rights, development, the environment and the concerns of women and children, while new definitions and vocabularies were also forged. For these measures, huge amounts of donation and government aid were collected. This had an immediate impact on all the developing countries, including India. A new NGO culture took root, along with the imported vocabulary, working methods and money. In this decade, a lot of emphasis was placed on finding issues, analysing their causes and highlighting them. Alongside, the character of the media also changed. New streams of media, such as those on human rights issues, developmental and environmental journalism, etc. were born.

Towards the final years of the 1990s and the beginning of the new millennia, the focus was more on solving the issues with traditional methods. For instance, getting the laws enacted, implementing them, putting pressure on governments to implement welfare schemes for schools, hospitals, employment, housing, etc. through organisations and movements. But in the final years of the last decade, a new need was felt. The need for original and new solutions, based on outcomes and evidence, in addition to their collation and exchange.

Not only in our country but all over the world, people are busy looking for alternative solutions – whether these are related to development, markets, energy depletion, environmental protection, climate change or issues related to human rights. Emphasis is being laid on finding new methods of advocacy. Against this backdrop, NGOs have created their own space in policy and decision-making in governments, international institutions and the corporate world. Entrepreneurship in the social sector is being promoted.

In the NGO space, we have not yet reached a stage where social problems receive ample highlighting, which is still needed in many respects. Media and foreign charities have played a role and helped here, but there is a contradiction as well. No deadline can be set for the solution to any problem, especially when it is connected with cultural or systemic reasons. On the other hand, new issues keep cropping up everyday. And then there is an abundance of funding for those issues. Most of the organisations and movements of today are the product of this.

Overall, there is a marriage of convenience between mass movements and the NGO culture. Perhaps this is what is fashionably called civil society today. Even the biggest, most powerful and corrupt politician must face his voters at least once every five years when he is held accountable. Union leaders are accountable to their members and the corporate leaders to their consumers and shareholders. But the accountability of the civil society, whether it is honest or corrupt, is to whom is something that is difficult to say. How many public organisations and social institutions exist that practise democracy? How many are transparent in character? Especially in financial matters.

These NGOs start dreaming of seats in the assemblies or the Parliament once they get a little funding from abroad, use new communication techniques or get contacts with the media to generate a small crowd (or sometimes, large crowds). But how many activists have succeeded in mainstream politics, who used to run movements for farmers, labourers, Dalits, tribals, fishermen, women, environment, displacement, land, corruption, etc.? Barely any. But those who indulge in communal politics vis-à-vis – Dalits, tribals and minorities – are reaping the benefits of power.

Some important movements are still being run on certain issues. No doubt, some of them are backed by very honest and dedicated activists. But the majority have a very narrow view and a singular standpoint. What is more, the dependence on foreign aid has crippled most of them. The lifeline of some movements itself is very short. In contrast, those who are a little successful or have been able to trumpet their success, have cornered those issues as their sole possession. They encash that success or their specialist image and spend many years in comfort in this way. They spend most of their time giving speeches, appearing on TV debate shows as experts, travelling from one place to another by air, to so-called spread the cause.

There is an urgent need today for these mass movements leaders to do some brainstorming, self-criticism and honest analysis. There are elements of deep sensitivity, human values and spirituality in their objectives, aims, attractive slogans and dreams. Whether they believe it or not, values such as equality, justice, unity, participation, non-violent spirit, sensitivity, tolerance, nature love, etc. are nothing but a reflection of Godly qualities. The erosion of these values from organisations and movements is the biggest reason for their perversion, fission and defeat.

□□□

(—June 2012)